THE VILLAGE OF HIGHGATE (THE PARISH OF ST. PANCRAS, PART I), BEING THE SEVENTEENTH VOLUME OF THE SURVEY OF LONDON, BY PERCY W. LOVELL, F.S.A., AND WILLIAM McB. MARCHAM

AMS PRESS

NEW YORK

John Boydell 1780

A NORTH VIEW OF THE CITIES OF LONDON AND WESTMINSTER WITH PART OF
HIGHGATE.   TAKEN FROM HAMPSTEAD HEATH, NEAR THE SPANIARDS

LONDON COUNTY COUNCIL

SURVEY OF LONDON

ISSUED BY THE JOINT PUBLISHING COMMITTEE
REPRESENTING THE LONDON COUNTY COUNCIL
AND THE LONDON SURVEY COMMITTEE

UNDER THE GENERAL EDITORSHIP OF

SIR GEORGE GATER *(for the Council)*

WALTER H. GODFREY *(for the Survey Committee)*

VOLUME XVII

THE VILLAGE OF HIGHGATE

(THE PARISH OF ST. PANCRAS, PART I)

PUBLISHED BY THE LONDON COUNTY COUNCIL
THE COUNTY HALL, LONDON, S.E.1
1936

Reprinted from the edition of 1936, London

First AMS edition published in 1971

Manufactured in the United States of America

International Standard Book Number:
Complete Set: 0-404-51650-5
Volume XVII: 0-404-51667-X

Library of Congress Catalog Card Number: 76-37851

AMS PRESS INC.
NEW YORK, N.Y. 10003

THE VILLAGE OF HIGHGATE (THE PARISH OF ST. PANCRAS, PART I), BEING THE SEVENTEENTH VOLUME OF THE SURVEY OF LONDON, BY PERCY W. LOVELL, F.S.A., AND WILLIAM McB. MARCHAM

iv

MEMBERS OF THE LONDON SURVEY COMMITTEE

THE FORMER PRESIDENTS OF THE COMMITTEE WERE—
THE LATE LORD LEIGHTON, P.R.A.
THE LATE RT. HON. AND RT. REV. DR. CREIGHTON, LORD BISHOP OF LONDON.
THE LATE MOST HON. THE MARQUESS CURZON OF KEDLESTON, K.G., G.C.S.I.,
G.C.I.E.

President

THE RT. HON. THE EARL OF CRAWFORD AND BALCARRES, P.C., K.T., F.S.A.

Honorary Members and Subscribers

The Rt. Hon. LORD ALDEN-HAM.
THE SOCIETY OF ANTIQUARIES OF LONDON.
THE ROYAL INSTITUTE OF BRITISH ARCHITECTS.
THE ARCHITECTURAL ASSOCIATION.
THE INCORPORATED ASSOCIATION OF ARCHITECTS AND SURVEYORS.
C. R. ASHBEE, M.A.
THE ATHENÆUM.
Miss HELEN BARLOW.
P. A. BAYMAN.
BOYLSTON A. BEAL.
HUGH BEAVER.
WALTER G. BELL, F.S.A.
THE BIRMINGHAM PUBLIC LIBRARY.
THE BISHOPSGATE INSTITUTE.
A. H. BLAKE, M.A., F.R.HIST.S.
ALFRED C. BOSSOM, M.P., F.R.I.B.A.
ARTHUR BROWN.
THE UNIVERSITY OF CALIFORNIA.
MOIR CARNEGIE.
THE WORSHIPFUL COMPANY OF CARPENTERS.
Miss A. G. E. CARTHEW.
H. J. CHETWOOD, F.R.I.B.A.
THE BRENTFORD AND CHISWICK PUBLIC LIBRARIES.
THE CHURCH HOUSE LIBRARY.

The Rev. P. B. CLAYTON, F.S.A.
Sir CYRIL S. COBB, K.B.E., M.V.O.
Captain E. E. COLQUHOUN.
THE COLUMBIA UNIVERSITY.
THE CONSTITUTIONAL CLUB.
W. W. CORDINGLEY.
THE COURTAULD INSTITUTE OF ART.
Captain A. C. CRAWFURD.
The Most Hon. The MARQUESS OF CREWE, K.G.
THE CROYDON PUBLIC LIBRARIES.
Major W. W. DOVE, F.S.A.
EUSTACE ERLEBACH.
RICHARD L. GIVEEN.
THE GOLDSMITH'S LIBRARY, UNIVERSITY OF LONDON.
LADY GRAY.
THE GUILDHALL LIBRARY.
RICHARD WALDEN HALE.
E. STANLEY HALL, F.R.I.B.A.
RICHARD HARRISS, A.R.I.B.A.
ARTHUR F. HILL.
THE INSTITUTE OF HISTORICAL RESEARCH.
Mrs. ALDERSON HORNE.
Mrs. E. J. HORNIMAN.
W. T. HUGO.
CONSTANT HUNTINGTON.
The Rt. Hon. The EARL OF IVEAGH, K.P., G.C.V.O., F.R.S.
Mrs. DENYS KING-FARLOW.
F. A. KONIG.
The Hon. LADY LAWRENCE.

G. C. LAWSON.
Miss PAULINE LEFTWICH.
The Rt. Hon. The VISCOUNT LEVERHULME.
H. W. LEWER.
LADY LOCKYER.
THE LONDON LIBRARY.
THE LONDON AND MIDDLESEX ARCHÆOLOGICAL SOCIETY.
THE LONDON SCHOOL OF ECONOMICS.
The Hon. Mr. JUSTICE LORT-WILLIAMS, K.C.
GILBERT H. LOVEGROVE, F.R.I.B.A.
MARY COUNTESS OF LOVELACE.
The Rev. WILLIAM MAC-GREGOR, F.S.A.
J. L'ESTRANGE MACKIE.
THE MANCHESTER PUBLIC LIBRARIES.
THE MANCHESTER SOCIETY OF ARCHITECTS.
Mrs. JOHN MARKOE.
LEONARD MORGAN MAY, F.S.A.
THE METROPOLITAN PUBLIC GARDENS ASSOCIATION.
G. VAUGHAN MORGAN.
JOHN MURRAY, F.R.I.B.A., F.S.A.
THE NEWBERRY LIBRARY, CHICAGO.
THE NEW YORK LIBRARY.
RICHARD NICHOLSON.
R. C. NORMAN.

v

The Oxford and Cambridge Club.

The Free Library of Philadelphia.

The Carnegie Library, Pittsburgh.

Sir D'Arcy Power.

Arnold Danvers Power.

The Public Record Office.

E. A. R. Rahbula, M.C., O.B.E., A.R.I.B.A., F.S.A.

Colin E. Reader.

The Reform Club.

Cecil Harold Ridge.

Harold A. Rutt.

The John Rylands Library.

The Shoreditch Public Library.

Frederick Simms.

G. C. Simpson.

Sion College.

Mrs. Vernon Smith.

W. J. Songhurst.

R. T. D. Stoneham.

Sir Andrew T. Taylor, F.S.A., J.P.

Hamilton H. Turner.

The Library, University College.

The Victoria and Albert Museum.

Noel P. W. Viner-Brady, F.S.A.

Lewish Huth Walters.

The Library of Congress, Washington.

The West Ham Public Libraries.

Mrs. Wharrie.

Miss M. J. Wilde.

H.M. Office of Works.

John E. Yerbury, F.R.I.B.A.

Active Members

Oswald Barron, F.S.A.

W. W. Begley, F.R.Hist.S., L.R.I.B.A.

J. W. Bloe, O.B.E., F.S.A.

W. W. Braines, B.A.(Lond.).

A. E. Bullock, A.R.I.B.A.

C. J. P. Cave, F.S.A.

G. H. Chettle.

A. W. Clapham, C.B.E., F.B.A., F.S.A.

Miss E. Jeffries Davis, F.S.A.

The Rev. E. E. Dorling, F.S.A.

J. J. Edmunds.

H. W. Fincham, F.S.A.

Thomas F. Ford, F.R.I.B.A.

G. Gordon Godfrey.

Mrs. Ernest Godman, A.R.E.

Philip Hudson, A.R.I.B.A.

B. R. Leftwich, M.B.E., F.R.Hist.S., F.S.A.

W. McB. Marcham.

A. R. Martin, F.S.A.

E. C. Nisbet.

Francis W. Reader.

Francis R. Taylor, L.R.I.B.A.

T. O. Thirtle, A.R.I.B.A.

A. H. Thomas, LL.D., F.S.A.

George Trotman, L.R.I.B.A.

R. E. Mortimer Wheeler, M.C., D.Litt., F.S.A.

Edward Yates, F.S.A.

Walter H. Godfrey, F.S.A., F.R.I.B.A., *Editor for the Committee.*

Professor Geoffrey Callender, F.S.A., F.R.Hist.S., *Honorary Treasurer of the Committee.*

Percy W. Lovell, B.A., A.R.I.B.A., F.S.A., *Secretary of the Committee,* Lancaster House, St. James's, S.W.1.

SUBSCRIBERS TO THIS VOLUME

James Anderson.
L. C. and H. E. Attkins.
Auctioneers' and Estate Agents' Institute.
F. O. W. Bamberger.
E. Barrs.
Battersea Public Library.
T. P. Bennett.
Bethnal Green Public Library.
Louis Blanc.
Arthur T. Bolton, F.S.A., F.R.I.B.A.
R. H. B. Bolton.
Sir A. H. Bodkin, K.C.B.
C. W. Bower.
Andrew Bowerley.
R. H. Brandt.
Burghley Central School for Girls.
C. J. Burckhardt.
Frederick Vango Burridge, O.B.E., R.E.
Camberwell Public Library
Channing School, Highgate.
Chelsea Public Library.
H. W. J. Chipchase.
Sir Arthur Crosfield, Bart., G.B.E.
Deptford Public Library.
Miss E. Gladys Dickinson.
Miss Esmé Dicks.
Neville Dixey.
K. S. Dodd.
Mrs. M. W. Drysdale.
Miss V. A. Duval.
J. J. Edwards.
H. L. Farrer.

Peter Ferguson.
Finsbury Public Library.
Fulham Public Library.
W. B. Gabriel, F.R.C.S.
Greenwich Public Library.
Wm. J. Grimshaw.
Hackney Public Library.
Hampstead Public Library.
Misses C. and E. Hardy.
S. Houston Hardy.
E. Vincent Harris, A.R.A.
L. J. Haskins.
Highgate Literary and Scientific Institution.
Holborn Public Library.
Miss E. S. Hollis.
Hornsey Public Library.
Charles H. R. Horwood.
Miss Horwood.
Geoffrey Hutchinson.
Inner Temple Library.
C. H. James.
Kensington Public Library.
Miss King.
Stephen Lacey.
Lambeth Public Library.
Mrs. George Lea.
Oswald Lewis.
E. A. Lintelo.
Kenneth T. Lomas, D.S.O.
R. J. McNeill Love, F.R.C.S.
George W. L. Marriott.
Middle Temple Library.
Dr. J. C. Nicholson.
Misses Owen.
G. W. Pearse.
John William Pearson.

W. Potter-Mackenrot.
Sydney E. Preston.
Prickett and Ellis.
J. B. Priestley.
John Ravenshaw.
F. Ruffell-Smith.
A. W. Russell.
St. Pancras Public Library.
Victor Saville.
Arthur Dalton Sharp.
Shoreditch Public Library.
Mrs. G. E. Smith.
Mrs. Ironside Smith.
Southwark Public Library.
Stepney Public Library.
S. A. and Lady Marjorie Stirling.
Stoke Newington Public Library.
Lady Stokes.
Ella M. Terry.
Lockett Thomson.
Harold C. Tompkins, F.L.A.
Mrs. Turnbull.
F. J. Varley.
Victoria Public Library, Melbourne.
Wandsworth Public Library.
Dr. Grace Watson.
Arthur Waugh.
Westminster Public Library.
R. S. Whipple.
E. Williams.
Dr. Woollard.
Woolwich Public Library.

CONTENTS

APPENDICES

DESCRIPTION OF THE PLATES

x

ILLUSTRATIONS IN THE TEXT

HERALDIC ILLUSTRATIONS
SUPPLIED BY REV. E. E. DORLING

xvii

PREFACE

THE Survey Committee has long contemplated the production of this volume on Highgate, and Mr. Percy Lovell, our Secretary, and Mr. W. McB. Marcham have been collecting the material for many years. We are fortunate in having their collaboration, for Mr. Lovell has been intimately acquainted with the beautiful houses that have made this one-time hamlet so attractive, and Mr. Marcham has studied its court rolls and local records down to the smallest particular. Historically, the village is interesting as an example of a very early residential neighbourhood, developing by reason of the beauty and other natural advantages of its site, and acquiring an individuality not derived from the usual parochial or manorial centre. Highgate is an outlying part of the extensive parish of St. Pancras, and although the chapel of its Grammar School (situated just within Hornsey) was used as a place of burial and even assumed, for a time, an unofficial parochial character, it was not until recent years that a church was built and Highgate became a separate ecclesiastical parish. The area occupied by the village was part of the Manor of Cantlowes, the endowment of the prebend of that name in St. Paul's Cathedral, a donation of the pre-Conquest period. Its name and those of Kentish Town and Ken Wood are still open questions for the philologist, and they are probably not related to one another. It is interesting, however, to note that succession in the Manor of Cantlowes was by gavelkind, a custom closely associated with the Kingdom of Kent.

The architecture of Highgate derives its interest not only from the beautiful surviving examples of late 17th and early 18th century buildings, but also from the problems afforded by many of its vanished houses. Dorcester House had an almost unique plan for an Elizabethan dwelling. Ashurst House may have been a final evolution from the Banqueting House where Lord Bacon died, and its successor in the grounds of Arundel House. Its latest form, together with the skilful designs for the Hospital founded by William Blake, raises an intriguing question of authorship. Among the existing examples of fine architecture the mansion of Ken Wood, with its splendid Library by Robert Adam, is easily the most notable.

In this volume of the Survey the Joint Publishing Committee of the London County Council and the Survey Committee have introduced certain changes in order to reduce the weight of the book and to decrease its bulk, which in recent issues has assumed uncomfortable dimensions. The letterpress is printed on a lighter paper, and the illustrations occupy both sides of the paper. It is hoped that this change may commend itself to the public and make the Survey less formidable to house and easier to handle.

Acknowledgment of very kind assistance must be made to the owners and occupiers of the various properties described, and also to the Ecclesiastical Commissioners, the Iveagh Trustees and to many others who have assisted with information or illustrations, whose names appear in the text and elsewhere.

WALTER H. GODFREY.

THE VILLAGE OF HIGHGATE (PARISH OF ST. PANCRAS, PART I)

INTRODUCTION

THE area of the metropolitan borough of St. Pancras (2,694 acres) is practically coterminous with the pre-1899 civil parish. In Norman times the parish included land eastward to Clerkenwell, from which it was divided by the river Fleet, where Warner Street and Farringdon Road are now. A few hundred acres now in St. Marylebone, part of the manor of Rugemere, were also in St. Pancras. A rough estimate gives 3,300 acres as the area at the time of the survey of 1086, entered in Domesday Book as follows:

"Ralph, a canon, holds Rugemere. It was assessed for 2 hides. The land is 1 carucate and a half. There is 1 plough in the demesne and (another) half plough can be made. Wood for hedges, and (rendering) 4 shillings. This land is worth 35 shillings; in the time of King Edward 40 shillings. It was, in the time of King Edward, and is now, in the demesne of the canons."

"The canons of St. Paul's hold Tothele. It was always assessed for 5 hides. The land is 4 carucates. There are 3 ploughs and a half, and another half can be made. There are 4 villeins and 4 bordars. Wood for 150 pigs; and 20 shillings for the herbage. With all its profits it is worth 4 pounds; the same when received; in the time of King Edward 100 shillings. The manor lay, and lies in the demesne of St. Paul's."

"At St. Pancras the canons of St. Paul's hold four hides. [Cantlowes.] The land is 2 carucates. The villeins have only 1 plough, and another plough can be made. Wood for hedges. Pasture for the cattle, and (rendering) 20 pence rent. There are four villeins who hold this land under the canons, and 7 cottagers. With all its profits it is worth 40 shillings; the same when received; in king Edward's time 60 shillings."

"At St. Pancras Walter, a canon, of St. Paul's, holds one hide. The land is one carucate. There is one plough and 24 men who render 30 shillings per annum. This land lay, and lies, in the demesne of the Church of St. Paul."

An estimate of the population at that distant date may be made from the figures given by assuming that each of the 53 men represented a family of five persons, which gives a total of 265. If to these we add slaves, servants, officials and retainers it appears fairly safe to say that the total population of St. Pancras at the time of William the Conqueror did not exceed 300. This number may be contrasted with the present population of 200,000. There is no reason to think that the density of population in the rural parishes of Middlesex in the 11th century exceeded a few hundreds. We know that as late as 1674 the neighbouring parish of Hornsey, with a comparable area, had about 800 inhabitants.

In the present volume on Highgate we are mainly concerned with the manors of Tottenhall and Cantlowes, both endowments of prebends in St. Paul's Cathedral. All the northern part of the parish lay within these two manors, the boundary between them being the road now variously named High Street, Camden Town, Kentish Town Road, Highgate Road and West Hill. From Merton Lane the dividing line ran near the site of the road now called Fitzroy Park as far as the point where it turns eastward towards The

I

Grove, at Highgate. From that point the boundary ran northwards to the parish boundary which it joined immediately eastward of the site now occupied by Beechwood. Cantlowes lay to the east and Tottenhall to the west of this line. The manors were seldom " in hand," but were leased by the prebendaries for three lives, that is, until the death of all three persons named in the lease, but the leases were always renewed by the insertion of a new life when one dropped out. In addition to the court baron belonging to every manor, the lords of each of these manors owned the Court Leet, which met yearly for the appointment of parish constables and other officers and exercised a certain control over sanitary matters, nuisances, etc., and had jurisdiction in matters affecting the king's peace. The Court Baron dealt with the titles to land within the manor, and its rolls constitute a complete land-registry so far as copyhold land is concerned.

From a survey of the manor of Tottenhall made in the time of Henry VIII[1] we learn that the lessees of the demesne lands (or home farm of the manor), who then paid a yearly rent of £38, had also to supply the Prebendary every year with three good loads of hay, carried into the manor place at their own expense, or pay 15s. instead. In the leases the manor was always described as the prebend, manor or lordship of Tottenhall or Tottenham Court in St. Pancras or Kentish Town, and also the woods and fuel lying besides Highgate, parcel of the said prebend. This phrase " woods and fuel " meant, in the words of the above-mentioned survey, " a wood att Higate parcel of the said manor and prebend which the prebendary kepith in his owne handes conteyning by estimacon two hundreth acr' of ground or more." It can be identified with Sherrick's Farm, mentioned in this volume under Ken Wood (p. 126). In the year 1314 the woodward, Henry Slademan, having charge of the wood called " Schyrwyk " was removed from office.[2] In 1650 there were five pieces of pasture called Sherrick Wood (48 acres), Sherrick Wood (50 acres), and Sherrick Wood (10 acres 1 rood), all rented by Nathaniel Syddens.[3] The farm-house stood on the road side (when Hampstead Lane followed the parish boundary) slightly to the north of the site now occupied by Beechwood, where Lady Southampton's house stood at the end of the 18th century. The old farm-house in 1650 had four lower rooms, two chambers and two garrets.

The manor house of Tottenhall stood on the east side of Hampstead Road, between Tolmer Square and Euston Road. In 1757 Euston Road was made across the demesne land of this manor between Hampstead Road and the present parish church of St. Pancras.

The manor continued in the hands of the Crown after the reign of Henry VIII, subject to payment of an annual rent to the Prebendary and fines on renewal of the lease from time to time. A sub-lessee in 1609 was William Cholmeley of Highgate, who had a lease for 31 years from that date, and mentioned in his will[4] that he, as steward of the manor, had £22 or £23 in hand from fines, due to the Crown. In 1650 Thomas Harrison of London bought the manor from the Commonwealth[5] and in 1655 also purchased the Crown interest.[6] In 1661, the Crown having recovered possession, granted

2

the manor to Sir Henry Wood, an officer of the royal household, for 41 years, on account of £500 owing to him by the late king for board wages in lieu of diet.[7] The reversionary interest belonging to the Crown was granted to Isabella, Countess of Arlington, wife of Henry Fitzroy, 1st Duke of Grafton, a son of Charles II by Barbara Villiers, Duchess of Cleveland. She died on 7th February, 1722-3, and her son Charles, 2nd Duke of Grafton, obtained from the Prebendary on 18th July, 1723, a fresh lease for three lives. The periodical renewal of these leases for lives was terminated by an Act of Parliament in 1768, which vested the freehold in Charles Fitzroy, brother of Augustus Henry, 3rd Duke of Grafton, subject to a ground rent of £300 per annum. Their widowed mother married James Jeffries, esquire. The freehold land belonging to the manor covered 254 acres 3 roods and 17 perches, and Mr. Fitzroy (afterwards Baron Southampton) also acquired the profits arising from the Courts Leet and Courts Baron.

Regarding Cantlowes there is a record[8] that in the year 1546 William Leyton, gentleman, " Prebendary of the Prebend of Cantlowes alias Kentishe Towne alias Cantelers," with Edward, Bishop of London, and the Dean and Chapter of St. Paul's, granted to King Henry VIII, the said Prebend.

Whatever the significance of this grant, the manor certainly remained in the ownership of succeeding prebendaries, and was leased by them for lives. The holding of the Courts Leet and Courts Baron, however, was sometimes kept in their own hands by the prebendaries. The manor house of Cantlowes stood on the east side of the King's Road, where that thoroughfare is now crossed by the railway, near Randolph Street. It was described in 1649 (on the Commonwealth Survey) as consisting of a little courtyard, a porch entry, hall, parlour, kitchen, milk house, a little yard, a brushing room, two pairs of stairs, two little rooms next the parlour, built with timber, an orchard, a fair garden with a brick wall on the south, a base yard, barn and two stables, cart house and little pingle, containing 3 acres 1 rood, then leased to Richard Gualter at £16 a year, together with fields which extended over the land now bounded by King's Road, Kentish Town Road, High Street, Camden Town, and Crowndale Road. The total area of the demesne lands was 213 acres. The lessee had to provide meat, drink and entertainment for one dinner for the steward, bailiff and three or four friends, and feed for their horses. This would be on the occasion of their holding manor courts. The Prebendary was entitled to the first crop of three acres of meadow.[9]

The four villeins in Cantlowes mentioned in Domesday Book were predecessors of the copyhold tenants who afterwards held all the land within the manor from the parish boundary on the north to the freehold land on the south, that is, near Leighton Road. Inheritance in the manor was by gavelkind, that is to say if a copyholder died intestate his land did not descend to his eldest son but to all his sons equally (if he had more than one), and in the absence of a son to all the daughters equally. If two or more persons holding copyhold wished to have it divided up amongst them so that each owned his own portion separately, a committee of the copyholders would divide it up into parts of equal value and lots would be cast to determine the ownership of each.

3

THE VILLAGE OF HIGHGATE

The historical notes in this volume do not claim to constitute a History of Highgate, but contain as many authenticated facts as possible concerning the buildings described and the sites on which they stand. A complete history would require the inclusion of the portion of Highgate lying in Hornsey, which is outside the County of London and is therefore beyond the scope of the Survey. These notes will be found to throw an interesting light on the families and personalities connected with the village. The human element is brought out in many entries in the Court Leet records, of which a few specimens may be selected as follows : In 1658 William Mollineux, Henry Lee, Rodigon Portman and others were each fined 20s. for selling ale in black pots being less than measure appointed by the statute, while others were fined for selling ale and beer without a licence. An alehouse keeper named John Buckland was fined 40s. for allowing unlawful gaming in his yard, namely play at " cloythcailes " otherwise Nine Pins. The churchwardens and constable were each fined 10s. because they had failed to give notice in church, on the Sunday after Easter, of days fixed for parishioners to " endeavour themselves to the amending of the highways." At the same court a disturbance was caused by William Peirce of Kentish Town who abused the jury for fining him and " made a great noise by talking aloud about unnecessary things," so that it was impossible for the steward and jury to hear each other speak and the business was interrupted. " Although the steward did then in a friendly manner admonish the said William Pierce " he persisted and was fined 40s. for his " uncivil gestures, scoffing, clamorous and impertinent speech," the said sum being " far less than his demerits required." In 1668 it was found that the inhabitants were wanting a Pair of Shooting Butts and that the Stocks at Highgate were decayed. In 1673 Sir Thomas Hooke (of Cromwell House) was fined for allowing his drain to run in the highway in a ditch belonging to the manor of Cantlowes, to the common nuisance. In this year also, the Pound at Highgate was found to be decayed. The parish officers in 1701 were each fined 20s. for not erecting and repairing a pair of stocks and a ducking stool. The proprietors of the Hampstead Waterworks were also fined £10 for allowing their water pipes to leak on to the highway.

Highgate Grammar School, founded by Sir Roger Cholmeley, was situated in Hornsey (outside the parish of St. Pancras and the County of London), and its site is not within the area covered by this volume. It is, however, intimately connected with the inhabitants of Highgate, and has an important bearing on its ecclesiastical history. Old Highgate was never a parish, although the chapel belonging to Sir Roger Cholmeley's Free School developed into what virtually served as a chapel of ease for both Hornsey and St. Pancras, and the school itself declined to the status of an elementary school attached to the chapel. Their relative positions were reversed through a successful agitation which led to the judgment in the Court of Chancery in 1826 which declared that it was not a chapel of ease and that the public had no right there. Henceforth the endowment was restored to its original purpose and Sir Roger's foundation developed into a great public school,

4

while the formation of a District Chapelry by Order in Council and the erection of St. Michael's Church in 1832 provided for the spiritual needs of Highgate. Although it was not a civil or ecclesiastical entity the village was a little community with a life of its own, which, indeed, in some measure it yet retains, despite its being merged in the surrounding urban area. Until the erection of St. Michael's Church, burials took place in the chapel and in its burial ground, and the chapel possessed its own registers.

Sir Roger Cholmeley, formerly Lord Chief Justice of the King's Bench, is the historical personage whose name is best known in Highgate. He founded the " Free Grammar School of Sir Roger Cholmeley, knight " in 1565, and was buried at St. Martin's, Ludgate Hill, on 2nd July in the same year. It is disappointing that the court rolls for that period are not available to determine the exact site of his house. It will be seen from the historical notes that Cholmeley owned land at the north end of Waterlow Park, as well as the site of Holly Terrace and the former Holly Lodge estate, together with land now included in the grounds of Witanhurst. He also owned property on the Hornsey side of the High Street (including Townsends Yard) and at Crouch End. We are, therefore, left to surmise the exact location of his house. The relevant facts are too numerous to work out here, but it may be tentatively placed on the site of Fairseat, or thereabouts. Jasper Cholmeley, esquire, of Worcestershire, J.P., and Quorum of Middlesex, Clerk of the Writs, to whom Sir Roger appears to have bequeathed his Highgate property, and who died on 31st October, 1586, aged 48, mentions in his will[10] a tenement which he purchased of John Martyn "*next my orchard*" (see p. 90). If this means next the orchard attached to his residence, it is fairly certain that he lived in the house containing 15 hearths, occupied in 1665 by Major Gunstone, represented to-day by Fairseat.

Cholmeley

Finally, a note on the object and scope of this Survey may be of assistance to our readers. When originally started in 1894 its object was to draw attention to the architectural and historical monuments of bygone generations primarily with a view to arousing a desire for their preservation. The scope of the Survey was limited roughly to monuments dating up to the end of the 18th century that were still standing in the year 1894. The volumes were therefore in the nature of a register, with brief historical notes on the more important buildings. With the closer co-operation of the London County Council the historical side of the work has developed far beyond the dreams of the original founders. In the present volume rather more has been said about the 19th century than is usually the case, but no attempt has been made to deal with that period exhaustively. Much more can be found in the pages of Mr. John H. Lloyd's *History* and in the Heal and Potter Collections.

REFERENCES.

1. P.R.O., S.C. 11/50.
2. Brit. Mus. Add. MSS. 42,294.
3. P.R.O., E.320. L.24.
4. Will of William Cholmeley. P.C.C. 9 Crane.
5. P.R.O., C.54/3545 (no. 38).
6. P.R.O., C.54/3815 (no. 4).
7. P.R.O., C66.2967 (no. 7).
8. P.R.O., E322/48.
9. Eccles. Com. 243,155.
10. Will of Jasper Cholmeley. P.C.C. 17 Rutland.

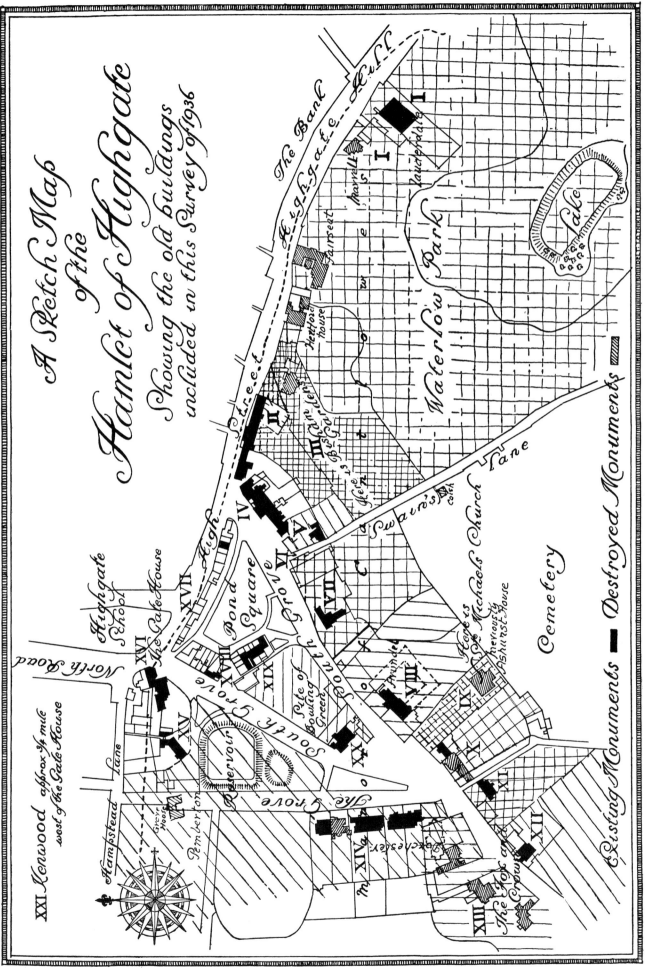

A Sketch Map
of the
Hamlet of Highgate

Showing the old buildings
included in this Survey of 1936

The Bank

Highgate — Hill

I

I

Harvells

Fairseat

Waterlow Park

Lake

Hertford House

Street

II

The Gardens

St Michael's Church Lane

Swain's

High

IV

V

VI

Grove

VII

Hope's

St Michael's Church Lane

VIII

Pond Square

South Grove

Site of Bowling Green

previously Ashurst House

Cemetery

Highgate School

The Gate House

XVII

XVI

Grove

XIX

North Road

Hampstead Lane

Pemberton Row

Reservoir

XV

Grove House

The Grove

XX

X

IX

III

XI

XIV

Hillcrescent

XIII

The Crown and

XII

Existing Monuments ▬ Destroyed Monuments ▨

XXI Kenwood approx ¾ mile
west of the Gate House

This plan does not attempt to represent Highgate at any particular date. The roman numerals correspond to those of the respective sections of the book.

I—LAUDERDALE HOUSE AND WATERLOW PARK

Ground Landlord.

The property was formerly copyhold of the Manor of Cantlowes, but was enfranchised in 1856, and is now in the ownership of the London County Council.

General Description and Date of Structure.

That a house of some size occupied this site in the latter years of the 16th century is certain, and the names connected with it will be found in the historical notes that follow. Although very much altered it is easy to recognise a large part of the fabric of the original building, but it is impossible to determine its first plan. The entrance is now in a range facing Highgate Hill and looking north-east, and the basement walls here are built of two-inch bricks in English bond, and are undisturbed. At right angles is a long range facing south-east, looking over the gardens. It is of two storeys, the upper projecting beyond the lower, and the oak timbers of the roof are in good preservation. It is probable that this was the " long gallery " of the Elizabethan house, and in its lower external wall is still to be seen a good oak doorway of the period with stop-moulded frame and square head. This doorway now frames a modern inscription recording the gift of the house to the London County Council. It is not certain that the doorway is in its original position. A later wing facing south-west, with the upper storey carried on columns, balances that to the north-east, and gives the house the appearance of having been a half H plan, but a basement (not now built over) on the north-west side may indicate that the house was originally quadrangular or open on the south-west, instead of, as now, the north-west side. The long ground-floor room looking to the south-east is now panelled, partly with panels found *in situ*, and partly with similar wainscot found in other parts of the house. It is all of late 16th-century type: small panels, moulded styles with butt joints, and chamfered and moulded rails. In the internal wall is a four-centred arched doorway, within a square moulded frame of Elizabethan date, the spandrels on one side being carved with a simple strap-work design (Plate 9).

The house must have been largely altered by John Maitland, 2nd Earl and 1st Duke of Lauderdale, in the time of Charles II. The fine stair in the angle between the north-east and south-east ranges is of this date, and may have taken the place of an Elizabethan stair in the same position. It is of sturdy dimensions with panelled strings. The moulded handrail mitres over the newels excepting the two upper ones which have slightly shaped caps. The balusters are of twisted pattern. Several of the original doors remain on the stair and the one by which the hall is entered has an arched frame with semicircular head. This appears to have been adapted either at this or a slightly later period from a replica of another doorway in the hall, which has radiating panels in the upper half dating from the first half of the 17th century.

The staircase is lit by an elaborate and beautifully designed lantern

7

light, octagonal in plan, its vertical sides being formed of eight panels with enriched bolection mouldings of bold proportions. The junction with the ceiling is marked by a plaster cove, enclosed in mouldings and filled with excellently modelled fruit and flower in high relief (Plates 10 to 12). The cornice has a carved egg-and-tongue enrichment without an upper fillet. The light itself is a simple but effective octagonal cone on a low drum of 18th-century ironwork.

It is probable that the original hall of the house was either in the destroyed north-west range or in the position of the present entrance hall, since the overhang of the south-east range precludes the possibility of its being placed there. The entrance hall is panelled with large panels of 17th- or 18th-century type, some being fielded. At the north-west end is an elaborate recess, finely carried out in carved and panelled oak (Plates 6 and 7). The external frame is formed by two fluted pilasters with Corinthian capitals supporting an entablature, the cornice of which is mainly composed of a large cavetto covered with carved ornament. The architecture is also enriched, and each member breaks round the projecting blocks above the pilasters, and a key block, in the centre, with carved soffit. The interior of the recess is occupied at dado height by a shaped and moulded shelf of Sicilian marble, and in the floor below is evidence of a drain. The recess is lined with marble below the shelf, and above by panelling between a centre pilaster, twin angle pilasters, and two more, one at each edge of the reveals. The ceiling of the recess is higher than that of the room, and an entablature, similar to that of the outer frame, and equally enriched, is carried round at the higher level. One of the capitals (shown on the left in the section, Plate 6) has been made up from a small carved drum. The whole recess is beautifully finished and was probably designed as an elaborate sideboard, when the room was used as a dining-hall. It is possible that the panels at the back were at one time made to open, in which case it would have been used as a serving hatch to the kitchen to the north. In the late 18th century the house underwent further changes. The two columns of Greek Ionic type, now in the entrance hall, are balanced by a pair of similar columns at the junction of the south-east and south-west wings, and it would seem that the whole garden range on the ground floor was converted into a long apartment, with pairs of columns at either end of the internal wall. The upper storey was at the same time prolonged over a colonnaded loggia on the south-west, the windows were replaced by sashes of the period, and the roofs were furnished with pediments. The details of the doors, windows and shutters inserted at this time are characteristic of the very end of the 18th and the beginning of the 19th century. To this period no doubt can be ascribed the classical scene of Briseis being led away from Achilles, executed in plaster, which fills the space over the fireplace in the entrance hall.

The entrance has a porch supported by two columns of the Doric order with full entablature, and the gates on Highgate Hill are of wrought iron hung to brick piers. In the garden to the south-west of the house is a brick wall, having a recess with four-centred arched head; and to the south-east are

8

some 18th-century wrought-iron gates hung to brick and stone piers with well-carved stone vases as finials (Plate 12).

The building was taken over by the London County Council in 1889, and put into good repair. A low modern range that closed the north-west side was taken down, and with it an unimportant veranda, which had been inserted to prolong the loggia on the south-west. Careful plans were made at the time, and alterations to the interior and its panelling and fittings are fully recorded. The entrance hall is now a shelter for the public using Waterlow Park. The long ground-floor space on the south-east is used as a refreshment room and the upper floors give residential accommodation for the Council's staff.

CONDITION OF REPAIR.
    Good.

HISTORICAL NOTES.
    Waterlow Park is formed from the grounds attached to three houses, Lauderdale House, Fairseat, and Hertford House, the last mentioned being taken down by the London County Council after Waterlow Park was presented to them in 1889. The donor, Sir Sidney Hedley Waterlow, was Lord Mayor of London in 1872-3, and died on 3rd August, 1906.
    When Sir Roger Cholmeley founded his Free Grammar School at Highgate in 1565, Roger Martin, esquire (afterwards Sir Roger, Lord Mayor in 1557-8), was appointed one of the foundation governors. He died on 24th December, 1573, and his brother, John Martin, citizen and haberdasher of London, was elected a governor on 23rd February, 1578,* in place of Alderman Sir John Langley. John Martin[1] and Margery his wife, on 1st February, 1582, surrendered to Jasper Cholmeley and Margaret his wife a tenement and garden in Highgate, late in the tenure of Robert Dickins, deceased, and then (1582) of Richard Goatley, carpenter, between the tenement of widow Sell on the south, and the garden of Jasper Cholmeley, gentleman, on the north, with a way along the pale of Jasper Cholmeley near the tenement, by and across 15 acres of land of Edward Stafford, esquire (held in right of his wife), to the spring in Pond Field, part of the said 15 acres, called the Conduit Head, four feet wide, with the right to take water to the said tenement in leaden pipes. Jasper Cholmeley is described in the will of Sir Roger Cholmeley as his " servant " (i.e. clerk), and Sir Roger bequeathed to him the manor of Renters in Hendon and other lands. As will be shown on pp. 19 and 24, the land northward of Lauderdale Park belonged, in fact, to Sir Roger Cholmeley, and we may guess, although it is no more than a guess, that the tenement thus conveyed to Jasper Cholmeley formed part of the present Waterlow Park. Moreover it is possible that this was the tenement on which John Martin gave a rent-charge of 20s. per annum to the Grammar School. This bequest was invalid in law and Jasper Cholmeley replaced it by a charge on his manor of Renters, in Hendon.
    The earliest occupier of " Lauderdale House," or rather the site on which it stands, so far identified in the court rolls, was Richard Martin, citizen and goldsmith of London, son of Sir Richard Martin (Lord Mayor, 1589 and 1594). He married as his second wife Anne, sister of Sir William Bond (see below). The successive owners thereafter were as follows :

c. 1589-99.   John Povey of Barnards Inn, whose wife was Anne, daughter of John Trott of Colney Hatch, draper. He probably lived here before 1599, since on 27th December, 1589, he had been elected a Governor of the Grammar School in place of Owen Lloyd, one of the foundation governors, who had died in France. His father, John Povey, citizen and embroiderer of London, had six daughters[2] by his first wife, Alice (who died 17th October, 1553), and 14 sons and four daughters by his second wife, Elizabeth (who died 20th June, 1594). John Povey (the son) died in June, 1599, leaving the estate to his only child, Katherine, the wife of William Bond. To the Grammar School he bequeathed 20 nobles towards furnishing a library.[3]

    * New style has been adopted throughout unless two years are shewn.

THE VILLAGE OF HIGHGATE

1599-1617.   William Bond, who held in right of his wife, Katherine, was knighted on 23rd July, 1603, and nominated Alderman of Farringdon Ward on 22nd August, 1605. Refusing at first to serve, he was committed to Newgate " til he conform himself." In 1611 he added 10 acres of pasture to the gardens of Lauderdale House, which he bought from the sons of Frances Southcote, widow of Robert Southcote. He was the son of Sir George Bond (Lord Mayor, 1587) and brother of Richard Martin's wife, Anne. The genealogical table (p. 145) shows these family relationships.

On 22nd June, 1610, Lady Arabella Stuart, cousin of King James I (and, failing heirs of James, the next in succession to the throne), married Sir William Seymour, grandson of the Earl of Hertford. The king had forbidden this alliance, which might have produced claimants to the throne, on grounds of royal descent, and, when he heard of it, instantly committed her to the custody of the Bishop of Durham, and sent Seymour to the Tower. In March, 1611, her journey with the Bishop to Durham had to commence. On the 14th of that month she wrote[4] to the Privy Council, protesting that she was so weak that even a journey to a place agreeable to her would be the cause of her death, and asking for time to recover her strength. Her request was not granted, and the Lords of the Council sent a letter addressed to Sir William Bond at Highgate, asking him to lend a couple of rooms for her in his house for a night, since she would not be able to reach Barnet, where she was to stay. She arrived at Sir William Bond's house on the 15th, and the Bishop reported[5] to the Council that when taken out of her litter between ten and eleven o'clock, she was very faint and " as wet as if she had been taken out of the Thames." On the advice of the doctor she remained in bed the next day. The Bishop said that he himself was somewhat distempered, but he understood that Sir William Bond " had a very especial care both of her and of such as were about her." No doubt the lady was ill, but she evidently gave the worthy bishop a great amount of trouble, and when the Council sent Sir James Croft to help him, he wrote : " I humbly thank God, his Majesty and your Lordships for sending my ancient Oxford acquaintance Sir Croft to free me and my men." Lady Arabella remained at Highgate for six nights, removing to an inn at Barnet on 21st March, and arriving there between four and five o'clock. In reporting their arrival the Bishop added a postscript to his letter as follows : " May it please your Lordships to take notice (as in my former I made bold to acquaint your Lordships) of the kind usage which Sir William Bond and his lady gave to the honourable Lady and her followers, even to the last hour of their departure." Lady Arabella at this time was 35 years of age, but her husband was only 22 ; he died, as Duke of Somerset, in 1660. The fate of his wife was less happy. After staying at an inn at Barnet for 11 days she was moved to the house of Thomas Conyers, esquire, at East Barnet, on 1st April, when the Bishop went north to Durham. On 3rd June she escaped from East Barnet and got on board ship, but was captured, and died in the Tower on 25th September, 1615, having lost her reason.

The following record[6] of expenses incurred by the government during her stay at Highgate is interesting :

> " For diet at Highgate for 6 days from 15th to 21st March, 1611, £18 5s. 3d.
> For the stable at Highgate for 6 days £9 17s. 10d.
> For lodging some of the retinue of Lady Arabella and the Bishop at Highgate 20s.
> For divers persons who took pains at Highgate £7 12s. 6d."

Dr. Thomas Moundford, the physician, received 30s. a day, and there were also, of course, riding and posting charges and the servants' wages.

1617-25.   Sir William Bond died at Conquett, in Brittany, in 1617, and his widow, Dame Catherine Bond, held the property. At the time of her death the eldest son, John Bond, was of age, but his brothers, Thomas and Richard, were under age. In accordance with the custom of the Manor of Cantlowes, which, like that of the adjoining Manor of Hornsey, was gavelkind, the three sons were admitted as tenants in common, and John Bond immediately sold his third share to Sir Henry Hobart (who died in 1625), but his brothers retained their shares until 1632.

1625-32.   The estate conveyed to Sir Henry Hobart of Blickling, Norfolk, knight and baronet, Lord Chief Justice of the Court of Common Pleas, was described as " a messuage, garden, etc., in Highgate, and 26 acres of land, formerly in the occupation of Richard Martyn, junior, citizen and goldsmith of London, afterwards of John Povey and late of Sir William Bonde and Dame Catherine his wife, and two tenements and garden plots formerly in the several tenures of John Mundaie and William Ridgewaie, then of Alice Sell, widow, and Thomas Gillett, and afterwards of Richard Rockwell and Lewis Hughes; and ten acres of meadow. . . ." It will be observed that "widow Sell" was mentioned in the conveyance of 1582, cited previously. In a pamphlet published in 1636, John Taylor, the "water poet," mentions "at Highgate, at the Mermayd, Mary Sell," but the Mermaid was on the opposite side of the road, in Hornsey, and widow Sell is mentioned as there in 1645.

In his will,[7] dated 20th July, 1625 (proved 7th March, 1626), Sir Henry Hobart mentions that he had bought the third part of his house from John Bond, esquire, and that the legal formalities in connection with the purchase had not been completed. His wife was Dorothy, daughter of Sir Robert Bell, Chief Baron of the Exchequer, who probably continued to reside at Highgate after her husband's death. In his *History of Highgate*, Mr. Lloyd has printed a letter addressed to her at Highgate on 28th February, 1626-7, by Richard Glover from the town house of the Hobarts in the parish of St. Bartholomew's, Smithfield. He seems to have been one of the lawyer-clerks of Sir Henry Hobart, and was one of the four trustees admitted at the manor court to the estate surrendered by John Bond. In the letter he tells her "S^r — Richardson was this day sworne Chiefe Justice of the Comon Pleas: my Lord Keeper in his Speech told him that he was now to succeed one in the place who was as noble just upright honest and worthy a Judge & as patient hearer as ever satt in that place [i.e. her late husband] and therefore he had a good example to follow w^h many other good speeches." There are three entries in the Register of Highgate Chapel concerning the Hobart family: On 27th September, 1636, Nathaniel, son of Sir Nathaniel Hobart (son of Sir Henry) and Anne his wife, was baptised. On 17th March, 1633-4, the Hon. Lady Elizabeth Lisle, wife of John de Lisle, daughter of Sir Henry Hobart, was buried. On 13th April, 1667, Elizabeth, daughter of Sir Nathaniel, was buried. Sir Henry Hobart, from whom the Earls of Buckinghamshire are descended, died on 26th December, 1625.

Hobart

1632-41.   On 3rd June, 1632, Thomas Bond and Richard Bond conveyed their respective third-shares to William Geere of All Hallows, Honey Lane, citizen and draper of London, and Sara his wife, who acquired the remaining third in 1638 from the trustees of the Hobart family. He was sometimes called "Captain William Geere," being, no doubt, a captain in the City Train Bands, and is referred to as Captain William Geere in subsequent proceedings under the Commonwealth. He had two daughters,[8] Sara, baptised on 16th March, 1619-20, at All Hallows, and Mary, baptised there on 7th September, 1623. Sara married on 22nd March, 1640-1, Thomas Howe of Gray's Inn, gentleman, then aged 26, the son of Thomas Howe of South Ockendon, Essex, esquire. Her sister, Mary, married Sir Robert Payne of Barton Stacey, Hants, who lived at Arundel House (p. 50). Their father appears to have been married twice, since they are referred to as half-sisters[75]. Whether the transaction next recorded should be regarded as a sale of the house or a mortgage appears debatable.

1641-4.   By deed dated 10th June, 1641, Mary, widow of Alexander, 1st Earl of Home, eldest daughter of Edward Sutton (alias Dudley), 9th Lord Dudley, agreed with William Geere to pay down £1,000 and another £700 by instalments. If she paid £1,700 the property was to become hers absolutely, but she had the option of giving him a year's notice to repay her £1,700, the property then reverting to him. She died in September, 1644, at St. Botolph's, Aldersgate, leaving two daughters, Anne, Countess of Lauderdale, and Margaret, Countess of Murray.

Maitland Earl of Lauderdale

1644-51.   We now come to the occupants whose name has become permanently attached to the house. Anne, Countess of Lauderdale, was the first wife of John Maitland, 2nd Earl of Lauderdale, who was born on 14th May, 1616, and succeeded his father as 2nd Earl in 1645. Fighting on behalf of King Charles I in the civil war, he was taken prisoner at the battle of Worcester in 1651, and imprisoned in the Tower for nine years, until the restoration of Charles II. On 17th May, 1649, John Ireton, Sheriff of London, obtained a lease of the premises from the

11

Earl of Lauderdale and Anne, his wife. On 5th September of the same year he laid information[9] that the Earl of Lauderdale, a " delinquent," had an estate real and personal at Highgate, and Captain William Geere had money and goods in his hand due to the said Earl. Consequently the property was " sequestrated " by the Commonwealth government. After considerable argument it was decided [10] that the lands had been mortgaged to the Countess of Home by William Geere for £1,700, and if he repaid this sum to the government the sequestration would be discharged. He paid the money to the Treasury and the sequestration was discharged on 4th February, 1652. Therefore he was sole owner of the unencumbered estate. The money was handed over to John Ireton, who (as appears from a later recital on the court rolls of the manor) bought the estate from William and Robert, sons of William Geere, but the date of his purchase is not mentioned.

Ireton

1652-60.　　　There is very little doubt that John Ireton lived in the house until the Restoration. He was a son of German Ireton, and was baptised on 17th October, 1615. He became an alderman of Bread Street Ward on 16th September, 1651, M.P. for London in 1653, Master of the Clothworkers' Company in 1652, and a Governor of Sir Roger Cholmeley's Free School at Highgate on 14th June, 1656. In the register of the Chapel it is recorded that on 10th August, 1655, was buried a still-born child of Alderman Ireton. Ireton was Lord Mayor of London in 1658-9. On 1st May, 1660, a few days before the restoration of the monarchy, he conveyed the house to Sir Edward Ford. John Ireton appears to have been confused by some writers on local history with his more celebrated brother, Henry Ireton, who married Bridget, the daughter of Oliver Cromwell, and died at the age of 40 in 1651. John Ireton was excepted from the Act of Indemnity, but not as to life. He died in 1690.

1660-71.　　　On 30th July, 1660, John, Earl of Lauderdale, on behalf of his wife, daughter of the Countess of Home, petitioned the House of Lords to be restored to the possession of the property alleged to have been " taken possession of in 1649, by John Ireton, Alderman of London, who as Lord of the Manor would not permit Lady Lauderdaill to proceed in claiming her property, but tore up her plaint, saying ' Her husband was a traitor to the State, and should have no lands there.' . . . In 1651 Alderman John Ireton, pretending that the lands in Highgate belonged to the petitioner, who for his loyalty was then deemed a delinquent, obtained a grant of them from the Usurper, and has ever since enjoyed the same."[11] On 12th July Sir Edward Ford had been admitted at the manor court on the surrender of John Ireton, and the first step towards reversing this entry was to verify the previous records showing the admission of Lady Lauderdale's mother, in 1641, and the admissions of her daughter after her death, in 1648. Here a difficulty arose because the original rolls had disappeared during the confusion of the civil war, when the manor of the Prebendary of Cantlowes had been sold by the Commonwealth to Richard Utber, draper, and the Prebendary on resuming possession had not recovered all the rolls. The lawyers duly produced the copies held by the Earl, and these were accepted by the manor court and enrolled for record in 1662. One of these original rolls, that for 1648, is in the possession of Frank Marcham. The assessment for the hearth tax dated 1665 shows the Earl of Lauderdale rated for 26 hearths, and the same in 1674. There is an interesting entry under date 28th July, 1666, in Pepys' *Diary*,* describing how he drove out to Highgate with Lord Brouncker to visit Lauderdale at his Highgate house. He heard there some Scotch airs for the first time, and does not seem to have been much impressed by them.

---

*" Thence with my Lord (Brouncker) to his coachhouse and there put in his six horses into his coach, and he and I alone to Highgate. . . . Being come thither we went to my Lord Lauderdale's house to speake with him about getting a man at Leith to joyne with one we employ to buy some prize goods for the King ; we find (him) and his lady and some Scotch people at supper. Pretty odd company ; though my Lord Bruncker tells me, my Lord Lauderdale is a man of mighty good reason and judgement. But at supper there played one of their servants upon the viallin some Scotch tunes only ; several, and the best of their country, as they seemed to esteem them, by their praising and admiring them ; but, Lord ! the strangest ayre that ever I heard in my life, and all of one cast. But strange to hear my Lord Lauderdale say himself, that he had rather hear a cat mew, than the best musique in the world ; and the better the musique, the more sicke it makes him ; and that of all instruments, he hates the lute most, and next to that, the baggpipe."

12

SIR WILLIAM PRITCHARD

On 11th October, 1669, Mr. Graham, servant to the Earl of Lauderdale, was buried at Highgate. The Earl was made Secretary of State for Scotland, had a seat in the famous Cabal Ministry, was created Duke of Lauderdale in 1672 and died at Tunbridge Wells on 20th August, 1682, worn out by debaucheries and the anxieties of constant intrigue. His character and career are too well known for detail here. The Countess Anne died at Paris in 1671, when her only daughter, Mary, succeeded.

1671-7.   There is no doubt that the Earl of Lauderdale possessed Lauderdale House in right of his wife as long as he lived, but some elaborate legal transactions were carried through after her death with the evident intention of getting a clear title for a purchaser. The beneficial owner, Mary, wife of the Right Hon. John Hay, Lord Hay of Yester, only daughter of Anne, late Countess of Lauderdale, surrendered to " Jerman " Ireton in 1674, and he mortgaged the estate in 1675 to John Sympson of the Inner Temple, for £618, when it was described as formerly the inheritance of William Geere, Michael Geere and Robert Geere, sons of William Geere. Then Margaret, Countess Dowager of Murray (aunt of the above Mary), released her right to " Jermin " Ireton, in 1677. In 1674, Sir Edward Ford being then dead, his daughter and sole heiress, Catherine, and her husband, the Hon. Ralph Gray, esquire, had surrendered to " Jermin " Ireton of Gray's Inn. Thus " Jermin " Ireton had become possessed of all possible rights in the estate. He was the son of John Ireton, and the two, father and son, conveyed it in 1677 to William Mead, citizen and merchant tailor of London.

1677-88.   In 1680 William Mead sold the house to John Hinde, citizen and draper of London, for £2,000. Five years later John Hinde also bought the house then on the site of Witanhurst (p. 72), but was declared bankrupt in 1686. The trustees in bankruptcy held Lauderdale House until 1688, when they sold it to Sir William Pritchard.

1688-1705.   Like William Mead, Sir William Pritchard was a member of the Merchant Taylors' Company. He was elected alderman of Bread Street Ward on 27th June, 1672, became Lord Mayor in 1682-3, and was elected M.P. for London in 1685-7, 1690-5, and 1702-5. In 1695 and 1701 he was an unsuccessful candidate for Parliament. He was arrested at Grocers' Hall and detained six hours in 1684 by the Whig Sheriffs, against one of whom, Papillon, he subsequently obtained at a trial before Judge Jeffreys, " to the amazement of all," £10,000 damages, which, however, he released in 1688, when he drank his opponent's health. He was displaced as alderman in August, 1687, with Turner and four others, for " opposing the address for liberty of conscience," but on 4th October, 1688, was placed in the chair when the Lord Chancellor attended for the restitution of the Old Charter of the City. He lived in stirring times and took an active part in current politics. That he was highly esteemed by the Merchant Taylors' Company is shown by their paying £125 to Sir Godfrey Kneller in 1687 to paint his portrait and that of Sir William Turner, to hang up in their Hall. At Great Linford, Bucks, where he was buried with great ceremony, is the following monumental inscription : " In the Vault underneath lies interr'd the Body of Sr. William Pritchard, kt. and Alderman and some time since Lord Mayor of London. A most excellent Magistrate of exemplary Virtue and goodness. He was one of the City's Representatives in sevl Parliaments and President of St. Bartholomew's Hospitall where he erected a convenient apartment for cutting of the stone. And built & endowed a School house and Six Alms Houses in this Parish. Hee departed this life the 18 Feby. 1704 in ye 74th year of his age."[12]

Sir William Pritchard, who appears to have been the last owner-occupier of the house, married Sarah, a daughter of Francis Cooke of Kingsthorpe, Northants, who in her will, dated 26th April, 1707, bequeathed £800 to various charities of which about £22 10s. is disbursed yearly to ten poor maids of the hamlet of Highgate, or to widows if no old maids can be found.

1705-19.   Richard Uthwatt and Daniel King, nephews of Sir William Pritchard, next owned the house, in accordance with the terms of his will.[13] At this time the occupier was Edward Pauncefort, esquire, a civil servant, of whom it is mentioned that the plate of Highgate

Chapel was double gilt at his expense in 1705. He was elected a Governor of the Grammar School on 29th March, 1712. In 1718 he was Joint Cashier of the Excise, and afterwards Treasurer of the Revenue of the Excise, Yeoman of the Jewel Office, etc. His wife, Rebecca, daughter of Sir Samuel Moyer, Bart., died on 2nd November, 1719, aged 42. In his will[14] he directed his executors to buy out of his personal estate, lands of the clear yearly value of £60, to hold them in trust to pay £30 a year to the six poor widows living in the almshouses lately erected by him at Highgate (still standing in Southwood Lane), and to pay £10 a year to the Reader of Highgate Chapel, and to pay the residue to the Charity School for Girls at Highgate lately built at his charge. His executor, Mr. Robert Pauncefort, in July, 1751, paid £1,500 in discharge of this legacy. The almshouses founded by Sir John Wollaston and Pauncefort and the Girls' Charity School, form one uniform building, the whole of which was erected by Mr. Pauncefort, he having rebuilt the six old almshouses on the same plan with the six new ones of his foundation.[15] He also gave by will to the Sons of the Clergy Corporation as much money as would buy lands of the clear yearly value of £100, and declared such purchase should be in full satisfaction of £2,000 bequeathed to them by his late wife's will.[16] He died on 4th July, 1726. In St. Michael's Church is the monument (removed from Highgate Chapel) which he set up to the memory of his wife (see p. 57).

1719-54.   Richard Uthwatt died in December, 1719, aged 61, and was succeeded by his second son, Thomas Uthwatt (the elder son John having died in 1712). " This polite and accomplished gentleman, who had travelled through France and Italy, and had been High Sheriff for this county, having been at times disordered in his mind, cut his own throat, and died a few hours after, at his own house in this parish [i.e. Linford, Bucks]. He left an only daughter behind him the wife of Matthew Knapp of Little Linford, esquire."[17] He was buried on 8th August, 1754. The names of the lessees and occupiers at this time have not all been recovered, but we find that in 1752 the lease of Lauderdale House was assigned by Sir Thomas Burnett, Judge of the Common Pleas, to William Allix of Tower Hill.[18]

1754-7.   Thomas Uthwatt was succeeded by his nephew, Henry Uthwatt, esquire, of Lathbury, Bucks, son of his brother Richard. He married on 12th June, 1750, Frances, daughter of Sir John Chester, Bart., of Chicheley, and died in London of consumption on 22nd December, 1757, aged 26. The lease of the house was assigned in 1756 by Martha Draper of Highgate, spinster, and Edward Wharton of St. Paul's, Covent Garden, to Ann Crastayne, it being then described as a capital messuage in Highgate, formerly in the possession of Edward Pauncefort, and then of Edward Price and Matthew Langley. The last named was elected a Governor of the Grammar School on 9th February, 1746-7. In the Register of the Chapel is recorded on 18th November, 1752, the birth of Thomas, son of Mr. Matthew and Mrs. Elizabeth Langley of St. Pancras, oilman, followed by a record of the infant's burial on 30th November. Matthew Langley died on 9th June, 1758.

1757-94.   Henry Uthwatt having died without issue, the property came to the daughter of his uncle, Thomas Uthwatt (d. 1754) mentioned above, because there was no male heir of the Uthwatt family. She was Catherine, wife of Matthew Knapp (Sheriff of Bucks in 1767), whom she had married in June, 1750. Her husband, who was born in 1728, died in 1782, aged 54.[19] Like her father, she was of unsound mind, and her affairs were managed by her two daughters, Sophia and Harriett, until her death on 15th February, 1794. They were living at Portugal Street, Hanover Square, in 1788, when they had licence to lease the house to Thomas Woodroffe Smith of Great St. Helen's, merchant, for 21 years, the late occupier being mentioned as John Cobb.

1794-5.   Sophia Knapp succeeded under her mother's will. According to the Land Tax Assessments, Messrs. Kirton and Sheldon were occupiers from 1794 to 1808, Petrie and Scott from 1809-10, it being empty in 1811. William Gittens kept a school there for many years after 1812. In 1795 Miss Knapp died.

1795-1841.   Harriett Knapp, sister of Sophia, succeeded. She was born on 3rd February, 1760, and died on 7th January, 1841. In 1830 she had licence to lease to William Gittins for 21 years, evidently a renewal of his previous lease.

Knapp

1841-89.   On the death of Miss Harriett Knapp in her 80th year the estate passed to her coheirs, John Leonard Knapp (1767-1845), and Matthew and John, the two sons of his brother, the Rev. Primatt Knapp (1764-1838), (Harriett Knapp's uncle, Primatt Knapp, was the father of John Leonard Knapp and the Rev. Primatt Knapp). John, mentioned above as brother of Matthew, appears as John Knapp, M.D., of Edinburgh, in 1845, when he sold his fourth-share to his cousin, Arthur John Knapp, son of John Leonard Knapp. At the same time John Leonard Knapp conveyed his two fourth-shares to his son, who thus obtained three fourths; the remaining fourth belonging to Matthew. On 24th June, 1865, Matthew Knapp of Little Linford, and his cousin Arthur John Knapp, conveyed the Lauderdale House estate to Sir Sidney Hedley Waterlow. On 16th December, 1889, Sir Sidney Waterlow presented the estate to the London County Council, together with Hertford House, the site of " Andrew Marvell's Cottage," and his lease of Fairseat, for the benefit of the public for ever.

To continue the story of the lessees, Mr. Gittins gave up his school before the expiration of the lease mentioned above. In 1839 the house was occupied by Mr. Yarrow, as shown by the following extract : " I also found on my first arrival in London a profitable engagement as a literary assistant to Mr. James Yarrow, a retired Unitarian minister, an amiable elderly gentleman, and a rusty old scholar, who had devoted the latter end of his life to the compilation of a work on The Art of Weaving amongst the Ancients, a ponderous work crammed with Greek, Latin and Hebrew quotations, in which the co-operation of an ordinary amanuensis and copyist would have been unavailing. Mr. Yarrow was a wealthy man, or had married a wealthy wife ; the latter, still youngish, made her hospitable home in Highgate, formerly the abode of Charles II's Nell Gwynne, a quaint old mansion, unaltered for two centuries,—the centre of a social circle, where she delighted in bringing together the young of both sexes, trusting to the instincts of natural selection, and the power of music, dancing and champagne suppers for results in which she declared she neither ' marred nor made.' In spite of all disclaimers, the house at Highgate was immensely popular as a matrimonial mart of the most honourable description."[20]

Some time after this Lauderdale House was the home of Richard Bethell, Lord Westbury. He was born at Bradford-on-Avon on 30th June, 1800. At Oxford he graduated when he had just completed his 18th year, taking a first class in classics and second in mathematics. He boasted that from the age of 17 he supported himself entirely by his own exertions, his father, Richard Bethell, M.D., of Bristol, being unable to afford him monetary help. In 1823 he was called to the Bar. In 1840 he became Q.C. He entered Parliament in 1851 and brilliantly promoted many measures of law reform. In 1861 he became Lord Chancellor and Baron Westbury. Of his judgments it is said that our " law reports contain no more perfect examples of precise and lucid statement, of concise reasoning, or of polished English ; and no judge has ever striven more persistently than did Lord Westbury to bring every question to the test of principle, and to restrain within due limits what seemed to him the excessive authority of precedents." He was forced to resign his Chancellorship in 1865, it being found that his lax and inattentive regard to the public interests in the administration of his department had conduced to some irregularities in making appointments to office. He died at his house in London on 20th July, 1873. He married firstly, in 1825, Ellinor Mary, eldest daughter of Robert Abraham, by whom he left seven children, and secondly, on 25th January, 1873, six months before his death, Elinor Margaret, third daughter of Henry Tennant of Cadoxton, Glamorganshire.

The last tenant was James Yates (1789-1871), unitarian and antiquary, who was born in Toxteth Park, Liverpool, on 30th April, 1789. In 1832 he succeeded John Scott Porter as minister of Carter Lane Chapel, Doctors Commons, London. He finally left the ministry, and an account of his many activities and writings will be found in the *Dictionary of National Biography*. At Lauderdale House he had a noble library and a fine collection of works of art. " His hospitality was profuse (though his own habits were of the simplest) and his conversation, aided by his marvellous memory, was full of interest. Few men of small stature had a more courtly dignity ; his power of caustic remark was all the more effective from the unvarying calmness of his measured speech." He died at Lauderdale House on 7th May, 1871, and was buried at Highgate Cemetery on 11th May. He married (about 1820) Dorothea, daughter of John William Crompton of Edgleston, who survived him without issue.

THE VILLAGE OF HIGHGATE

Sir James Pennethorne's House.

From the map of *circa* 1804 (Plate 1) it will be seen that a house and garden numbered 75, with a pond (76) and field (77) formed a portion of what is now Waterlow Park at the beginning of last century. Stephen Dowell had come into occupation of this estate in 1801 and held it until 1810. It was referred to in the conveyance from Sir Sidney Waterlow to the London County Council in 1889 as " a tenement since converted to a messuage called Elms Court (but then pulled down)," and must be identical with a messuage " late in the occupation of Mrs. Catherine Knapp " which her daughter, Sophia Knapp, had licence to lease in 1795 to Meyrick Field of Mill Street, Hanover Square, upholsterer, for 14½ years. The inference is that Mr. Dowell held from or under Mr. Field. According to the land tax assessments Robert Sutton followed Mr. Dowell in 1810, and William Addison, schoolmaster, who tenanted Englefield House from 1821 (see p. 26), moved here some time between 1825 and 1831. Thomas Howe had a lease of it for 21 years from Miss Harriett Knapp in 1830. In the conveyance of 1845 from Dr. John Knapp to his brother, however, this " tenement " is described as " late in the occupation of Dr. Benjamin Duncan, since of Addison and now of Thomas Howe." In 1856 the description is similar, but " *late* of Thomas Howe." This makes Dr. Duncan the predecessor of William Addison, whereas we have Robert Sutton shown from 1810 onwards. Several explanations might be suggested to explain the apparent difficulty of Dr. Duncan and Mr. Sutton appearing simultaneously as occupier, but the point is better left to await the result of further research. Dr. Duncan kept a school between 1816 and 1826 in a house on the site of the present Channing House School, opposite. A print of this school house appears on page 223 of Lloyd's *History of Highgate*, showing also the long building which still stands in front of Betchworth House. The schoolhouse (not the long building) was rightly said by Prickett to have been pulled down in 1825, and wrongly stated by him to have been the " last remaining wing of Arundel House "—to the utter confusion of local history for many years.

The best-known occupant of the house with which we are dealing was Sir James Pennethorne (1801-1871) the architect. He was born at Worcester on 4th June, 1801. He and his brother, John, served their articles with John Nash, whose wife was first cousin to their father, Thomas Pennethorne. James Pennethorne was placed under Augustus Pugin to study Gothic architecture in 1822 and travelled on the Continent from 1824 to 1826. As principal assistant to Nash he directed the West Strand, King William Street and other metropolitan improvements. He planned New Oxford Street, Endell Street, Cranborne Street and Commercial Street, but many of his projects were rejected or cut down by the short-sighted policy of the Government. After 1840 he was wholly employed on public works and designed Victoria Park (1841) and Battersea Park (1846). In 1852 he drew up a scheme for a great park in North London to be called Albert Park, but this was not carried out. His last work was the University of London in Burlington Gardens, Piccadilly. He was knighted in November, 1870, and died suddenly from heart disease on 1st September, 1871, at his residence, Worcester Park, Surrey. He was buried at Highgate.

"Andrew Marvell's Cottage."

Until pulled down in 1868 an old house of Elizabethan character (*see* Plate 13) stood a little to the north of Lauderdale House. Its exact position is now marked by a stone built into the wall fronting the road. This stone is one of the steps which originally led to the garden. The name of Andrew Marvell does not appear on the court rolls, and no documentary evidence has been found to justify the firmly held tradition that he lived there. This must have been the house assessed in the Hearth Tax Rolls in 1662-75 at seven hearths, and occupied by George Pryor, esquire, a London merchant. He acquired the southern portion of the Cholmeley estate (see p. 24) in 1641, when William Cholmeley, esquire, surrendered to him conditionally a messuage in Highgate with a barn, garden, orchard and field of four acres, and a yard adjoining the barn aforesaid, late in the tenure of Whorewood, and a barn and barnyard near adjacent, late in the tenure of Paker. The surrender became absolute in 1647, and the equity of redemption was finally released in 1658 by William Cholmeley, late of Highgate, esquire, only son of Edward Cholmeley, and grandchild and heir of William Cholmeley, late of Highgate, deceased. The estate included the four houses shown in the hearth tax return as occupied by George Pryor, Major Thomas Gunstone, Robert Lea and Paul Sindery (afterwards Mr. Felkin).

16

Dorothy, a daughter of George Pryor, was buried at Highgate on 29th August, 1644. Pryor was elected a Governor of the Grammar School on 5th June, 1658, and lived here until he died at the age of 80.[21] The three daughters of George Pryor were married to three brothers, viz. (1) Mary to Charles Izard of London, (2) Martha to Richard Izard, citizen and grocer of London, and (3) Elizabeth to Ralph Izard of London, grocer. Ralph Izard and Elizabeth had three sons, (1) Ralph Izard, whose wife was Dorothy, afterwards of Charlestown, South Carolina, (2) Benjamin Izard, whose wife was named Elizabeth, also later of Charlestown, and (3) George Izard of London, gentleman. The family was afterwards of considerable note in America. These three sisters had a brother, Charles Pryor of Edmonton, who married Mary, daughter of Jeremiah Richardson and widow of Thomas Hollier, who died on 23rd May, 1700, leaving a son George Pryor. Miss Mary Richardson, after she became Mrs. Pryor, inherited from her father in 1678, property on the opposite side of the road, in Hornsey, including Northgate House, No. 130, and Ivy House, No. 128, Highgate Hill, two beautiful houses which happily still remain.[22]

George Pryor's dwelling house passed under his will to his daughter, Martha, the wife of Richard Izard, citizen and grocer of London, by whom it was conveyed in 1681 to Ann Morgan, late of Southwark, widow, with remainder to Thomas and John, sons of Thomas Morgan, late citizen and grocer, deceased. She had licence to lease for 21 years. In 1697 she conveyed it to John Hardrett, citizen and merchant taylor of London. In 1715 he settled it on himself and Elizabeth Moseley, widow, in trust for Rebecca Hamilton, wife of Charles Hamilton, merchant, of London. Two years later Mrs. Hamilton conveyed it to Elizabeth Tovey, of St. Martin's, widow.

This house next appears in the ownership of Flexmore Dakins, esquire, a lawyer, who was admitted to Gray's Inn on 23rd May, 1719, as son and heir of Charles Dakins, gentleman, of Gray's Inn Lane. He died on 19th August, 1734, at the age of 44, and was buried in Hornsey churchyard.[23] Dakin's successor was Mary Charnells, spinster, his cousin, under whose will, proved in 1737, the house went to her cousin, Robert Charnells of Newton in the Thistle, Warwick, attorney-at-law.[24] He sold it, in 1754, to Thurston Ford, citizen and founder of London. In 1755 it passed from him to Richard Draper, serjeant-at-law, who died on 7th January, 1756, in the 61st year of his age.[25] His sister, Martha Draper, spinster, succeeded, the premises being then described as a "capital messuage heretofore in the occupation of Flexmore Dakins, afterwards of Mary Charnells and now of — Pardo." Catherine Harrison and Mary Harrison, spinsters, of Copford, Essex, were admitted in 1776 as heiresses of Martha Draper, and Mary Harrison became sole owner on the death of her sister in 1793. In this year she conveyed the property to John Wilkinson of Woodford, Doctor of Physic, and Mary Edwards was admitted under his will in 1820. William Walker was the occupier from 1817 to 1820, followed by Sarah Walker and then by Miss Elizabeth Walker, the latter being tenant when Mrs. Mary Edwards sold it in 1849 to Matthew and Arthur John Knapp, owners of Lauderdale House. Mr. Duckham was the last tenant.

Fairseat.

The house formerly standing on the site of Fairseat was described on the death of George Pryor as a messuage in the occupation of Nathaniel Herne, with five acres of pasture and four bays of barn, late in the occupation of Humphrey Kettle. The last named was a brewer, who lived on the site of No. 4a, North Hill, Highgate. It will be seen (Appendix II, p. 139) that a house rated at 15 hearths was occupied in 1665 by Major Gunstone (wrongly written Grinstone), which was empty in 1674, Thomas Gunstone being noted as owner. He may have owned a leasehold interest, but his name does not appear as a copyholder and his "ownership" in that sense may be disregarded. Although the house of Nathaniel Herne is not described as lately occupied by Gunstone, it could have been no other. It came to George Pryor's daughter, Mary, wife of Charles Izard. Sir Nathaniel Herne, the occupier, was elected a governor of the Grammar School on 17th June, 1675, in place of George Pryor. He was a member of the Barber Surgeons' Company ; sheriff in 1674-5 ; knighted 2nd August, 1674 ; alderman, 1676 ; M.P. for Dartmouth, 1679 ; Deputy Governor of the East India Company, 1672-4, and Governor 1674-6 and 1678-9. He lived in Old Jewry, as did his brother, Sir Joseph Herne. He died on 10th August, 1679, aged 50. He married Judith, daughter of Sir John Frederick, Lord Mayor of London, and had, with other issue, a son, Frederick Herne, whose daughter, Judith, married at Hampstead, in 1704, William, 2nd Earl of Jersey. From him is

Herne

17

descended the family of Burchell-Herne of Bushey Grange, Herts.[26] His monumental inscription at St. Olave's in Old Jewry reads " a man of great worth and character in this city, and most extensive charity, especially to poor seamen, and for the education of their children."

Elizabeth Stratford, widow, was the occupier in 1709 when Thomas Andrews of Highgate, gentleman, bought the estate from the sons of Ralph Izard and Elizabeth his wife, sister of Mrs. Mary Izard. Thomas Andrews married Sarah, daughter of John Townsend, citizen and soapmaker of London, owner of the adjoining Hertford House. Their son, Townsend Andrews of St. Martin-in-the-Fields, was buried at Highgate on 14th May, 1737. The Rev. Townsend Andrews, Vicar of Ashwell, son of the last named, was granted in 1769 a licence to lease the premises, then in the occupation of Sir James Hodges, knight. In 1795 the Rev. Townsend Andrews conveyed the house to Sarah Belcher of Chislehurst, widow, and the five acres of land hitherto attached to it to Robert Mendham, esquire (of Bisham House). The next owner was Charles Brunsden, esquire, followed by his widow, Sarah (see map), who died 19th January, 1802, aged 44.[25] In 1802 it was acquired by William Bloxam of Lombard Street, stationer, in whose family it still remains. He married Elizabeth, daughter of Henry Isherwood,[25] and had nine sons and daughters. William Bloxam was appointed a Governor of the Grammar School on 21st February, 1802, and died on 6th August, 1814, aged 68. The tenant in 1826 was Robert Lucas. Three of Bloxam's daughters, the Misses Jane, Louisa and Emily Bloxam, leased the house on 25th August, 1865, to Sir Sidney Hedley Waterlow. In 1871 they conveyed it to their nephew, William Tucker Bloxam of No. 1, Lincoln's Inn Fields, by whom it was enfranchised on 17th September, 1925.

Waterlow Bart.

Hertford House.

This house, marked Dr. Sandys on the map (Plate 1), is represented in the Hearth Tax assessments by a house with seven hearths in the occupation of Paul " Sinderye," and a house on the south occupied by Robert Lea, having four hearths. From his will, dated 30th March, 1668, and proved 25th February, 1668-9 ([27]), it appears that Paul Sindrey was a citizen and vintner of London, possessed of considerable wealth. He had a brother, John, and three sisters, Mary Hayler, Abigail Vesey and — Haynes.

In 1704 Charles Izard was admitted to the premises, which were described as two messuages heretofore in the tenure of Paul " Syndrey " and Robert Lea and a parcel of land adjoining the field late of Humphrey Kettle between the brick wall of the garden formerly of Richard Felkin and a messuage then of Richard Gower. Richard Felkin was the successor of Sindrey and " the parcel of land " had been staked out from the field and allotted to the house in 1676, when George Pryor's estate was divided amongst his daughters. Richard Gower's house was Bisham House (No. 64 on the map on Plate 1). In the following year Charles Izard sold Hertford House to John Townsend, citizen and soapmaker of London, whose son-in-law, Thomas Andrews, acquired the neighbouring house (Fairseat) in 1709.

On the death of John Townsend in 1725 his grandson, Townsend Andrews, had the house under his grandfather's will, it being then occupied by his mother, Sara Andrews, widow, who also occupied the house formerly tenanted by *Francis* Lee. Townsend Andrews died in 1737, leaving a widow, Catherine, and a son, afterwards the Rev. Townsend Andrews. The latter seems to have got into difficulties for he surrendered his property in January, 1795, to trustees for the benefit of his creditors. In the following May the trustees conveyed Hertford House to Thomas Sandys, of Highgate, surgeon. In 1800 Sandys and his wife, Anne, conveyed the premises to Joseph Foster of Highgate, surgeon and apothecary, when it was stated that the two houses were now used and occupied as one, an alteration which, in fact, had probably been made as early as the year 1725. Joseph Foster conveyed the property in 1802 to William Mitchell of Turnwheel Lane, London, sugar factor, from whom it passed in 1805 to William Walker of Gravel Lane, Houndsditch, sugar refiner. In 1808 Walter Carruthers, esquire, acquired it from Mr. Walker and conveyed it in the following year to John Pennell of Totteridge, esquire. After 1816, when Mr. Pennell died, it was owned and occupied by his daughter, Margaret, and her husband, Dr. Bernard Geary Snow. James Hickson, esquire, lived there in 1869, when it was acquired from the trustees by Sir Sidney Hedley Waterlow.

18

II—NOS. 17, 19 AND 21, HIGH STREET
(THE GOULD CHARITY ESTATE)

GROUND LANDLORD, LEASEHOLDER, ETC.

These houses were originally copyhold of the Manor of Cantlowes but were enfranchised in 1862. They are now the Gould Charity Estate, which is administered by the Governors of Highgate School. They are in the occupation of:

No. 17 Mrs. H. D. Oxley.
No. 19 Mr. Frank Southgate.
No. 21 Messrs. A. T. and L. C. Attkins.

GENERAL DESCRIPTION AND DATE OF STRUCTURE.

These houses were built in 1733, replacing the older houses referred to below. The builder's name was Robert Harrison. They constitute a row of three houses of three storeys with a basement and attic, and an extension to the east which seems to have been planned from the first as a shop, its upper floors being an enlargement of No. 17. The plans (Plate 15) of the houses are otherwise identical, namely a room back and front flanked by the entrance passage and stair, the only other variation being the small " powder closet " projection to the west of No. 21 which overlaps Englefield House.

The entrance doors, which have hoods and console brackets, are approached by steep flights of stone steps, the windows have arched heads and the two storeys are separated by plain brick bands. A slight brick cornice and parapet mask the eaves, and the tiled roof has flat-topped dormers. Above the doorways the windows are replaced by recessed brick panels (Plate 16).

The staircases (Plate 17) have continuous strings and turned balusters, the newels being shaped into dwarf columns. The strings and balustrades are in the same plane, forming a triangular space at their intersection which is panelled instead of being fitted with balusters of diminishing size. The ground and first floors are panelled throughout with large deal panels and a dado range. The doors are chiefly two-panelled. The opening from the entrance hall to the stair is flanked in each case by a pair of pilasters.

CONDITION OF REPAIR.

The three houses are all in a good state of repair.

HISTORICAL NOTES.

These three houses stand on land that at one time belonged to Sir Roger Cholmeley, the founder of Highgate School, and from him came to William Cholmeley, esquire (see pedigree, App. VI). In November, 1636, William Cholmeley leased to John Glover of Lincoln's Inn, esquire, a messuage in the occupation of John Flood, Richard Wall and Anthony Holland, and a barn and barnyard and a parcel of waste. This messuage stood on the site of the houses now belonging to the Gould Charity. John Glover severed a great part of the barnyard from the barn and added it to the waste ground, afterwards erecting a brick wall in place of the former palings across the waste, which he converted to a garden and orchard, planting it with " all manner of choice fruit trees " at a cost of at least £1,000.[28] On 20th November, 1640, Cholmeley conveyed the land to trustees for John Glover, who bequeathed it by his will dated October, 1648, to his wife Johanna. She afterwards married William Vaughan of Gray's Inn on 1st May, 1656.

In 1658 the estate was settled on Johanna Vaughan (late the wife of John Glover) and her son, Richard Glover, esquire, shortly before her death. Richard Glover came into possession in 1659, when he had licence to lease to Richard Gower for 31 years. Johanna[29] was the daughter of Francis Dorrington of London, merchant (by Hawes his wife, daughter of Simon Horspool, citizen and draper of London), third son of Matthew Dorrington of Stafford and Winifred his wife, daughter of Reginald Home. Her aunt, Elizabeth (d. 7th February, 1621-2, *s.p.*), a sister of Hawes, married Alexander Kinge, Auditor of the Exchequer (d. 6th January, 1617-8), lord of the manor of Bibsworth in Finchley.

In 1667 Richard Gower surrendered the three houses to his wife, Anne, and her heirs. The description in the Court Rolls then given is extremely detailed and reveals the fact that John Glover laid out the ground and built the wall referred to above. It is as follows : " three messuages or cottages formerly in the several tenures of Richard Wall, Anthony Holland and John Lloyd and now of Richard Gower, and a barn and barnyard near the aforesaid messuage or cottage, formerly in the occupation of Parker, widow, deceased, and now of Richard Gower, at Highgate, and a brick wall which divides the premises now surrendered from the premises and garden now in the tenure of Richard Gower (afterwards Bisham House, on the site of the present Bisham Gardens) and the soil on which the brick wall stands, and a parcel of ground lying in the garden last mentioned containing from the stone in the wall aforesaid lettered ' N-Glover ' 28 feet to the stone in the quickset hedge lettered ' SW-Glover ', 92 feet to the stone in the wall of the garden on the west lettered ' W-Glover,' and a passage which — Cholmeley, esquire, deceased, heretofore had for horses and carts to the field in his tenure, which adjoins the orchard now in the occupation of Richard Gower on the south in the barnyard aforesaid, which field is now in the occupation of George Pryor, gentleman."

Anne, the wife of Richard Gower, esquire, was buried at Highgate on 10th May, 1687, and her husband, who died on 12th December, was buried there on 14th December, 1688. Their daughter, Elizabeth, had married Edward Gould of London, merchant (afterwards Sir Edward), and the estate was held in trust for her under her mother's will.[30] She died on 8th March, 1712-3, and was buried in Highgate Chapel on 14th March. With her sister, Anne, she inherited a considerable landed estate in Stoke Newington,[31] part of which is now contained in Abney Park Cemetery. Sir Edward Gould died on 26th September, 1728, aged 80, when, in accordance with the will of his late wife, the estate passed to three trustees nominated by the Rev. Edward De Chair, Rector of St. Pancras, by deed dated 4th August, 1729.

Gould

The three trustees so appointed were Francis Annesley of Green Street, William Bridges of Highgate, esquire (who lived in a house on the site of Holly Terrace), and Edward Stanton of Highgate, gentleman (who is recorded as paving the altar of Highgate Chapel with black and white marble at his own cost). They leased the property to Robert Harrison of Highgate, bricklayer, on 9th June, 1733, for 87 years,[32] the late tenants then being Andrew Brookes and Michael Roberts. The trustees, therefore, until the year 1820 had little control over the property, and their functions were virtually limited to receiving the reserved rent and distributing it according to the trusts of Lady Gould's will, as follows : " To distribute the issues and profits among such poor inhabitants of the village of Highgate, whether lying in Hornsey or St. Pancras, as shall not receive any public alms or collection from their respective parish and shall to the discretion of such trustees appear to be most proper and fit objects of relief and charity."

Robert Harrison, who owned considerable house property in different parts of Highgate, dying on 3rd August, 1744, left his leasehold estate to Mary and Sarah Lane, daughters of his niece, Bridget Wheeler.[33] In the wall of No. 17 is a stone tablet inscribed

L

S M

1745

obviously referring to Sarah and Mary Lane. Harrison built the houses now standing, and a moiety was leased in 1756 to Henry Anderson of the Inner Temple by Mary Lane and her sister Sarah, then the wife of John Arnold, a lawyer of Staple Inn. The tenants were Bridget Wheeler (mother of Mary and Sarah), Noah Nason and William Marshall. In the following year Mary married Thomas Reynolds of Highgate, carpenter. In 1764 the other moiety, for the remainder of the lease, was assigned to Morris Spurling of Highgate, gentleman, by the executor of John Arnold, together with Thomas Reynolds and Mary his wife and her widowed sister Sarah.[34] It passed to Philip Acton of St. Marylebone, gentleman, in 1773.[35]

William Belcher, esquire, Benjamin Price and William Bloxam were admitted trustees on 25th April, 1810, and on 24th April, 1821, Robert Isherwood and Richard Nixon took the places of Messrs. Price and Bloxam, deceased. In 1859 the trustees were William Dodge Cooper Cooper of Toddington Manor, Dunstable (who had formerly lived in the house now called the House of Mercy on North Hill), and Harry Chester of Rutland Gate, Hyde Park, esquire. In 1861 Harry Chester and the Rev. William Weldon Champneys, Parson of St. Pancras, transferred the trust to Charles John Bloxam, esquire, of Lincoln's Inn Fields, George Abraham Crawley of Whitehall Place, esquire, and John Lawrence Tatham of Lincoln's Inn, esquire, the lessees then being Thomas Broadbent, at £24 per annum, Mary Redfern, at £22, and Nathaniel Sibley, at £24, whose leases dated 28th February, 1844, were for 21 years, expiring at Michaelmas, 1862.[36]

III—BISHAM HOUSE (SITE) AND ENGLEFIELD HOUSE, NO. 23, HIGH STREET

GROUND LANDLORD, LEASEHOLDER, ETC.

Englefield House, which was originally copyhold of the Manor of Cantlowes, now enfranchised, is owned by, and is in the occupation of, Dr. Francis Allen.

GENERAL DESCRIPTION AND DATE OF STRUCTURE.

Bisham House stood until 1884 south-east of the Gould Charity property (see Section II), within grounds which at one time included the present Englefield House, and extended from the High Street to Swain's Lane (see Plate 3). The house gave their name to Bisham Gardens. A reference to the plan (Plate 15) will show how Englefield House is interlocked with its neighbours on each side and the natural inference would be that it filled the gap between them after they were built. It is, however, probably earlier than either, since its detail belongs to the first quarter of the 18th century and its plan may be probably explained by the fact that the adjoining houses have been rebuilt, those to the east being traceable in the Court Rolls as early as the middle of the 17th century.

Englefield House has a frontage of close on 30 feet and at the back it is some 2 feet less, the space lost by the overlapping of the powder closet in No. 21 being compensated by its own projection on the east beyond No. 25. The front section of the plan is divided into two equal parts, that on the left on the ground floor being the entrance hall and on the right a sitting room, while above are two bedrooms. This leads to an interesting arrangement of the front elevation (Plate 18) which is symmetrical on the first floor with four windows—two to each room—flanked by recessed brick panels at each end. On the ground floor the entrance door, with a pedimented head on brackets and panelled pilasters, is beneath the second window from the left but appears central since to the left of the door the single upper window is replaced by a double window separated by a mullion only. This makes it necessary to omit the left-hand brick panel while retaining that on the right. The first-floor treatment, however, appears again in the basement.

The door is approached by a flight of seven steps, and the basement windows are mostly above ground. A chamfered plinth course, a projecting band of brickwork, with moulded bottom course at first-floor level and a prominent wood-blocked cornice at the eaves, are the chief features of the elevation. The cornice returns on itself on the left side. The roof is tiled and was furnished with two dormers, with flat tops hung with sash windows now replaced by a continuous range. The main window frames are practically flush with the brickwork, which has rubbed brick arches and flush quoins. The chimney on the left has been heightened to master the roof of No. 21.

The garden elevation is similarly treated and has the same eaves cornice. Its three windows on each floor light one room, to the east of which

22

is the stair, now masked by a modern projection. The " powder closet " of No. 21 blocks the light from a small room adjoining the stairs which on the first floor has been thrown into the front room to form a recess.

In the interior the stair (Plates 19*a* and 21) is of early close-string design with square newels (with pendants) and turned balusters. The rooms generally are panelled and many of the doors are of two-panel type. The back room on the ground floor is a remarkably fine example of an early Georgian interior (Plates 120 and 121). It has a bold

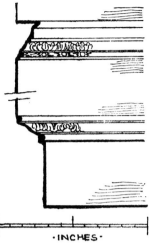

·INCHES·

cornice with dentilled bed mould, and walls furnished with fielded panels, carved dado rail and skirting. The fireplace end of the room is elaborately designed. The mantelpiece and overmantel are richly carved with foliage and strings of fruit and flowers with a seated Cupid in the centre of the frieze, festooned with draped swags. All the mouldings are enriched and the external angles of the chimney breast have husk ornament. Of little less elaboration are the doors of the room, which number four, one on each side of the fireplace (leading to cupboards), the entrance door and one communicating with the front room. They are all of six panel with egg-and-leaf mouldings, bold egg-and-tongue architraves and pedimental overdoors, with richly carved frieze and mouldings. The last named has in addition a small bust within the pediment.

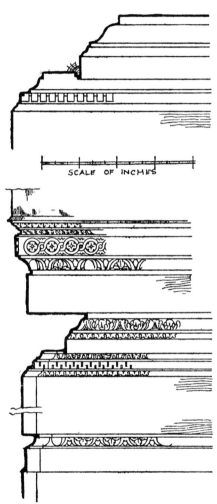

SCALE OF INCHES

In one of the bedrooms is a fireplace with a bolection moulded wood surround of a date not later than the early part of the 18th century. In the opening is fitted a magnificent example of a hob grate of the Adam period, of duck's-nest pattern enriched with fan-shaped reeding and husk ornament, the central point being occupied by a sphinx in an elliptical panel (Plate 19*b*).

THE VILLAGE OF HIGHGATE

CONDITION OF REPAIR.

Good.

HISTORICAL NOTES.

In the middle of the 16th century Sir Roger Cholmeley, the founder of Highgate School, owned all the land between High Street and Swain's Lane, southward to the grounds of Lauderdale House and northward to South Grove (excluding Angel Row and the Angel). The southern portion, including " Andrew Marvell's Cottage " and what later became the estates of Hertford House and Fairseat, descended, as described before (p. 16), to William Cholmeley, gentleman, great-grandson of Jasper Cholmeley, the legatee of Sir Roger.

The site of the three houses to-day belonging to the Gould Charity, Nos. 17, 19 and 21, High Street, also descended, as we have seen (p. 19), to William Cholmeley, but the remainder of Sir Roger's land, northward of the present Waterlow Park, was conveyed by him to Richard Hodges, one of the Foundation Governors of his school. The frontage of this land is now occupied by houses numbered 3 to 15 (odd) and 23 to 33 (odd). In 1553 Sir Roger conveyed to Richard Hodges of Highgate, gentleman,[28] a messuage, barn, garden and half an acre of land adjoining the messuage. Twelve years later Richard Hodges and Joan his wife obtained from Sir Roger[28] a cottage late in the occupation of Margaret Wilkinson, widow, and 1 acre 34 perches called " powles," abutting on the said cottage and barnyard east, on Swain's Lane west, on a close in the occupation of Sir Roger Cholmeley south, one head abutting on the common highway called the Green (South Grove).

Richard Hodges remained a Governor of the Grammar School from his first appointment on 7th June, 1565, until his death on 10th October, 1572. Another Governor was William Hodges of Highgate, gentleman, from 16th June, 1581, until his death on 9th January, 1581-2. The land of Richard Hodges came to his niece, Ann Grant, in 1599,[28] when she was the widow of Thomas Widmore of Hughendon, Bucks, gentleman, who died on 20th May, 1586, leaving two sons, Richard Widmore and Nicholas aged 17.[37] In 1610 Anne Widmore, widow, and Nicholas Widmore took out a licence to lease a tenement to Thomas Russell, yeoman, for 21 years, afterwards converted by him into four tenements. There was also another house, occupied by John Glover, which he leased in 1635 from Nicholas Widmore, after the death of Anne Widmore. This was Bisham House, or its predecessor on the same site.

Widmer

Nicholas Widmore lived at Old Thame, in Oxfordshire. In 1641 he conveyed his land to Sir Robert Payne on condition that if Sir Robert failed to pay him £100 a year for the remainder of his life, the land should revert to Widmore. In 1654 Sir Robert Payne mortgaged the estate to Robert Holt, along with Dorchester House, which he also owned (see p. 88). In the account of Sir Robert Payne under Arundel House (see p. 51) it will be seen that he died in embarrassed circumstances, which may account for his falling into arrear with his payments to Nicholas Widmore, with the result that Widmore proceeded to claim possession.[38] This endangered the interests of the mortgagees, and Robert Holt's daughter, Sara, with her husband, William Roberts (both under age), had to enter an action in Chancery, alleging that the £100 a year had been paid for 17 years and was now only three-quarters of a year in arrear, which they were willing to pay to Widmore for Sir Robert Payne. They got judgment in July, 1658,[39] to stay the forfeiture on condition they paid into court or to Widmore the £75 owing. The parties evidently came to terms, Widmore foreclosed, and surrendered his rights to William Roberts and Sara his wife in the next year.

As stated before, the occupier of Bisham House after 1635 was John Glover. He must have been the John Glover mentioned as Steward of the manor of Cantlowes in 1648, when Alderman John Warner, Mayor of the City of London, was lord of that manor. Richard Gower succeeded Glover as lessee, obtaining a lease for 31 years from Robert Holte in 1657[28] and acquiring the ownership of the estate from William Roberts and his wife in 1661. His father was Colonel Thomas Gower of Highgate, a Governor of the Grammar School from 1st October, 1658, until his death in 1676, when he was buried at Highgate. Other burials there, as recorded in the Register, are those of Susan, daughter of Mr. Richard Gower, 9th July, 1670; Penelope, daughter of the same, 28th August, 1670; Thomas, son of the same, 25th April, 1671; Mrs. Anne Gower, wife of Richard Gower, esquire, 10th May, 1687; and Richard Gower, esquire, 14th December,

24

1688. The hearth tax assessed on this house in 1665 was on 11 hearths and was payable by Richard Gower.

Richard Gower was succeeded by Edward Gould of London, merchant (afterwards Sir Edward), in right of his wife Elizabeth, daughter of Richard Gower, whom he married at Highgate on 17th September, 1683 (see p. 20). In St. Michael's Church, Highgate, is a memorial cartouche to Sir Edward Gould removed from the old chapel. It is described on p. 55. In addition to this estate in St. Pancras Sir Edward, in 1709, acquired the " Duke's Head " on the Hornsey side of the High Street and 16 acres of land behind it, which, on 11th August, 1713, he settled on himself and Frances Monoux his " wife designate." In her will, proved 5th April, 1738, Dame Frances Gould of Gloucester Street, St. George the Martyr, Middlesex, gave to Edward Gould (the eldest son of Mrs. Jane Gould) " all my goods in the inventory belonging to my house at Highgate that is now let to Mrs. Decostey, and two hundred pounds." The house referred to was in Hornsey, on the 16 acres of land mentioned before.

Sir Edward Gould was succeeded by his great-nephew Edward Gould of Mansfield Woodhouse, Notts (1703-75), son of Edward Gould of Highgate (1677-1721), son of James Gould, China merchant (1641-80), brother of Sir Edward. Edward Gould of Highgate in 1701 married Jane, daughter of Sir Francis Pemberton of Grove House (see p. 93). He died on board the *Montague* in the East Indies, leaving a widow aged 41 and a son aged 18. Mrs. Edward Gould was buried at Highgate on 7th March, 1746-7.[40]

Edward Thoroton Gould of Mansfield Woodhouse, only son of Edward Gould, was the last of the family to own this estate. Three years after the death of his father he sold to Robert Mendham, esquire, a messuage formerly in the occupation of Richard Gower, esquire, afterwards of Sir Edward Gould and now of Robert Mendham, with 1 acre 2 roods 26 perches of land. It will be observed that this area very closely corresponds with the amount of land conveyed by Sir Roger Cholmeley to Richard Hodges, namely a garden and ½ acre plus 1 acre 34 perches, together 1 acre 2 roods 34 perches. Included in Hodges' land was a small area on the north-west, now occupied by Church House, No. 10, South Grove (see p. 34), and the site of Nos. 23-33, High Street, on the north-east.

Robert Mendham, a merchant in Walbrook, was elected a Governor of the Grammar School on 10th April, 1796, and died on 7th April, 1810, aged 77, leaving a son, John Mendham, who conveyed the estate in 1813 to John Pennell (the owner-occupier of Hertford House), who immediately conveyed it to Charles William Hick, who was a hatter, of Cheapside, and also owned property in Southwood Lane, north of the Baptist Chapel there.

Charles William Hick and Rebecca his wife, who had occupied the house, in 1817 conveyed it to Peter Heywood of the Royal Navy. He was a midshipman on board H.M.S. *Bounty* when the crew mutinied against Captain Bligh. His aunt, Mary (daughter of Thomas Heywood, esquire, a Deemster of the Isle of Man), married Admiral Thomas Pasley (1734-1808), who was created a baronet for his gallant conduct on the First of June, 1794, when he commanded a division of the fleet. In his will Captain Heywood mentions the portraits of his parents and of his uncle, Sir Thomas Pasley. In Highgate Cemetery is the following monumental inscription : " In memory of / Frances Heywood, / widow of Cap^n Peter Heywood, R.N. / She died Octr 28th, 1863, aged 81. / Also of / Cap^n Peter Heywood, R.N. / One of the Midshipmen on board / H.M.S. 'Bounty,' Cap^n Bligh. / He died February 10th, 1831, aged 58. / His remains are deposited in the vaults / Under the Old Church, Highgate. / Requiescat in pace /." Captain Heywood bequeathed the house to his wife.[41]

In 1832 Joseph Gardiner, esquire, leased the house from Mrs. Heywood and ten years later became the owner. He died on 2nd August, 1853, leaving it to his wife, Harriet Gardiner.

Englefield House.

This house was conveyed by Edward Thoroton Gould to William Pilton of Piccadilly, wireworker, in 1783, as a messuage late in the tenure (amongst other premises) of Mrs. Terry, and " now of — a schoolmaster," with a garden. The " other premises " referred to were a small messuage, coachhouse and stable, occupied in 1879 by Mr. Charles Sparrow, now No. 29, a house at the end of the yard which is entered by a passage between No. 27 and No. 31.

25

THE VILLAGE OF HIGHGATE

The " schoolmaster " mentioned as tenant in 1783 was John Rosier, who was still the occupier in 1794 when Mrs. Anne Pilton succeeded on the death of her husband. In 1799 she sold the house to Thomas Ensor and it continued in the ownership of his descendants until purchased in 1884 by the late Thomas Horsley of South Grove, baker.

On the death of Thomas Ensor in 1820 it came to his son, James Ensor, who was of Brill Terrace, Somers Town, in 1808, of College Street, Camden Town, in 1813, of Totteridge in 1823 and of Hammersmith when he died on 18th January, 1868, in his 80th year.[25]

Thomas Ensor appears to have occupied the house from 1794 to 1819 and was followed successively by William Addison, schoolmaster (from 1821), Mrs. Millington and Miss Millington, the last mentioned being the occupier in 1884.

IV—NOS. 33-5, HIGH STREET, THE ANGEL TAVERN AND ANGEL ROW AND RUSSELL HOUSE (NOS. 1-9, SOUTH GROVE)

GROUND LANDLORD.

All these houses were originally copyhold of the Manor of Cantlowes.

GENERAL DESCRIPTION AND DATE OF STRUCTURE.

The houses fronting the High Street have no special features though at one time the backs presented a picturesque appearance, while the Angel Tavern itself after successive alterations has been practically reconstructed in recent years.

Angel Row also, to-day, is of no great architectural importance. Nos. 1 and 2 have weather-boarded backs to the first floor, while No. 8, though smaller than its neighbour No. 9 (Russell House), contains a very beautiful little staircase with turned and shaped balusters constructed round a well less than two feet square, with but a single baluster to each portion of its close string and two half balusters against the square newel posts. A detail of this stair is reproduced on Plate 23.

No. 9, South Grove (Russell House), is of three relatively low storeys, three windows in width, the entrance door occupying the position of the westernmost window on the ground floor. The house probably dates from the early part of the 18th century, and is possibly a little older than Church House, which adjoins it, but the street front, which is of half-timber construction, has been cemented over and treated in a manner which belongs to the end of the century (Plate 24*a*).

The door case (drawing, p. 31), with pilasters, horizontal entablature and architrave, rising in the centre of the frieze, is probably of the earlier date. The back overlooking the garden (Plate 24*b*) has a gable which has been altered in shape by the inclusion of an additional upper window, but its original form was probably that of its neighbour to the east seen in the same view.

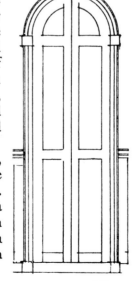

THE VILLAGE OF HIGHGATE

The entrance hall is panelled, with the staircase at the farther end, approached through a square opening spanned by a beam supported by square fluted pilasters similar to those on either side of the front door. The front room on the ground floor is also panelled in the style common in the early 18th century. There is a cupboard, illustrated on p. 27, with semicircular head and shaped shelving adjoining the fireplace.

CONDITION OF REPAIR.
Good.

HISTORICAL NOTES.
The frontage originally comprised in the Angel and Angel Row estate extended from No. 33, High Street to No. 9, South Grove, both inclusive. The available records provide a continuous succession of owners only from 1610, but the following entries of nearly four and a half centuries ago so clearly refer to this site that they deserve reproduction here. In 1489 John Wyking surrendered at the Cantlowes Manor Court for himself and his wife a cottage, curtilage and enclosed garden at " Highgate Grene " called the " Cornerhous," described as " lying between the land of Giles Eustace on the west and the king's way (High Street) on the east, abutting north on Highgate Grene (South Grove) and south on land of John Leeche." The reversion was to Giles Eustace. Six years later Giles Eustace died, bequeathing to his daughter " a tenement in which John Wyking dwelleth " with another tenement next it inhabited by Henry Kyrkby. His will, made on 2nd and proved on 10th April, 1495 (Appendix I), shows that Eustace held considerable landed property in the parishes of St. Pancras, Islington and Hornsey. An interesting bequest is that of 6s. 8d. to " Richard Baker, heremyte of the Chapel of Hygate." Eustace's land in Hornsey lay to the east of Southwood Lane. His three sons died childless and their sister, Alice, outlived them and came into the property. She married Thomas Harte and was ancestress of Sir Eustace Hart of Highgate, knight, who died on 18th September, 1634, and was buried at St. Benet's, Paul's Wharf, in the City of London.

As early as the year 1610 the site was occupied by the inn and a row of cottages, the owner being William Steere, citizen and skinner of London. In 1611 he conveyed it to George Humble, citizen and leatherseller of London, in whose family it remained for 158 years. The occupiers then were William Steere, John Cranmer, William Partington, Michael Merrall, William Smith, William Trynnoel and Owen Cope. In that year it consisted of eight cottages and eight gardens, but in 1769 it is described as an inn, three cottages in the High Street and six in South Grove. The original houses must have stood farther back from the road because several grants of the waste in front of them were made. In 1671 Richard Nickes of London, brewer, the lessee under the Humble family, was granted a piece of the waste before his two messuages, containing from east to west 36 feet and from north to south at the east end 18 feet, in the middle 16 feet and at the west end 14 feet. Again, in 1692, Stephen Humble was granted a piece of waste before his tenements there, extending from the rail before the messuage in the occupation of Weekes to the corner posts of the rail of his inn, called the Angel, towards the east, containing from east to west 6½ poles and from north to south 18½ feet. Finally the ground in front of Nos. 2 to 8 was enclosed up to the present frontage in 1831.

The lessee of the inn in 1723 was James Crompton, senior, innholder, and three of his neighbours were named Robert Munday, Widow Heybourne and Thomas White. Crompton assigned his 40-year lease to his son, James Crompton, junior, of Highgate, carpenter, in 1725. The inn was then referred to as the Angel, formerly the White Lyon. In 1745 the tenant was Widow Neale, her predecessor being George Neale, deceased, and the three houses in High Street were occupied by Edward Wilton, Wallis, and William Quench. Six cottages faced South Grove, in the occupations of George Wilkinson, Anthony Wells, John Musine, and Widow Browne, one then empty, had previously been occupied by Samuel Eames. The whole estate was sold in 1769 in lots by the coheiresses of the Humble family, viz. Sara, wife of Samuel Taylor of Bygrave, Herts, and Catherine, wife of William Mason of Nortonbury, Norton, Herts. Thereafter we are able to trace the story of each house separately.

Humble

28

ANGEL ROW

No. 33, High Street was in the same ownership as the Angel from 1769 until at least as late as 1876. Some of the tenants were : William Bowstread, seedsman (1769) ; James Bristow, *circa* 1812 ; Thomas Stedman, plumber ; Mrs. Woodland, 1876.

No. 35, High Street. This formed two houses in 1769 occupied by Samuel Feary, shoemaker, and later by —— Allcock, shoemaker. It was purchased in that year by John Southcote of Highgate, in Hornsey, esquire, who died without issue in 1779, when his two brothers, Thomas and George, succeeded. They left it to their wives, by whom it was sold to James Sutton, shopkeeper, in 1801. In 1832 Hannah Eedes, widow, was admitted under the will of Edmund Slaughter, by which time the houses had become one, and were occupied by William Clarke, fishmonger. She sold the property in 1833 to John Matthias Clark, fishmonger.

No. 37, High Street, The Angel. In 1769 this house was bought by Andrew Aspden of Old Street, St. Luke's, ivory turner. It was then in the possession of John Southcote, esquire. In 1772 when Andrew Aspden died the property passed to his son, John, also of Old Street, ivory turner. The subsequent owners were : Jennet Jones and Mary, wife of Thomas Poole, daughters of John Aspden, 1828 ; John Dunning, 1829 ; Thomas Townshend, 1841 ; John Ogle, 1856. The tenants during this period were—John Baret, 1770-4 ; Jeremiah Lister, 1774 ; Thomas Baker, 1777 ; Thomas Sheppard, 1778 ; James Bristow, 1808-14 ; Richard Houlder, 1817 ; Anthony Richardson, 1818 ; Richard Yeo, 1819-24 ; William Rowe, 1825 ; Thomas Stedman.[42]

No. 2, South Grove. Elizabeth Austin and Eleanor Austin, grocers, bought this house in 1769, and occupied it until 1772, when Elizabeth died and her sister became sole owner. She died on 18th November, 1792, and it passed to the three daughters of her brother, Edward Austin, who had died on 31st December, 1791. One of the three sisters was Mrs. Elizabeth Bolton, widow, who, in 1794, married James Nathaniel Prickett, shopkeeper. From them it passed to Samuel Yexley of Highgate, victualler, in 1801, and to his widow, Elizabeth, a few months later, who leased it to George Hipwell for 14 years in 1816. She died in 1829, leaving it to Mary Fitch, her niece, who died in 1871 leaving a daughter, Sarah Fitch, who died on 25th November, 1879. —— Yexley owned the " Coopers Arms " now No. 48, High Street.

No. 3, South Grove. From 1769 to 1794 this house was owned by the proprietors of No. 2, passing to Eleanor Austin in the latter year under the will of her aunt Eleanor. The occupier in 1769 was Rothwell, a coachbuilder ; in 1780, John Dorsett. In 1782 it was empty. Joseph Chandler was there from 1808 to 1818, followed by Joseph Houghton. Eleanor Austin, the owner in 1794, at once conveyed it to Charles Marion Welsted of Kimbolton and it passed from him to Jeremiah Mangaar in 1805, the tenant still being Mr. Houghton. In 1821 it passed to his widow under his will, and on her death to Sarah Berny Thomas, wife of David Thomas, and Anne Leigh, wife of Philip Leigh, her daughters. Sarah Berny Thomas died on 12th February, 1858, without issue, and Mrs. Leigh died on 9th October, 1846, leaving two sons, both silk factors, one being Lewis Leigh of South Glastonbury, Hartford, Connecticut, U.S.A. They sold it, in 1860, to John Newman of No. 19, Tavistock Terrace, Holloway, gentleman, who died in 1879.

No. 4, South Grove. This house was bought in 1769 by the tenant, Doily Chandler, baker, being then described as two houses adjoining, with the oven and out offices. When Doily Chandler died, in 1772, his mother, Jane Chandler, succeeded him. At her death, in 1779, it passed under his will to his two sisters, Rose, wife of James Gray, and Elizabeth Wilson. In 1808, Mr. and Mrs. Gray ceased to occupy the premises and conveyed the house to John Hernon of King Street, Covent Garden. From him it was acquired in 1834 by John Fisher. The Fisher family were occupiers from 1809 and owners from 1834. Robert Edward Fisher of Kew Gardens, who came into possession on the death of Isabella Fisher, the surviving trustee, sold it in 1920 to Thomas Frank Horsley, Frederick Horsley and Stanley Horsley, trading as T. Horsley and Sons, bakers

29

and confectioners. Thus the house has been occupied and used as a baker's shop from at least as long ago as 1769 until the present time.

Nos. 5, 6, 7, South Grove. No. 5 was bought in 1769 by Joseph Copeland and William Watts, butchers, the occupiers, and Nos. 6 and 7, then occupied by Mr. Musine, whitesmith, by William Watts alone. Joseph Copeland died in 1771, William Watts thereafter being sole owner of the three. No. 6 and No. 7 seem to have been occupied together. In 1804, after the death of William Watts, his son, Joseph Watts, became the owner and conveyed the houses to Charles Lyne in the following year. The occupiers of No. 5 were Elizabeth Clarke in 1779, Stephen Preston, 1794 to 1819, and then John Clarke. Nos. 6 and 7 were occupied by William Watts in 1779, and leased by him in 1789 to Charles Lyne. He was followed by Thomas Lyne, 1817-8; Widow "Line," 1819-23; and Mary Lyne in 1824. Thomas Fleming (a trustee, who had been admitted in 1825) conveyed to William Horrell a seventh share in the premises in 1852, and the remaining shares during the next three years, so that by 1855 Horrell was in possession of the whole. He died on 14th September, 1867, leaving the property to his nephew Henry Lyne Dixson of Little Sussex Place, Hyde Park Square, licensed victualler, and to Henry Smith Styan. It was then in the occupation of Arthur Fry, butcher, and Samuel Hill, gardener (two houses). The estate of Charles Lyne comprised also cottages in Swain's Lane and houses in York Place, Nos. 43, 55, 57, etc., High Street.

No. 8, South Grove. This house was bought in 1769 by George Stow of St. John's Street, brushmaker, the occupier then being Elizabeth Werden, grocer, who remained there until 1779. In 1779 it was acquired from John Stow by John Davis of Islington, carpenter, and by him conveyed to Richard Walklin, gardener, in 1781. His only son succeeded on his death in 1818, and mortgaged the premises to John Ramsbottom, who foreclosed in 1823 and conveyed it to the son of the mortgagor, Richard Hartley Walklin, and Martha his wife. In 1828 it was sold to John Paul Woolley of Staines, gentleman, who leased it to J. C. D. Jenkins for 21 years. John Matthias Clarke acquired it in 1844 from Sarah Woolley.

Russell House, No. 9, South Grove. This house, the last and most interesting of the row, was bought in 1769 by John Southcote of Highgate in Hornsey. On his death in 1779 his two brothers succeeded, the occupier then being William How, who was followed by Thomas Sandys in 1794. The brothers both predeceased their wives, who sold the house in 1801 to Elizabeth Thorne, wife of Richard Thorne of Rathbone Place, St. Marylebone, coachmaker, the tenant then being the Rev. Edward Porter, who was pastor of the Congregational Church in Southwood Lane and died in 1812.[43]

In 1810, Mrs. Thorne, then being a widow, leased the house to Hyman Hurwitz of Highgate, schoolmaster, for 50 years at £42 per annum.[44] He will be noticed more fully in connection with Church House, No. 10. Mr. Hurwitz held the lease for only two years, assigning it in 1812 to Thomas Price of Kingsgate Street, Holborn. Mrs. Elizabeth Thorne bequeathed the house to her niece Elizabeth Rogers, after the death of her mother, Hannah Rogers, which happened on 27th August, 1829. Elizabeth Rogers came into possession in 1835 and died on 22nd September, 1872. The tenants following Thomas Price were Mesdames Cuttell and then —— Marks.

Elizabeth Rogers bequeathed the house to John Edward Hopkins of Hollybush Cottage, Bethnal Green, gentleman, and another. Hopkins died on 1st March, 1886, when John Barry Hopkins of No. 10, Wildash Road, East Dulwich, succeeded.

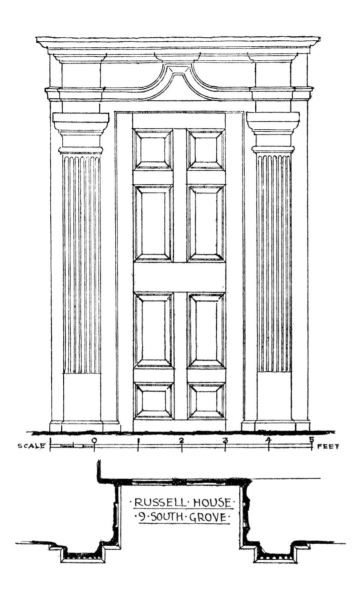

SCALE |———| 0 | 1 | 2 | 3 | 4 | 5 | FEET

·RUSSELL·HOUSE·
·9·SOUTH·GROVE·

V—CHURCH HOUSE (NO. 10, SOUTH GROVE) AND SITE OF THE HIGHGATE LITERARY AND SCIENTIFIC INSTITUTION

GROUND LANDLORD AND LEASEHOLDER, ETC.

The house was formerly copyhold of the Manor of Cantlowes but has been enfranchised and is now owned by the Highgate Literary and Scientific Institution and is in the occupation of Mr. J. Isaacs.

GENERAL DESCRIPTION AND DATE OF STRUCTURE.

Church House has a fine brick front five windows in width and three storeys in height above a basement. It is distinguished by the segmental heads not only to the brick arches over the openings but to the window frames themselves. The entrance is placed in the centre and has a good example of a wooden doorcase (Plate 29 and drawing below), with Ionic columns and pediment, which is practically a replica of that at Moreton House. The entrance hall is panelled throughout and has a dado rail and moulded wooden cornice all painted, the stair being approached through a semicircular-headed opening with panelled soffit springing from a fluted pilaster on either side. Similar panelling lines the staircase walls. The stair ascends in two flights (dog-leg fashion) from floor to floor, and has cut strings and carved brackets, while the turned and shaped balusters are grouped two

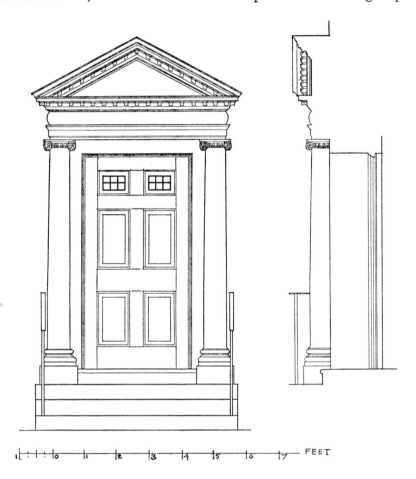

to a tread, each having the small intermediate block that became usual in the reign of George I. The newels are fluted columns, with moulded caps and bases, over which the moulded handrail breaks to form a square capping. All the principal rooms are panelled.

The plan of this house, which is L-shaped (see measured drawing, Plate 25), provides for two little additional rooms on each floor which were probably intended for dressing rooms or powder closets projecting from the

33

C

adjoining bedrooms, and these add to the interest of the garden elevation (Plates 26 and 27*b*).

The front garden is enclosed with a dwarf wall with railings, and the entrance has a good wrought-iron gate hung to panelled sides with iron scroll-work (see measured drawing, Plate 92). Over the side panels and centre is a wrought-iron overthrow with scrolls and there are brackets attached to the railings. In addition there is a heavy arched bar surmounting the whole, intended to carry the lamp bracket. The house is fully illustrated (Plates 25 to 30).

CONDITION OF REPAIR.
Good.

HISTORICAL NOTES.

As shown in the notes to Bisham House (p. 24), the site of Nos. 10 and 11, South Grove originally belonged to Sir Roger Cholmeley and part came into the hands of Nicholas Widmore of Old Thame, Oxfordshire. He conveyed in 1665 to Hugh Dorrell of Old Thame, and Merrell his wife, a messuage in "Swines Lane," which they in turn conveyed in 1683 to John Welbe, citizen and grocer of London, who also obtained at that time the grant of a piece of waste lying before two messuages, containing from east to west 60 feet, from north to south at the east end 22 feet and at the west end 30 feet. This was evidently at the eastern corner of Swain's Lane (west of Church House), now the site of the Highgate Literary and Scientific Institution and the cottage behind. In 1698 the messuage had become two messuages, one in the occupation of Sisera Lambert and the other then vacant but lately occupied by Charles Prior, gentleman, and a parcel of land before the messuages, heretofore purchased of Hugh Dorrell, esquire, and a parcel of waste before the houses, and a pump. John Welbe died in 1698, and his wife, Mary Welbe, described in her will as of St. John's, Wapping, died in the year following, leaving her daughter, Mary,[45] two copyhold messuages in Highgate, one in the possession of Daniel Coachman, and the other late of —— Pryor, esquire, and now of herself, with the free use of the pump standing in a partition pale, and the well thereunto belonging for both the said messuages. This will was dated 8th March, 1699, and proved 30th March, 1699, the executor being widow Welbe's father, Robert Marcy. Mary Welbe, the daughter, married Joseph Hurt of Maidstone, brazier. They conveyed the houses in 1711 to William Brown, citizen and skinner of London (who lived in a house on the site of No. 16, South Grove).

William Brown died on 29th October, 1715, leaving to his grandson, William Brown, "two new purchased messuages in the occupation of Aaron Sparling and John Monk which I lately bought of Joseph Hurt and Mary his wife, near my dwelling house at Highgate."[46] William Brown, son of this William Brown, succeeded in 1752 and immediately conveyed the two houses to Peter Storer, by whom they were bequeathed to his sister, Sidney, the wife of John Hawkins. Peter Storer lived in the adjoining Church House, which had originally been in all probability part of the Cholmeley estate, but of which the earlier history has not been traced.

The actual site of Church House seems to be represented by a cottage and little yard leased in 1611 to John Panton, esquire, for 21 years, by Thomas Westfield, clerk, who owned it in right of his wife. He was rector of Hornsey from 1615 to 1637 and afterwards Bishop of Bristol. He died on 25th June, 1644, and was buried in the Cathedral.[47] The reversion belonged to Sarah Birchinshaw, widow, the sister of Mrs. Westfield, whose daughter, Sarah, married Robert Storie, citizen and clothworker of London. Sarah died before her mother, and left a daughter, Anne, who was five years of age when her grandmother died in 1621.

Westfield

In 1638 Anne Storie conveyed the cottage to John Parker, citizen and haberdasher of London, who is recorded in 1659 as being then long since dead. In that year his two daughters, Mrs. Johanna, the wife of Mr. Robert Wilson, and Mrs. Elizabeth Parker, conveyed it to the tenant, Richard Wright, yeoman, whose predecessor was William White. From an incidental mention of Richard Wright in 1646 when he was ordered to scour his ditch at Highgate Hill it appears likely that he then lived in this cottage. He died in 1666, leaving a widow, Anne, and three sons under age, Edward, aged 17, John, aged 16, and Joseph, aged 13.

Mrs. Wright took for her second husband Owen Lewis of Highgate, yeoman, and when her eldest son, Edward Wright, came of age in 1670 he conveyed his third share to his stepfather. In 1672 Mr. and Mrs. Lewis, with her second son, John Wright, then of age, conveyed a third share to John Storer of Highgate, clerk. In 1674 the youngest son, Joseph Wright, on coming of age conveyed his third share to John Storer of the Middle Temple, son of the first-named John Storer. John Storer was a clergyman of the Church of England, who matriculated at Emmanuel College, Cambridge, in 1633, took his B.A. degree in 1637 and M.A. in 1640. He was curate at Doddinghurst, Essex, 13th October, 1637, Lecturer at St. Giles, Cripplegate, 18th March, 1641-2, vicar of Barking, 5th March, 1646/7, and Rector of Beckenham, Kent, 19th October, 1647. He married on 1st January, 1644-5, Joanna, daughter of John Christmas. Four of his children were baptised at Beckenham, viz. John in 1651, Elizabeth in 1653 and another Elizabeth, and Peter, on 3rd November, 1657. Calamy says that during his eleven years' stay at Beckenham he was well beloved though he sometimes met with rudeness from such persons as despised the ministerial office. He was appointed rector of St. Martin Vintry in Upper Thames Street, 23rd June, 1658. At the Restoration he became Lecturer at Stowmarket, Suffolk. This appointment he resigned before St. Bartholomew's Day, 24th August, 1662, because he would not accept the Act of Uniformity, which came into force then. Preferment in the Church being at an end for him, he came to Highgate and was licensed to keep a school there, on 17th April, 1672.[48] In 1678 the two Storers surrendered a messuage in the tenure of Robert Poulson of Highgate, to Robert Massey of London, joiner, on condition that he did not build or allow to be built any building to the prejudice of them or the obstruction of their view. Robert Massey, with Joanna, his wife, immediately surrendered a half of the above, then in the occupation of John Storer, senior, clerk, to the said John Storer, and the other half to his son, John Storer. Apparently this indicates either a division of John Storer's dwelling house, or the erection of another adjacent to it.

John Storer of the Middle Temple was born at Beckenham in Kent, was Sizar at Christ's College, Oxford, at the age of 16 on 8th July, 1668, and was admitted to the Middle Temple on 2nd February, 1671.[49] He succeeded in 1717 on the death of his father and immediately, with his wife, Elizabeth, surrendered to Peter Storer of the Inner Temple, gentleman, his son. John Storer, clerk, appears regularly on the " Homage " of the manor court from 1672 to 1689, as " John Storer, gentleman." Then there is a break of eight years before " John Storer, gentleman " again appears. He continued to sit on the Homage fairly often until 1714. Evidently the Rev. John Storer died about 1689, and the John Storer who appears from 1697 to 1714 was his son.

Peter Storer married Anne, only daughter of Christopher Ansty, a widow, who had a daughter, Ann Ansty Wetherby, by her former husband. The daughter married Gilbert Bearblock, as appears from the record of a surrender made by Peter Storer, son of the above, in 1754. In addition to the house formerly belonging to the two John Storers, Peter Storer acquired from the trustees of Mrs. Frances Bromfield, wife of Peter Bromfield, in 1736, a messuage, coachhouse, stables and garden, and a parcel of waste before the house, late the estate of John Wynn, gentleman, deceased. Mrs. Bromfield was formerly the wife of Mark " Winn " of St. Mary, Newington Butts, soapmaker, by whom she had two sons, John and Mark, under age in 1699, when their father was dead. The house came to her under the will of her son, John Wynn, of Highgate, gentleman, who died in July, 1730, leaving her his freeholds in Peckham and Bermondsey Street, Southwark, as well as his copyhold at Highgate by way of satisfaction for the great expenses she had in the Court of Chancery in order to get him during his minority under her care and out of gratitude for her tender care of him during several illnesses.[50] Her former husband, Mark " Winn," had been admitted on the surrender of John Welbe of London, grocer, in 1692, the house being then described as a messuage on the east of " Swines Lane " in the occupation of Christopher Foster, apothecary. In his will dated 13th May, 1699, and proved 1st June, 1699,[51] Mark Wynn mentions this as " the copyhold I had of Capt. Thomas Welbye of East Smithfield," at a cost of £300. The signature to his will was proved by Thomas Hall of St. George Martyr, Surrey, goldsmith, who said he was formerly a partner with the testator in the office of " Bayliffs of the Hundred of Brixton." John Welbe of Whitechapel, gentleman, had been admitted in 1682 on the surrender of Robert Massey of London, joiner, to a messuage in the occupation of Robert Poulson. Thus the records take us back to a house described in the same words as that owned by the two John Storers in 1678.

Peter Storer of the Inner Temple made his will on 30th March, 1749, and it was proved by his son, Peter, on 16th January, 1750. He desired to be buried in the chancel at Ashford, Middlesex, the funeral to be made with a hearse and one mourning coach with four horses each, without any ornaments or noise. To his wife he left for life the use of all his household goods, plate, linen and furniture in his dwelling house at Highgate except such of them as were Sir John Austin's or Mrs. Wright's, as well as £100. Also he gave her for life his farm at Old Ford. To his daughter, Martha, he gave £5,000 stock in the Bank of England and £50 ; to his daughter Sidney the like sum of £5,000 and £50. The remainder of his estate he left to his son Peter. This will was witnessed (with two others) by John Hawkins, afterwards the celebrated Sir John Hawkins, who married Sidney Storer on 24th March, 1753.[52]

The copyholds at Highgate inherited by Peter Storer the younger were a capital messuage (as in 1717) and a piece of waste granted to John Storer in 1689. In 1752 he acquired the two houses from William Brown mentioned before (p. 34), thus completing his ownership of the whole site now occupied by Church House, the Institution and the cottage behind. His will was proved on 9th August, 1759.[53] He desired to be buried in the chancel at Ashford near his parents. To his sister, Martha, wife of William Baker, esquire (of Rawston), he left his manor of Ashford, houses and land in Bethnal Green, Middlesex, Baddow in Essex, an estate in Bedfordshire, with all the plate, jewels, furniture, etc., in the houses. To his sister, Sidney, wife of John Hawkins, he gave his freeholds at Mile End, Old Ford Marsh, Bearbinder Lane and Church Lane in Middlesex, at Somerton in Suffolk and Cateaton Street and Lad Lane in the city of London, fee farm rents in various counties and his copyhold estate in Hornsey and Highgate. He mentions that John Hawkins was steward of his manor of Ashford. An interesting bequest to his " sister Baker " in addition was " the spring clock which is now in the back bed chamber of my house at Highgate, the repeating gold watch with the chased gold case thereto belonging and also the gold chased chain which hath a swivel fastened in the back part of it, the plain gold watch with the chain and ornaments which I commonly use therewith, the set of diamond shoe and knee buckles, the diamond stock buckle, the diamond buckle, for my shirt bosom, the diamond buttons for my shirt sleeves, my largest ring set with four great and two small diamonds." There was also a bequest to Mary Russell then living with him " as a grateful acknowledgment of her unwearied care and diligence in nursing and attending both my mother and myself to the prejudice of her own health and reputation " £3,000 Bank Stock and £300. In addition to several other substantial sums of money he left various amounts to Highgate people, viz. to Mr. John Pardoe of Highgate £100; to his neighbour John Southcots, esquire (who lived next door in Russell House) £100, and £200 to his wife ; to Archdeacon Yardley £100 ; to the Rev. Mr. Felton, Master of the Free School of Highgate, £100 ; to Robert Thomas, esquire, of Highgate, £100 ; to Mr. John Walklin, his gardener, £100. Storer had been elected a Governor of the Grammar School on 27th October, 1755, and he died on 8th August, 1759.

Thus Church House came into the possession of its best-known owner, John Hawkins, in right of his wife. He was born on 30th March, 1719, and was the youngest son of John Hawkins, carpenter and builder, and Elizabeth his wife, daughter of Thomas Gwatkin of Townhope, Hereford, gentleman. After qualifying as a surveyor he adopted the profession of the law and was employed by Mr. Peter Storer, whose acquaintance he made at the Academy of Ancient Music, and whose daughter, Sidney, as we have seen above, he married. The £5,000 which his wife had on the death of her father, augmented by the considerable property which her brother Peter Storer bequeathed to her, enabled Hawkins to retire from practice and devote himself to music and literature. He became Chairman of the Middlesex Quarter Sessions on 19th September, 1765, and was knighted. Leslie Stephen in the *Dict. Nat. Biog.* sums him up as " a man of coarse fibre, absurdly proud of ' my coach,' rough to inferiors and humble to men like Walpole, but not without solid good qualities." Dr. Johnson characterised him as " an honest man at bottom, but to be sure he is penurious and he is mean, and it must be owned he has a degree of brutality and a tendency to savageness that cannot easily be defended." His daughter, Laetitia Matilda Hawkins (who died unmarried at Twickenham on 22nd November, 1835, aged 75), published *Anecdotes*,

Biographical Sketches and Memoirs in 1822, in which she wrote (p. 139) : " My mother had, as I have stated, an only brother—a man whose name still lives in sweet hereditary remembrance in that part of Middlesex where we have copyhold property. Times then afforded a single man, with an un-incumbered landed property of £2,000 a year, to keep six carriage horses, and to live with a liberality equal to this. Mr. Storer, a perfect gentleman, kept up this style, but without ever suffering the smallest accumulation of debt ;—consequently he died rich. My mother had always been his favourite sister ; her lively temper and pretty person, together with the pains he had bestowed on her when hardly treated by her father because she was not a boy, had endeared her to him." Neither the style nor the matter of her books is particularly attractive but the following passage (p. 154) is interesting because it concerns Church House and its inmates. " My mother was born, I think, in or about 1726, and from her birth had lived on the very summit of Highgate Hill, and with a high road in view. She was at that period (the time of the '45 Rebellion) therefore of an age to be highly as well as deeply interested, in the event of so important a contest. She used to describe her father, who was a zealous Whig, as thoroughly dejected while matters were approaching to their crisis, and well recollected his burying two hundred guineas in his garden. She could describe all the scenery when the troops passed through to Finchley Common, and had even then before her eyes, the sumpter-mules and all the detail of the Duke of Cumberland's baggage."

Sir John Hawkins died on 21st May, 1789, leaving this property to his wife for life[54] and then to his son, John Sidney Hawkins. It has been usual to write of Sir John as a Highgate man, but it does not appear that he ever lived there. In 1782 he took out a licence to lease for 21 years, premises described as a messuage formerly in the tenure of Henry Playford and lately of David Duvaleoz, esquire, with the coachhouses and stables adjoining and also a yard and garden and small messuage behind the coachhouses formerly in the tenure of John Walklin and now of Cornelius. Sir John's brother-in-law, Peter Storer, left Mr. John Walklin, his gardener, £100, as mentioned before, and Sir John himself in his will mentions " the gardener's house adjacent thereto now inhabited by William Cornelius," the mansion house being then in the occupation of William Blamire. When Dame Sidney Hawkins came into the property in 1789 it was described as a capital messuage heretofore in the occupation of Peter Storer, etc., and a messuage then lately erected heretofore in the occupation of John Walklin, gardener, which ground abuts south on a garden heretofore in the tenure of —— Paul, esquire, and had formerly standing thereon a messuage and coachhouse (purchased by Peter Storer the elder) and land adjoining the dwelling house heretofore of Peter Storer the younger, on which ground formerly stood two messuages, formerly the estate of William Brown.

Dame Sidney Hawkins died in 1793 and her son, John Sidney Hawkins, then came into possession. He was born in 1758 and died on 12th August, 1842, in his 85th year at Lower Grove, Brompton, where he had long resided and was succeeded by his brother, Charles Sidney. According to Warwick Wroth, F.S.A., in the *Dict. Nat. Biog.*, he was " a learned antiquary whose talents were overshadowed by a sour and jealous temper." His library was sold in 1842. Of greater interest in the history of the house is Hyman Hurwitz (1770-1844), Professor of Hebrew in the University of London, who was born at Posen in Poland in 1770. He was a learned Jew who came to England about 1800 and conducted a private academy for Jews at Highgate, where he established a close friendship with Coleridge and corresponded with him. In 1828 he was elected Professor of the Hebrew language and literature at University College, London.[55] His tenancy of the house appears to have commenced in 1804, and to have lasted until 1820.[42] The landlord, John Sidney Hawkins, of Charlotte Street, Fitzroy Square, in 1821 granted to Hyman Hurwitz of Highgate, schoolmaster, for 17 years, a lease of Church House and a messuage abutting east and north in part on the before-mentioned premises (Church House), west on Swain's Lane and south on the garden belonging to the other premises. This latter was on the site of the Institution. It has been mentioned (p. 30) that Hurwitz took the place of the Rev. Edward Porter as tenant of the adjoining Russell House, No. 9, in 1810, but soon gave it up. Hurwitz (who died on 18th July, 1844) was succeeded as occupier by Leopold Newmigan in 1821[42] and who carried on the school. He was still there in 1831.

In 1839 the Highgate Literary and Scientific Institution was formed and entered into its present premises at the corner of Swain's Lane on 12th May, 1840.[56] When Charles Sidney Hawkins succeeded his brother as owner in 1842 the premises were described as a messuage, garden, coachhouse and stable formerly in the occupation of William Blamire, esquire, and the gardener's house adjacent thereto formerly inhabited by William Cornelius, esquire, "which coachhouse and stable has been some time since pulled down and upon the site thereof a certain messuage and building has been erected now called the Highgate Literary and Scientific Institution." This rebuilding is again mentioned in a lease granted on 22nd April, 1843, by Charles Sidney Hawkins to Kilham Roberts of Highgate, schoolmaster, for 21 years, of a dwelling house late in the occupation of Leopold Newmigan, as separated and parted off by a wall or wooden fence from a cottage and buildings formerly parcel of and held with the messuage, but now for the most part converted and used as a place of meeting of certain persons called the Highgate Literary and Scientific Institution.

A further lease of the Institution for 21 years was granted in 1861 by Charles Sidney Hawkins of Broughton, near Swindon, esquire, to William Gladstone of Fitzroy Park, esquire, Josiah Wilkinson of Fitzroy Park, esquire, and William Peter Bodkin of Merton Lane, esquire, where the premises are described as a messuage and buildings, etc., with a garden in front and a cottage behind, the said cottage being underlet to William Potter and then in the occupation of the widow of the late Jonathan Bower, stone mason, abutting on a messuage, garden and premises of Charles Sidney Hawkins leased to Henry Daniels. When the premises of the Highgate Literary and Scientific Institution and Church House, Nos. 11 and 10, South Grove, were enfranchised in 1897, Church House was stated to have been formerly in the occupation of William Bedmore and " now " of Robert Payne Grace. The story of the *Cow and Hare* on the site of which an unfounded tradition says the Institution was erected will be found in Section XI.

VI—SWAIN'S LANE

HISTORICAL NOTES.

This thoroughfare is mentioned as far back as the year 1492 as " Swayneslane," though the less euphonious form usually employed until last century was " Swines Lane." It was one of four parallel routes up the hill to the village, viz. West Hill, Bromwich Walk, Swain's Lane and Dartmouth Hill. Bromwich Walk never developed beyond a footpath and has disappeared. The use of Swain's Lane was mainly to provide access to the adjacent farm lands on either side and there were no dwellings in it except at a few yards from the upper end. In the year 1887 the London Cemetery Company acquired a group of cottages numbered 1 to 8, Swain's Lane, standing on a rectangular plot of ground on the western side, facing Waterlow Park opposite the moat. Here once stood the only house of note in the lane, belonging to Dr. Elisha Coysh. The owner in Queen Elizabeth's time was John Gilpin (see p. 42).[57] In 1609 William Gwercie (who had married Gilpin's widow), and Everard Gilpin, his son, conveyed to John Wetherley of Highgate, yeoman, and Margaret, his wife, a newly built cottage, a garden and half an acre in " Swayns Lane," late in the tenure of John Purton and Richard Blake. John Wetherley, by his will dated 21st November, 1631, and proved on 12th December, 1631, left to his wife " four cottages standing in Swines Lane," his son, William, was to have them after her death.[58]

Then a gap occurs in the record until we find Dr. Elisha Coish in 1657 in possession of a cottage and garden and a close adjoining containing half an acre in " Swines Lane " and a messuage adjoining the cottage, being formerly part thereof. In 1659 Dr. Coish had licence to lay pipes from " Swines Well in Swines Lane " to his house and to his other tenements there, for conveying water, about three yards from the well to the wall of the messuage. Lloyd in his *History of Highgate*, published in 1888, says : " The buildings were very ancient, of wood and plaster. The house was pulled down in 1760 ; the garden wall still remains." Lloyd quotes certain notes concerning Dr. Coysh : " This High Dutch physician—newly come over from Holland, where he resided all the time of the Great Plague in Amsterdam, and cured multitudes of people that actually had the plague upon them . . . was indeed a most charitable man to the diseased poor. . . . There is a case told of his goodness to thirteen poor people who were flying for their lives from London and Clerkenwell, and who intended to have gone north, away by Highgate, but were stopped at Holloway, as there the people would not let them pass, or not even suffer them to be in a barn for the night ; so they crossed the fields towards Hampstead, when Dr. Coysh having heard of their distress, he had them brought to his barns, and there attended to and fed them for two days ; he then saw them got safe to Finchley Common, where they intended to wait until they were in hopes the cold weather would check the infection." While receiving the narrative with reserve we may believe that it reflected the popular impression of the man. There seems no ground, however, for thinking that he was a Dutchman. One Roger Coise, citizen and grocer of London, living in Aldermanbury, mentions in his will, proved 24th March, 1579, his son-in-law, Richard Blake, and his brother, William Cois.[59] As we have seen, a Richard Blake was a tenant of these premises before 1609. Thomasine Coyce *alias* Coys, widow of the said Roger Coise, made her will on 9th January, 1593-4, five days before it was proved. She left £70 to her daughter " Susan Blage " (probably Susan Blake, wife or widow of the before-mentioned Richard Blake). This Mrs. Coyce was of Hackney and wished to be buried in Hackney Church.[60] Dr. Coish married Sara, daughter of John James, apothecary, of *Hackney*.

Dr. Elisha Coish[61] was born on 30th January, 1632, and baptised at St. Mary Aldermary. He was the son of Richard Coish, skinner. He was granted the degree of M.D. by Oxford University in 1657, and was admitted a Fellow of the College of Physicians in 1673, and died on 11th January, 1686, and was buried in St. Mary Aldermary. In his will, made 18th August, 1683, and proved 22nd January, 1686, he mentions that he had by deed in 1673 settled his estate on his wife, Sara, for life.[61] He married Sarah James on 5th October, 1656, at St. Mary Aldermary, and left four sons, James, Elisha, Richard and John, as well as a daughter Bridget. Of these John, the youngest, was to have his two copyhold messuages at Highgate, held of the Manor of Cantlowes. He also possessed leaseholds from the Corporation of London, on tenterground near the Dog House bequeathed to him by Hester Harrison, widow. She lived at Highgate in a house leased from Sir John Wollaston, on the site of Channing House School, and in her will [62] refers to him as her " friend Elisha Coysh, of St. Albones, Woodstreete, London, Doctor in Phisick."

John and James Coish died before their mother, and their brothers, Elisha and Richard, took the Highgate property after her death in March, 1703. Elisha Coish was dead in 1725, leaving a widow, Hannah, when his brother became sole owner. In 1740 Richard Coish was dead, leaving two sons, Elisha and Thomas, their Aunt Hannah being still alive. In 1761 Thomas Coish died, leaving the property to his wife, Rebecca, with remainder to his son Richard. She died in 1765. On 7th July, 1770, Richard Coish, then of Muswell Hill, with Loretta his wife, conveyed the property to John Rolls of Bermondsey, cowkeeper, who had married Richard's sister, Sarah. In 1801 it passed to one Finney Sirdefield. It is interesting to note that the John Rolls mentioned was the great-grandfather of John Allan Rolls of the Hendre and Llangattock, first Baron Llangattock.

In 1811 Finney Sirdefield had licence to lease two houses in Swain's Lane to Thomas Vincent, for 21 years. In 1834 Alfred Sirdefield succeeded under the will of Finney Sirdefield, the two houses having then become six. In 1858 Anna Sirdefield succeeded. She died on 4th November, 1882, and her executors sold the houses to the London Cemetery Company. Among the cottages standing in 1831 was one occupied as a police station.

GENEALOGY OF COISH AND ROLLS FAMILIES

Richard Coish, skinner, of Watling Street = Mary, died 27th January, 1672-3

Mary, married — Rye

Sara, dau. of John James of Hackney, apothecary. = Elisha Coish, M.D., b. 30th Jan., 1631-2. d. 11th Jan., 1685-6. Married 5th Oct., 1656, at Aldermanbury. Will dated 15th, and proved 27th March, 1703 — Will P.C.C., 2 *Lloyd*

James Coysh. Dead in 1697

Elisha Coysh, mercer. Married Hannah Fox, 12th Jan., 1692-3, at Aldermanbury. Her will proved 14th April, 1743, P.C.C. 103 *Boycott*

= Richard Coysh, citizen and fishmonger. Victualler, of the Drayman and Horses, Southwark. Will dated 17th Sept., 1735. P.C.C. 202 *Busby*

John Coysh. At Merchant Taylors School 1679-80. Buried 15th April, 1692

Bridget. Married

Rebecca. Lived at the Hen and Chickens p.h. in Camberwell. Will da. 30th Jan., pr. 4th Mar. 1765. P.C.C. 89 *Rushworth*

= Thomas Coish of Camberwell, butcher. Will dated 26th Jan., proved 3rd Feb., 1761. P.C.C. 48 *Cheslyn*

Elisha Coish of Bush Lane, wine cooper. Will proved 1751. P.C.C. 136 *Busby*

Sarah   Elizabeth

Sara = John Rolls of Bermondsey, cow keeper. Will dated 26th Aug., 1800, proved 27th Nov., 1801. P.C.C. 764 *Abercrombie*

Richard = Loretta Coish of Muswell Hill

Elizabeth married — Busby

John Rolls of Bryanstone Square and the Hendre, Mon. b. 30th Oct., 1776. d. 31st Jan., 1837. Will P.C.C. 407 *Norwich* = Martha Barrett. Married 27th Jan., 1803

John Etherington Welch Rolls. = Elizabeth Mary, dau. of d. 27th May, 1870 — Walter Long. Married 1833

John Allan Rolls of the Hendre, cr. Baron Llangattock, 30th Aug. 1892. b. 19th Feb., 1837, d. 24th Sept., 1912 = Georgina Marcia, 4th dau. of Sir C. F. Maclean. Married 1868. d. 1925

John Maclean Rolls, 2nd Baron 1870-1916

Hon. Allen Rolls, 1871-1916

Hon. Charles Stewart Rolls. b. 27th Aug., 1877. d. 12th July, 1910

VII—MORETON HOUSE (NO. 14, SOUTH GROVE), AND THE SITES OF NOS. 12, 13 AND 15, SOUTH GROVE

GROUND LANDLORD, LEASEHOLDER, ETC.

No. 14 was originally copyhold of the Manor of Cantlowes but has been enfranchised and is now in the ownership and occupation of Mr. K. S. Dodd.

GENERAL DESCRIPTION AND DATE OF STRUCTURE.

Moreton House is one of a pair of houses (Plate 31), its companion having been demolished, and is built on the characteristic local plan, namely a single room on either side of a central hall in which is the staircase, the arrangement being repeated on each floor with modern additions to the back (Plate 33). It will be seen from the historical notes that follow that the date of the house is 1715. The hall and stairway are panelled to the full height up to the first floor, and the ground and first-floor rooms to the west also retain their original panelling, while in the former there is an original cupboard beside the fireplace with semicircular-shaped shelving.

The room to the east of the hall and the one above it have been stripped of their early panelling and redecorated in the style of the latter part of the 18th century.

The exterior is of stock brick with red-brick angles, window heads and dressings (Plate 32). All the openings are square-headed, the centres ones having carved bracket ornament similar to those of Nos. 53 and 54, South Grove. Five out of the six windows to the left are dummies. The six-panelled entrance door is flanked by a pair of three-quarter columns of the Ionic order carrying a blocked entablature and pediment as overdoor. The brick string course at first-floor level is carried up over the centre to clear the pediment. The staircase, which is constructed in a rather confined space (see Plates 34 and 35), is of interest as a dated example since it affords a basis upon which to date the staircases in the neighbouring houses. In general construction it resembles the stair in No. 4, The Grove, except that it has two or even three curtailed balusters to the close string instead of a single one, the latter treatment being an earlier design.

HISTORICAL NOTES.

At the beginning of the 17th century the frontage between Swain's Lane on the east and Arundel House on the west was occupied by " a messuage yard, garden, orchard and close containing one acre," now represented by Nos. 12-15, South Grove. The property was in the tenure of Thomas Throckmorton, esquire, doubtless the Thomas Throckmorton of Congleton, Warwick, who died on 13th March, 1614, and who was the grandfather of Robert Throckmorton, who was created a baronet on 1st September, 1642. On 21st March, 1602-3, Thomas Throckmorton wrote to Sir Robert Cecil : " I received the letter from the Council this 21 March. It seems the bearer sought me in the country, where indeed I have made my abode here in Highgate the most part of this year for my urgent business about London. My house is infected with small pox. I was never more unable to travel from the aches that have fallen upon my limbs. I would humbly beseech liberty to remain here in my house for a time." As a Roman Catholic he was continually

41

Cooper

Holles

harassed by the laws then in force against adherents of the old faith. The letter from the Council which he mentions was a circular letter sent out by the Privy Council to various noblemen and others asking them to assemble unobtrusively in London. Queen Elizabeth died three days after this letter was written by Throckmorton, who was then about 70 years old.[63] This estate was conveyed in 1608 by William Guercie of Boyscott, Suffolk, esquire, and Everard Guilpin of Boyscott, a son of the late John Guilpin, gentleman, to Laurence Caldwell, citizen and vintner of London and Mary his wife. The John Guilpin mentioned was elected a Governor of the Grammar School on 22nd May, 1580, in place of William Lambe, a Foundation Governor. He died on 27th February, 1590-1, and it may be supposed that he lived in the messuage mentioned above. He held the office of clerk of the pleas in the Court of the Exchequer, and Thomasin his widow married William Guercy.[64]

Laurence Caldwell and his wife conveyed the property in 1610 to Nicholas Cooper, gentleman, son of John Cooper, scrivener, of St. Michael's, Cornhill, alderman of London, who had died on 3rd June, 1609. In 1619 it passed from Nicholas Cooper and his brother, William, to their sister, Elizabeth, the widow of John Jaques (died 1605). She died on 18th June, 1624, aged 49, leaving five sons and two daughters. Her brother, William, took this property under her will, subject to the payment of certain legacies to her children. William Cowper (or Cooper) of Ratling Court, Nonington, Kent (ancestor of the Earls Cowper), was born on 7th March, 1582, and was created a baronet on 4th March, 1641-2. He died on 20th December, 1664, his wife, Martha, a daughter of James Masters, whom he married in 1611, having died five years earlier.

The next owner was Sir Robert Payne of the neighbouring Arundel House (see p. 50), but the date of the conveyance is not available; it was probably about 1640. About this time the tenant was George Pryor, gentleman, who was elected a Governor of the Grammar School on 5th June, 1658, in place of Sir John Wollaston, deceased. His daughter, Dorothy Pryor, was buried at Highgate on 29th August, 1644. Later he lived on the site of Andrew Marvell's Cottage, the grounds of which were incorporated in Waterlow Park. In 1670 the owner of this and Arundel House was William Payne, who sold the whole property to Francis Blake. The tenant at that time (1670) was Benjamin Archer, and the hearth tax in 1666 shows him assessed on 10 hearths. In 1673 the house was occupied by " Esq. Kage."

In 1686 the Right Hon. Francis Holles of Ifield acquired the property from Francis Blake, subject to the yearly payment of £28. He evidently effected considerable alterations in the premises, then described as a mansion house, two gardens, an orchard, little stable, barn and great stable, heretofore in the tenure of Benjamin Archer, afterwards of —— Nelthorpe and now of Lord Holles, etc. Francis Blake again came into possession in 1688 and owned it until his death in 1694, when his son, Sir Francis Blake, succeeded. In 1715 Sir Francis Blake and Elizabeth, his wife, sold it for upwards of £500 to Roger Young, timber merchant.

Roger Young only lived a few months after his purchase, but when he died, on 2nd December, 1715, he had pulled down the outbuildings attached to this " very great and ancient mansion house " and built in their place and nearly finished two new brick houses, one being occupied at the time of his death. This cost him £480. He also owned some thirteen leasehold houses in " Blackfriars, Grubb Street and Spittlefields." As shown below, these two new houses occupied the westernmost portion of the frontage, therefore the house itself stood to the east of them on the site now occupied by the Congregational Church and Nos. 12 and 13.

Roger Young left four daughters and coheiresses, three of them being unmarried and the youngest being about ten years old. But for his untimely decease we should never have known the many interesting facts put on record through an action in Chancery brought by the three younger daughters against their mother in 1716 and in another Chancery action in 1727 by the mother and two of her daughters against another daughter and her husband. The Bill of Complaint in the first action[65] was filed on 19th December, 1716, by Martha, Margaret and Catherine Young, against Mrs. Martha Young, their mother, and Samuel Sanders and his wife, Hester, their sister, reciting their father's will and alleging that the defendants refused to pay the legacies. In the answer filed by the mother, Mrs. Martha Young, she points out that the daughters could not expect to have the full benefit of the legacies left them by their father because his purchase of this property and building on it had kept him bare of money, so that when he died he did not leave behind him so much as forty shillings in cash nor as much as £60 in exchequer bills, bank bills or debts, but on the contrary owed £150, of which £80 was to workmen and tradesmen for the new buildings.

The complaint was brought on behalf of Martha, Margaret and Katherine, infants, by Roger Young their uncle and " next friend," whence we may hope it was a friendly action for the purpose of getting the Court to authorise the widow and executrix to defer payment of legacies until the necessary funds had accumulated. There was an inventory of household goods and stock in trade given by Mrs. Young so informative regarding the furnishing of the house as to deserve to be set out in full.

" In the chamber one pair of steps and little room. Two bedsteads, one set of furniture, two feather beds, two bolsters, five pillows, two blankets, three rugs, one table, one glass, eight caned chairs, one caned couch, two chests of drawers, one pair of bellows, one close stool, one cradle.

In the parlour.
Two tables, five caned chairs, one looking glass, one clock, one grate and fender, seven pictures, two prints.

In the little chamber.
One striped camlet bed, one feather bed, and bolster, two blankets, one rug, one quilt, one table bedstead, one feather bed, and bolster, two blankets, one set of window curtains, two chairs.

In the best chamber.
One camlet bed, one feather bed and bolster, two pillows, three blankets, two quilts, two set of window curtains, two chest of drawers, one table, one looking glass, two sconces, ten chairs, one chest, one cupboard, three boxes, one grate and fender, shovel, tongs and two dogs, ten pair of sheets, five pair of pillowbeers, four table cloths, twelve napkins, twelve towels, some broken linen, all the deceased's wearing apparel linen and woollen, three rings, one watch, six knives and six forks.

In the kitchen.
One grate, shovel, fender, tongs and poker, one crane and spit, racks, a gridiron, one box iron and heathers, one jack, three spits, a shredding knife, seven candle sticks, one pair of snuffers, one mortar, two sconces, three boiling pots and covers, three saucepans, one firing pan, one warming pan, one table, five chairs, one cushion, one cupboard, a pair of bellows, some wooden, earthen and tin ware, fifteen pewter dishes, two pie plates, three dozen and nine plates, two pots, one funnel, three pottingers, two candlesticks, one silver tankard, one cup, two salts, seven silver spoons, one looking glass, one musket and sword, two escutcheons, two prints, some lumber.

In the yard and cellar.
One copper and iron work, one leaden cistern, all the brewing vessels tubs and pails, six hundred eighty two deals, two load of oak joists and quarters, thirty balks, two load and half of laths, three load of timber, four saws, some coals, wood and lumber."

All the household goods and stock in trade contained in this account were valued at £131 5s. 10d. Six rooms are thus accounted for, but, as will appear later, there were many more rooms in the old house let to various persons.

In the second action[66] the plaintiffs were Katherine Young, aged 16 (by her mother, Mrs. Martha Young), and the eldest daughter Hester (widow of Samuel Sanders of Blackfriars), and the defendants were their sister, Margaret, with her husband Thomas Pangbourne. In the interval of ten years many things had happened, which quite negative the idea of a " friendly " action. Martha had married one, James Ludlam, and been left a widow, her share had been bought by her mother, therefore only three daughters had then an interest in the property. The demand of the plaintiffs was for a partition of the estate, which was granted by decree on 10th November, 1729.[67]

Thomas Pangbourne, " hotpresser," married Margaret on 18th May, 1723, and bought from Mrs. Young a month later the fourth share formerly belonging to Mrs. Martha Ludlam, so that he now held one half share. The plaintiffs alleged that the estate was worth £100 a year, that Pangbourne inhabited part himself and let part at considerable rents. He had disposed of several parcels of land at great benefit and also converted several parcels of land to his own private use. Other parts by his own ill conduct and mismanagement had been empty and the tenants forced to leave. He had turned out several good tenants and thereby their tenements had stood empty for several years. They said he would not come to any fair partition of the estate nor allot them their two fourth parts and gave out in speeches that if they would not sell their shares at his price he would starve them out. In the framework of the lawyers' phrasing one can almost hear the two ladies breathlessly reciting their grievances. The answer of Mr. and Mrs. Pangbourne reveals an interesting state of affairs within the " very great and ancient mansion house " of Lord Holles. They set out the tenants as follows, from the date of their wedding.

Martha Young, widow, had three low rooms, one chamber, one coachhouse and one cellar belonging to the old house, and a garden, at £10 a year (" low rooms " mean rooms on the ground floor.) Some time after she left without notice.

Hester Sanders between Midsummer and Michaelmas, 1723, left without notice two chambers in the old house which she rented at £4, and they were unlet until Ladyday, 1725. She went to her mother's rooms (except one room then occupied by Richard Pangbourne, of London, hatter, father of Thomas Pangbourne, at £1) and paid £9 for them from Michaelmas, 1723, until the following Midsummer, when she left without notice and left them very much out of repair. At Ladyday, 1725, Susanna Pepys, widow, took the rooms at £4. The rooms first occupied by Mrs. Young and afterwards by Mrs. Sanders were taken by Richard Gadbury, gardener, at Christmas, 1724, at £10.

Richard Pangbourne occupied one large chamber and a cellar in the old house and a stable and garden, which garden he made at his own expense, at £6, and at Michaelmas, 1723, took another room at £1. On Midsummer Day, 1726, Richard Pangbourne's wife (Thomas's mother, unless his father had remarried) gave him notice, and he fixed a bill over the door of the house that the rooms were to let.

William Harding, a bridle cutter, had one large room at £3 10s. and had had the same ever since.

William Warminger, carpenter, had five low rooms and five chambers in the old house at £7, but Mrs. Sanders thought the rent was too low and Warminger agreed at Christmas last (1726) to pay 20s. more the first year and 10s. more each year until he paid £10.

Nathaniel Hall, junior, mason, had two rooms and a cellar in the old house at £4.

Jeremy Murden, labourer, rented the orchard behind the old house containing 1 acre at £4 till Ladyday, 1725, when Daniel King, baker, enclosed and rented a small part of it at 30s. a year and held it until his death, Murden paying 10s. a year less. Daniel King, it may be remarked, lived in the High Street on the southern corner of Townsends Yard, now No. 42.

James Crompton, junior, carpenter, had a timber yard near the house and a shed, at £4, and also built a shed for Pangbourne's chaise to stand in, at Pangbourne's expense.

Thus there were 19 or 20 rooms in the house in which at least a dozen adults lived, to say nothing of children.

The two new houses were built where a barn, stable and outhouses formerly stood. Anthony Mendez, merchant, occupied one at £25, until Ladyday, 1724, the house then remaining empty till Michaelmas, 1725, when Dennis Foy, coffeeman, took it at £20, being allowed £4 towards repairs.

Ralph Thompson, junior, soapboiler, had a lease of the other house, granted by Mrs. Martha Young to his father, Ralph Thompson, senior. He left at Christmas, 1723, and the house was empty for a year, when Henry Bradley, citizen and surgeon, of London, leased it for 21 years at £20 a year, payable quarterly. In the following Midsummer Pangbourne took over the lease.

Thomas Pangbourne said that he had frequently in a friendly manner offered to account to his sisters-in-law for their shares of the rents if they would allow for their shares of the expenses and, in particular, on 2nd January last, before they filed their Bill against him, made up separate accounts between himself and Mrs. Sanders and himself and Catherine, and sent it by his agent, but they refused to accept the balance or to allow for repairs. He claimed to have considerably improved the estate by his care and good management, but they on the contrary seemed inclined to allow it to go to decay and ruin by refusing to help with the necessary repairs. The dispute was settled, as stated before, by a partition of the estate, half going to Catherine Yorke and Hester Birch, and half to Thomas Pangbourne and Margaret. The mother, Mrs. Martha Young, appears to have died in 1750, for her will was proved in that year.

44

Moreton House, No. 14, South Grove.

The house occupied by Anthony Mendez, and later by Denis Foy, is represented to-day by Moreton House, No. 14, South Grove. The Court of Chancery was not expeditious and before the matter was settled in 1729 Catherine Young, who was aged 16 in 1726, had married Robert Yorke the younger, merchant, and her widowed sister, Hester Sanders, had married Robert Yorke the elder of Highgate, gentleman, as appears by their statements filed in May and October, 1728, respectively, doubtless indicating the approximate dates of their marriages.[68] It must have been the elder gentleman's previous wife who was buried at Highgate as " Mrs. Elizabeth Yorke late Pious Wife of Mr. Robert Yorke, in Hope of a glorious Resurrection December 1724."[25] Hester's second marriage did not last long, since she again appears as a widow and then, in June, 1731, as the wife of Robert Birch. The latter was an innholder of Huntingdon in 1737 and of Grantham in 1742. The detailed record of the portion allotted to Hester and Catherine as their half share is not available, but Robert Yorke and Catherine his wife in 1736 conveyed to Peter Storer what is described (in 1770) as a messuage formerly in the occupation of —— Foy, coffeeman, afterwards of Aaron Otto, and then of the Rev. George Hardy. From that date the ownership was the same as that of Church House (see p. 35) until the death of Dame Hawkins in 1794, when it passed under the entail to her son Henry Hawkins, esquire, who still owned it at the time of his death in 1842. Later occupiers[42] were Mrs. Winslow, Count Maltzan, Prussian Ambassador (1781), John Theurer, Susanna Lowther (*circa* 1794), Widow Marus (*circa* 1801), Mrs. Grant (1802-6), empty (1807-8), James Gillman (1809-22), —— Pott (1824-). Dr. Gillman moved to No. 3, The Grove in 1823.

Bisham Court, No. 15, South Grove.

The other house built by Roger Young, leased by his widow to Ralph Thompson, senior, and afterwards occupied by his son Ralph Thompson, soapboiler, is represented now by Bisham Court, No. 15, South Grove. It was conveyed by Thomas Pangbourne in 1752 to John Edwards, whose wife was the sister and eventually sole legatee of John Schoppens (see p. 58). The tenant in 1731 was Susanna Pepys, widow, in 1752 Elizabeth Carpenter, spinster, and in 1794 Mrs. Jones. From 1752 to 1820 the ownership was the same as that of Ashurst House (see p. 61). In 1830 the trustee of the Cave family conveyed the house to James Meharey of Fetter Lane, perfumier. It was then described as a messuage south of the Ponds in the occupation of Benjamin Richards, with the lofts or rooms over the stables or gateway belonging to the premises and a large garden to the south of the garden immediately adjoining the messuage, the said large garden being in the occupation of James Meharey and containing half an acre. It abutted east partly on " Swines Lane " and partly on premises lately occupied by Mr. Gillman and north partly on the garden of the house lately belonging to Mr. Gilman (No. 14, South Grove). For many years prior to 1808 the occupier was a Miss Jones, then followed by John Gates until 1819. It was empty in 1820-1 and Benjamin Richards first appears as occupier in 1822. He was there in 1831.[42]

James Meharey sold the house to Joseph Gardiner of Bisham House (see p. 25), and at his death on 2nd August, 1853, it passed to his widow, Harriet Gardiner.

Nos. 12 and 13, South Grove.

In order to complete the story of the whole estate the record of its remaining portion, lying between the Congregational Chapel and Swain's Lane, may be briefly given, as follows. Lætitia Matilda Hawkins, only daughter of Dame Sidney Hawkins, was admitted on the death of her mother in 1794, to " garden ground at the west corner of Swains Lane," which she had licence to lease in 1823 to George Stringer for 21 years. She died on 22nd November, 1835, unmarried, at the age of 77, when it passed under her will to her brother, Henry Hawkins, being then described a garden ground at the west corner of Swain's Lane and two messuages in the occupation of George Stringer and —— Fernee. The premises were again leased to George Stringer in 1838, for 21 years. At his death in 1841 they were described as a messuage formerly in the occupation of Susannah Loader, widow, and a garden at the west corner of Swain's Lane and two messuages. Later occupiers were —— Thoroughgood and —— Chipingfield.

VIII—SITE OF ARUNDEL HOUSE, OLD HALL (NO. 17, SOUTH GROVE), AND THE SITE OF THE LAWNS (NO. 16, SOUTH GROVE)

GROUND LANDLORD, LEASEHOLDER, ETC.

Old Hall was originally copyhold of the Manor of Cantlowes but has been enfranchised and is now in the ownership and occupation of Lord Rochdale.

GENERAL DESCRIPTION AND DATE OF STRUCTURE.

The site of Old Hall, and more particularly of its eastern neighbour, No. 16, South Grove, was occupied in the middle of the 16th century by a house belonging to the Cornwallis family which passed later to the Earls of Arundel. This house was believed to have occupied a site on the Bank which lies within the border of Hornsey. Its story, however, is to be found not in the records of Hornsey but in the Court Rolls of the Manor of Cantlowes, as will be seen from the historical notes which follow. The present building may contain some fragments of the early fabric, part of the basement of the north-east wing having brickwork of English bond. The existing structure consists of a centre block of three storeys flanked on one side by the one-storey wing referred to above and on the other by modern additions.

The plan of 1804 (Plate 1) shows a considerable range of buildings to the east of the main block of Old Hall and their general appearance can be gathered from a study of the houses shown on the skyline of the engraving of Ashurst House (Plate 41). There is also an engraving in the Potter Collection now in the British Museum which appears to have been taken from the prospectus of Messrs. Grignon & Hull's Academy (Plate 36*b*), which occupied the east wing of Old Hall and the house to the east, the site of which is covered to-day by a tennis court. From these drawings it is evident that the buildings were extensive and of Elizabethan character, and there is little doubt that they represent the remains of the actual fabric of Arundel House.

The main part of Old Hall dates from a rebuilding of 1694 but appears to have been refronted in stock brickwork with red bricks as dressings to the windows and external angles. The front (Plate 37) is symmetrically arranged with five sash windows on the first and second floors. There is an additional block or annexe to the north-east (slightly recessed from the face of the main building), which contains a second staircase. The centre of the front projects a few inches and in this is set a plain doorway with a modern porch.

The face of the building is relieved by a string course above the ground-floor windows and another which forms a slight cornice above the second-floor windows, over which is a plain parapet. The back elevation though considerably broken into by the two large projecting bays already noted shows several original windows with curved heads. Two central openings above the garden entrance have semicircular heads. There are brick string courses at the first- and second-floor levels and a small one just below the parapet to the main block only. The chimney stacks are at the sides of the house and the parallel roofs terminate in small twin gables. On one of these, to the south-west, is a rain-water head with the date 1691 with initials arranged thus $\begin{smallmatrix} 16 & A & 91 \\ W & & E \end{smallmatrix}$ for William and Elizabeth Ashurst, recording no doubt the rebuilding of the house at this period. Twenty years before this date from the evidence of the Hearth Tax Rolls (see Appendix II) the building which then occupied the site had been divided into two tenements. To-day, however, the two portions are restored to one occupation. It seems reasonable to suggest that the year 1691 saw its separation from the mansion house which at one time was occupied by the Earls of Arundel.

The plan (Plate 38) of the centre block now comprises a front hall running the full width, but in all probability it was at one time subdivided into a passage with flanking rooms. Towards the garden is a staircase hall with a room on each side, fitted with large modern bay windows. The one to the east is panelled in large squares with bolection mouldings, separated by plain square deal uprights which may be the remains of earlier panelling of the normal type. There is the usual cornice but below it is a plain frieze with a very small architrave moulding above the main panels. The doors, which are three in number, are of six-panel bolection moulded type with similar but very narrow panels above them. At one time a large conservatory led out of this room, but this has been replaced in recent years by a bay with canted sides round which the details of the panelling are continued.

On the first floor there is a typical 18th-century panelled room to the right at the head of the stairs over the ground-floor room just described. There are also some six-panelled doors with fielded mouldings somewhat similar to that in the main entrance to Russell House (No. 9, South Grove). The central stair seems to have been replaced by a modern one, but that in the east wing has spiral balusters, plain newels and continuous strings—probably of the late 17th century. There are one or two fragments of panelling of Jacobean date re-used in different parts of the basement, one being at the foot of the main stairs. There is also one 17th-century beam.

The entrance gate to Old Hall is an excellent example of 18th-century iron-work with elaborate scroll-work panels each side and an ornamental overthrow. The piers with ball finials have been cased in cement.

Although they are importations from elsewhere mention must be made, for the purposes of record, of the two magnificent panelled rooms that Lord Rochdale, the present owner of Old Hall, has fitted into the ground and first-floor apartments in the main block, with the circular bays overlooking the garden. The ground-floor room bears the date 1595 and was brought from an old inn on the quay at Great Yarmouth. It has a splendid modelled plaster ceiling. That on the first floor came from Rochdale in Lancashire. In addition to other woodwork the house contains to-day Lord Rochdale's famous collection of ancient painted glass consisting of 67 principal pieces of

Kemp Lord Rochdale

47

every period from the 13th to the 17th century. These were fully described by Mr. F. Sydney Eden in the *Connoisseur* for July, August and October, 1934.

HISTORICAL NOTES.

On the site now occupied by Old Hall, St. Michael's Church, Voel and (till recently) South Grove House, stood the celebrated mansion where Sir William Cornwallis lived during the reigns of Queen Elizabeth and James I, followed by Thomas, 2nd Lord Arundel of Wardour, and where Sir Francis Bacon, Lord Verulam, died in 1626. The frontage of the Arundel House estate extended from Bromwich Walk to Bisham Court. It is probably represented by a messuage, barn, stable, orchard and 3 acres of land conveyed to William Cornwallis, esquire, by Henry Draper in 1588, " late in the tenure of Richard Boyce " and in which Cornwallis (then Sir William) lived in 1610. In the same year, 1588, Cornwallis also acquired, from Sir Henry Cromwell and Susanna his wife, 10 acres of land, part of Broadmede. Some facts throwing light on the history of the estate may be found in the record of an action in Chancery[69] brought against him in 1603 by one Joan Sandbache, widow of Francis Sandbache, who claimed to have an annuity charged on some of the property. Her complaint was that Sir William had built on the land and so altered the old boundaries that she could not now identify the premises which had belonged to her husband. Sir William in reply stated that one Tarry dwelt in the messuage long since and built a new house, joining it to part of the old house, and was succeeded in ownership by one Warren, and he supposed that one or both of these two were responsible for altering the boundaries. Sir Henry Cromwell, who owned the property in right of his wife, sold it to him for £630, being £200 more than it was worth. Though not admitting liability Sir William stated that he had in fact paid her £3 6s. 8d. a year for many years. Then he offered £13 6s. 8d. in settlement, being four years' purchase, and " as much as her annuity was worth, even if her claim was good, because she was a very old woman and not likely to be of long continuance in this world." Her nephew, Martin, on her behalf demanded 15 or 16 years' purchase. The Sir Henry Cromwell referred to, who died on 7th January, 1603, was the grandfather of Oliver Cromwell, and married the daughter and heiress of Sir Ralph Warren, Lord Mayor of London in 1536-7 and 1544, who died in 1553. The reference to Warren in the pleadings of Sir William Cornwallis, given above, suggests that the property in Highgate belonged formerly to Sir Ralph Warren.

Cornwallis

Sir William Cornwallis was the eldest son of Sir Thomas Cornwallis, K.G., Comptroller of the Household to Queen Mary. In the year 1591 (10th March) he was elected a Governor of the Grammar School. His father died in 1604. Although we have the date (1588) of his purchase of his house at Highgate, there is a letter at Hatfield House[70] written by his father on 23rd July, 1587, to Lord Burghley. Queen Elizabeth paid visits[71] to Highgate on 11th June, 1589, 7th June, 1593, and in 1594, probably to Sir William Cornwallis. John Norden wrote in 1593, " At this place ——— Cornwalleys, Esquire, hath a very faire house from which he may behold with great delight the staitlie citie of London, Westminster, Greenwich, the famous river of Thamyse, and the country towards the south very farre." The house must indeed have been an attractive dwelling place, on the brow of the hill, with the village green in front to the north and the slopes of Highgate Hill behind with open country all the way to the city, affording a splendid panorama, Old St. Paul's being only some four miles away. William Cornwallis accompanied the Earl of Essex in his expedition against the Irish rebels in 1599 and was knighted at Dublin on 5th August, 1599. Notwithstanding the favour shown him by the Earl of Essex he is said to have been unfriendly behind the Earl's back. In the *Frere MSS.* is a note that on " Shroven Monday," 1601, six gentlemen were hanged for robbing Sir William " Cornwalleys." On May Day, 1604, King James I on his way to London on his accession to the throne visited Highgate, when he knighted Sir Basil Brook of Madeley, Salop. The royal guests were entertained by the performance of a masque written by Ben Jonson called *The Penates*, a private entertainment by Sir William Cornwallis of the King and Queen on the morning of May Day.

The first wife of Sir William Cornwallis was Lucy, one of the four daughters of John, Lord Latimer, by Lucy his wife, daughter of Henry, Earl of Worcester. She was buried at Brome, Norfolk, on 5th May, 1608. The estate was entailed on her four daughters : Frances, wife of

48

Sir Edmund Withipole, Elizabeth, wife of Sir William Sandes, Cornelia, wife of Sir Richard Farmer, and Anne, wife of Archibald, 7th Earl of Argyll, the last named being married at St. Botolph's, Bishopsgate, on 30th November, 1610. On 14th March, 1610, the four daughters surrendered their rights to their father at his Brick House in Bishopsgate Without, London, between the hours of 8 and 9 p.m., and he then conveyed the estate to Thomas, Earl of Arundel, and Dame Alathea his wife. Sir William took for his second wife, Jane, daughter of Hercules Meautys, and she afterwards married Sir Nathaniel Bacon, son of Sir Nicholas Bacon, who was half-brother of Sir Francis.[72] He died at Bishopsgate on 13th November, 1611.

Howard, Earl of Arundel

1610-32. Thomas, 2nd Earl of Arundel (1586-1646), was 24 years old when he became the owner of this house in Highgate. He was the only son of Philip Howard, Earl of Arundel, by his wife, Anne, coheiress of Dacre and Gillesland, and was born at Finchingfield in Essex on 7th July, 1586. His father died in the Tower on 19th October, 1595, attainted of treason. Thomas was then nearly 10 years old and he was carefully brought up by his mother, " a lady of great and eminent virtues," with his only sister, who died at the age of 16. By the attainder of his father he lost the family estates and titles, but was called Lord Maltravers by courtesy. On 18th April, 1604, King James restored him in blood and gave him his father's titles of Arundel and Surrey, but did not restore the estates. When 20 years old he married Alathea, third daughter and ultimately heiress of Gilbert Talbot, Earl of Shrewsbury (30th September, 1606) and, with the help of her fortune gradually bought back some of the family property, including Arundel House, London, for which he gave £4,000 in 1607. He went abroad for his health in 1609, travelling in the Low Countries, France and Italy, where he bought immense quantities of works of art. Horace Walpole called him the " Father of Vertu " in England, and his name is linked for all time with the Arundelean Marbles presented by his grandson to the University of Oxford. Like his wife, he was brought up a Roman Catholic, but on 25th December, 1615, was received into the English Church, to the great grief of his mother, who vainly tried to persuade him to return to the Romish faith. In 1616 (16th July) he was sworn a Privy Councillor. His circle of literary and artistic friends included Francis Bacon, Lord Verulam, two of whose visits to his house at Highgate are on record, the first made when Bacon was in the heyday of his prosperity ; the second when he was ill and in disgrace and went there only to die.

When Lord Arundel was away in Scotland with the King in 1617 Lady Arundel entertained Sir Francis Bacon, then Lord Keeper, with the two Lords Justices, the Master of the Rolls (Sir Julius Cæsar) and others to a grand feast at Highgate.[73] " It was after the Italian manner, with four courses and four table cloths, one under another ; and when the first course and table cloth were taken away the Master of the Rolls thinking all had been done, said grace (as his manner is when no divines are present) and was afterwards well laughed at for his labour." Seeing that he was the son of an Italian it seems curious that Sir Julius Cæsar should not have been acquainted with " the Italian manner." He was a son-in-law of Sir Nicholas Bacon, the half-brother of Sir Francis, and a very remarkable man. In the course of a long life he married four times, his first wife, whom he married in 1578, being Dorcas, sister of Richard Martin, goldsmith (of Lauderdale House) who died at Muswell Hill in 1595, and his third wife was Anne, daughter of Sir Nicholas Bacon, widow of Sir Robert Drury. The chart pedigree (Appendix IV) illustrates the curious way in which the occupants of Lauderdale House and Arundel House were connected with each other and with Sir Julius Cæsar (whose tomb is in the church of St. Helen's, Bishopsgate)[72] and with Francis Bacon. It may be remarked also that Bacon succeeded as Attorney-General Sir Henry Hobart, another owner of Lauderdale House. In 1621, when the House of Lords were considering the evidence against Viscount St. Albans for taking bribes whilst Lord Chancellor, Lord Arundel recommended that Bacon should not be summoned to the Bar of the House nor deprived of his peerage.

The story of Bacon's death is so well known that it requires no more than the briefest record here. He is alleged to have caught a chill while stuffing a dead fowl with snow to see whether it would not be thereby preserved from decay. Being too ill to go home to the Temple he stayed at Arundel House in Highgate, the Earl being absent from home. He was put into a bed duly warmed with a pan, but it was a damp bed, not having been used for a year, and he evidently developed pneumonia, of which he died in the arms of Sir Julius Cæsar on 9th April, 1626, at

D

the age of 65. On his death-bed Bacon sent the following letter to Lord Arundel, which shows that they were on intimate terms.

" My very good Lord,—I was likely to have had the fortune of Caius Plinius the elder, who lost his life by trying an experiment about the burning of Mount Vesuvius ; for I was also desirous to try an experiment or two touching the conservation and induration of bodies. As for the experiment itself, it succeeded excellently well ; but in the journey between London and Highgate, I was taken with such a fit of casting as I know not whether it were the Stone, or some surfeit or cold, or indeed a touch of them all three. But when I came to your Lordship's House, I was not able to go back, and therefore was forced to take up my lodging here, where your housekeeper is very careful and diligent about me, which I assure myself your Lordship will not only pardon towards him, but think the better of him for it. For indeed your Lordship's House was happy to me, and I kiss your noble hands for the welcome which I am sure you give me to it. I know how unfit it is for me to write with any other hand than mine own, but by my troth my fingers are so disjointed with sickness that I cannot steadily hold a pen." In communicating this letter to the *Gentleman's Magazine* in 1827, Mr. Basil Montague said he would be grateful if anyone could tell him the site of Lord Arundel's house. Some 85 years later Frank Marcham took the first step towards solving the problem by copying the relevant entry on the Court Roll of the Manor of Cantlowes, for 5th May, 1610, showing that the house was situated in the parish of St. Pancras, thus disproving the statement, first circulated by Frederick Prickett in 1842, that the house was on the Bank, in Hornsey. The only drawing so far discovered which bears the title of Arundel House is an engraving, formerly in the Gardner Collection, with a portrait of Lord Bacon inset below (Plate 36a). As already mentioned, however, in the architectural description above, the original house in its latest stage appears on two engravings, one of Ashurst House in 1710 (Plate 41) and the other of Messrs. Grignon & Hull's Academy, in the late 19th century (Plate 36b). These both show a long range, furnished with gables, which appears to have been the south front of the main part of the house towards Highgate Green. It is just possible that the Bacon view is really a representation of the elaborate Banqueting House, probably built by Lord Arundel, and which seems to have been converted into a residence by William Blake and ultimately became Ashurst House (*q.v.*). Plans of the house itself must surely exist somewhere, though so far it has not been possible to identify them. There is an interesting further field of research for students of Highgate history in looking not only for plans but also for the identity of the architect. The same suggestion applies to the adjoining Ashurst House and also to Lauderdale House.

1632–41.   In 1632 Thomas, Earl of Arundel, and Dame Alathea his wife conveyed this estate to Thomas Gardner of the Inner Temple and Rebecca his wife. He was the son of Michael Gardner, Rector of Greenford Magna, where he was baptised on 4th March, 1591. His mother was the daughter of Thomas Brown, a wealthy alderman of London, and his wife was a daughter of a merchant of London named Childe. In 1636 he was appointed Recorder of London, and a Governor of Highgate Grammar School on 6th May of the same year. Until the beginning of the Long Parliament he stood well with both King and Parliament, for he was admitted to the freedom of London by the Court of Aldermen on 6th October, 1640, and six weeks afterwards was knighted by the King. King Charles had intended him to be Speaker of the new House of Commons and Lord Clarendon describes him as being eminently qualified for the post, " he being a man of gravity and quickness, that had somewhat of authority and gracefulness in his person and presence," but he failed to secure a seat in the newly elected House of Commons. In 1641 he sold his Highgate property to Sir Robert Payne, who, like himself, was a royalist. Gardner was impeached in the House of Commons on 22nd March, 1642-3, for siding with the King, but the outbreak of the Civil War prevented further proceedings and he joined the King at Oxford before the end of the year and was discharged by the Court of Aldermen from his Recordership for absence from his post. Sir Thomas Gardner's two sons were killed in the war and he died at the age of 61 in 1652, being buried at Cuddesdon, in Oxfordshire.

1641–58.   Sir Robert Payne was the son of William Payne of Barton Stacey, Hampshire, and of Highgate, by Susan his wife, daughter of John May of Kent.[74] William Payne died on 9th October, 1628, when his son was 28 years of age. Robert Payne was appointed Sheriff

SIR ROBERT PAYNE

of Hampshire in 1631 and was knighted on 4th August, 1632. The following entries concerning his family are contained in the Register of Highgate Chapel:

1644-5　March 5. Susanna, daughter of Sir Robert Pane baptised. Buried 20 December following.

1646　July 1. William, son of Sir Robert Pane, baptised. Buried 11 July, 1646.

1647　October 16. Mr. William, son of Sir Robert Pane and Lady Mary Pane, baptised.

1649　August 18. Mary, daughter of Sir Robert Pane, baptised. Buried 8 April 1653 (M.I.)

1652　June 26. Lady Mary Pane, wife of Sir Robert Paine of Highgate, buried.

1654　May 19. Robert, son of Sir Robert Pane, buried.

1654　August 9. Susanna, daughter of Sir Robert Pane, buried.

1658　September 16. Sir Robert Pane, knight, buried in the vault in the yard.

1659-60　March 1. Mrs. Susanna Payne buried in the vault.

Payne

It will be seen that William Payne, the heir of Sir Robert, was aged 11 when his father died. His claim to be the lawful heir was challenged by one Robert Wayte, describing himself as " of Barton Stacy, gentleman," claiming that Sir Robert had married his mother, Patience Wayte, widow of Bartholomew Wayte, esquire, and stating that they had lived together as man and wife for 10 or 12 years. In the Bill of Complaint which he entered in Chancery[75] against Thomas Howe, esquire, on 29th June, 1660, he tells a most romantic story and was evidently a most unscrupulous liar. He alleged that Sir Robert made a will in his own hand dated 7th June, 1658, appointing him executor and therefore responsible for the maintenance of Sir Robert's mother, Susanna, and his son, William, and leaving £20 a year to Patience Wayte, etc., and he quoted verbatim a letter said to have been sent him by Sir Robert from the house of one Thoroughgood in Old Street, London, as follows : " Robert, I would have you send up my cows and horses by John Sneller as soon as you can, you had need send up the key of my house now, I may have my house robbed of my goods if you be not mighty careful. I would have you to sow what grounds you think fit. Pray Robert pay the poor men and the contribution ; you need not write to me for money for I love you too well to wrong you, nay, I have found you to be true and careful in all my business, and you have let me have money at all times when I was at want ; you have all my corn and other things at your command and whatsoever you do let or sell I will stand to, for I know I left you in debt when I came away, but let nothing trouble you therefore, if it please God to take me away before I come down into the country. I have laid a writing under my bed mat which you shall have, tied to the bed cords with a black ribbon ; there is that which will give you satisfaction for all your love you have had of me, but I do charge you to keep this as safe as your life and let not your own wife know of it. I rest your dear and loving friend Robert Payne."

Wayte said he received this letter on a Saturday about the middle of June, 1658, and sent the cows and horses on the following Monday by John Sneller. He alleged that Sir Robert died in August, 1658 (which is incorrect), and that before his death he sent for Wayte and held his hand for half an hour and wept to him and said he had done his mother and him much wrong, but hoped God and they would forgive him. He gave a detailed account of finding the will afterwards, tied with a black ribbon, etc., exactly as in the letter. (There is no trace of his having proved it in the Prerogative Court of Canterbury.) Finally he stated that Sir Robert maintained him, declared he was his son and employed him in the management of his Hampshire estates.

Whatever the position of Robert Wayte, he does appear to have obtained possession of some at least of the Hampshire property, since Thomas Howe in his answer says he was endeavouring to get possession on behalf of the heir, William, and that Wayte had committed great waste and spoil there. Thomas Howe was the son of Thomas Howe of South Ockendon, Essex, esquire, and was admitted to Gray's Inn on 12th May, 1637. He was aged 26 in 1641. He married (22nd March, 1640-1) Sara, daughter of William Geere of All Hallows, Honey Lane, citizen and draper of London, and his wife's half-sister was Mary, the wife of Sir Robert Payne, and mother of the infant William. Thus he was uncle by marriage to the boy, and was appointed his guardian at the manor court held on 9th June, 1659, after the grandmother Susanna was dead. In his answer to Wayte he denied that Sir Robert Payne made a will and made the astonishing statement that Thoroughgood's house was in fact a prison, into which he (Sir Robert) had been committed for debt

51

THE VILLAGE OF HIGHGATE

and " endeavoured to get out of the same with what speed he could," and after some months' imprisonment was permitted to go to his own house at Highgate hoping never to return to prison again. He pointed out that in these circumstances it is not probable that if he had made a will Sir Robert Payne would leave it behind him and never go to fetch it away, especially as he was often in London near the prison during the three months that elapsed between his coming out of prison and his death, which was about 8th or 9th September, 1658. (He was buried on 13th September.)[76] Howe also said that the keeper of the house " presently " (i.e. immediately) after the departure of Sir Robert turned out the room to air the curtain valance hangings, bedding and bed, and tightened the bed cord because it was loose, but no paper or writing was found. Sir Robert whilst in prison, and after coming out, declared his disaffection to the said Complainant and said he would go down to Hampshire to punish him for his " ill carriages and abuses to him." When his friends urged him to make his will he said it was time enough and he would do it hereafter. According to Mr. Howe, Sir Robert kept Wayte as a boy to run errands and for servile employment.

1658-70.   William Payne, esquire, son and heir of Sir Robert Payne. From a monumental inscription in Watford parish church,[77] it appears that William Payne, son of Sir Robert Payne, married Mary, daughter of Samuel Blackwell of Watford, and that she died on 27th July, 1669, aged 21. On 2nd August, 1669, he had licence to lease the Highgate property to his father-in-law, and in 1670 he conveyed the estate to Francis Blake of Highgate, esquire. It was then described as a capital messuage, etc., and two other messuages, etc., late in the occupation of William Payne and late of Samuel Blackwell, esquire, or his assigns, and formerly belonging to Thomas Gardner, esquire, Recorder of London, and Rebecca his wife. The Hearth Tax assessment for 1665 shows a house in the occupation of " Baron Turner " with 23 hearths. This was Christopher Turner, serjeant-at-law, son of Sir Christopher Turner of Milton Ernest, Beds., which gives us the name of an interim tenant, and was made third Baron of the Exchequer on 7th July, 1660. His father was knighted nine days later.

1670-91.   Francis Blake of Highgate, esquire. In 1674 the Hearth Tax shows, in place of Baron Turner's house, one of 10 hearths (reduced from 23 mentioned above), occupied by Mr. Johnson, and another of 11 hearths owned by Mr. Blake, but empty. Thomas Johnson, gentleman, occupied the house now represented by Old Hall, a portion of which, as we have already indicated, stands on part of the actual site of Arundel House, and the adjoining house, afterwards occupied by Elizabeth Cornish, must have formed a portion of the same structure, the explanation being that Arundel House was not at that time pulled down but simply divided into two houses. One of these was conveyed in 1674 by Francis Blake to Elizabeth Ashby and the other in 1691 to William Ashurst. There was also a third house on the estate, the Banqueting House (the site of St. Michael's Church), conveyed by Francis Blake in 1674 to Andrew Campion (see Section IX). Although these conveyances were made by the father, the houses were actually in the hands of his son, William Blake of Covent Garden, woollen draper.

A printed Almanack[78] published in 1655 mentions " the glorious invention of wind guns by E. Blake, the Governor of the new Hospital at Highgate." This was the Ladies' Hospital or Charity School (Plates 39 and 40) projected by William Blake for the education and maintenance of about forty fatherless boys and girls, to be supported by the voluntary subscriptions of ladies. The boys were to be taught the arts of painting, gardening, casting accounts and navigation, or to be put forth to some good handicraft trade and to wear a uniform of blue lined with yellow. The girls were to be taught to read, sew, starch, raise paste and dress, that they may be fit for any good service. Exactly what Blake achieved remains obscure, though he struggled for many years to establish this school, publishing a considerable amount of print as propaganda and finally landing himself in the Fleet as a prisoner for debt. From a print which he published entitled " A Delineation of the Ladyes Hospital at High-gate " (Plate 39) it appears that his own residence, afterwards the residence of Sir William Ashurst (see p. 60), stood on the site of St. Michael's Church. Referring to this he says it was " first only a Sumer's Recess from London, which, having that great and noble City, with its numerous Childhood, under view gave the first thought to him of so great a Design : intended now for Lodgings for Retyrement for Such as by His Maties Favour might be Governors of the Hospitall." The School itself appears

52

to have stood on the site of Old Hall. Dorchester House, on the opposite side of the Green, he acquired in 1682, intending it as a boarding house for the girls (see p. 90). That the Hospital was taken seriously by responsible people may be inferred from the bequest by John Bill of " Caine Wood " in his will dated 25th September, 1680, of £13 6s. 8d. " to be putt into the Register of the Ladyes Hospital founded by Master Blake at Highgate."[79]

1691-1724. As stated above, Francis Blake conveyed the western portion of Arundel House to William Ashurst in 1691. It was then described as a capital messuage in the occupation of Benjamin Richards, gentleman (except a garret belonging to Elizabeth Cornish), and two closes containing 13 acres, whereof one close abutted on the wall late of Elisha Coish, east (Section VI) and west on the garden of Sir William Ashurst, south on a close of the Hon. Francis, Lord Holles (Section VII), and north on the green walk adjoining the orchard of Elizabeth Cornish ; and the other close formerly containing 8 acres, then divided, and 5 acres converted to gardens and walks, extending to the wall of William Brown, citizen of London, on the north, formerly in the possession of William Blake, and the other 3 acres, remainder of the said 8 acres, now divided into two closes, abutting north on the last-mentioned garden, south on Traytors Hill, west on land of John Ives and east on Lord Holles' land ; and a parcel of waste adjoining north against the king's way on Highgate Green. The date 1694 found on a rainwater pipe indicates the erection of the building now known as Old Hall by Ashurst. Four years later Sir William Ashurst entailed the estate on himself, Elizabeth, his wife, and their heirs (1698) and Lancelot Stepney, merchant, is given as occupier. Dame Elizabeth Ashurst died on 14th March, 1724.

The later owners and occupiers of Old Hall were :

1724-5. William Pritchard Ashurst of Monken Hadley, son of Sir William Ashurst and Dame Elizabeth his wife. He conveyed it to Thomas Bayly, the tenant then being Brook Bridges, esquire.

1725-49. Thomas Bayly of Highgate, gentleman, who was elected a Governor of the Grammar School in 1728 and died on 17th June, 1749.

1749-75. Katherine, daughter of Thomas Bayly. Her second husband was George Langdale of Queen Square, St. George the Martyr, surgeon, she being Katherine Armitage, widow, before that marriage. At her death her husband sold the house to John Gorham, builder.

1775-1820. In 1782 John Gorham had licence to lease the house for 21 years, the occupier then being William Newdick. Gorham devised it to his nephew, Ebenezer Maitland, who with Mary his wife in 1802 conveyed it to Benjamin Price, who occupied the house at least as early as 1795, as shown by the Land Tax assessments. He died at Cheltenham on 4th November, 1820.

1820-22. Sarah, the daughter of Benjamin Price, wife of Sir John Maclean, bart. In 1820 and 1821 the house was empty. Sir John Maclean and Sarah his wife sold it in 1822 to Sir William Domville for £1,850.

1822-33. Sir William Domville, baronet. He served the office of Lord Mayor of London 1813-4 and presided during his mayoralty at a banquet given by the Corporation to the Prince Regent and the Allied Sovereigns on 18th June, 1814. He was created a baronet on 28th July following. He died on 8th February, 1833.

1833-47. Sir William Domville, baronet, son of Sir William. In 1837 he had licence to lease to Sir Robert Chester for 21 years.

1847-1911. In 1847 Sir William Domville, baronet, then of Southfield Lodge, Eastbourne, and Dame Maria his wife, conveyed the house to the Rev. Thomas Henry Causton, M.A., who was rector of St. Botolph's, Aldersgate, from 1824-38 and vicar of St. Michael's Church, Highgate, from 25th June, 1838, until his death on 15th May, 1854.[47] He served as a Governor of the Grammar School from 1828. His first wife, the Hon. Frances Esther, was buried at Highgate on 17th June, 1840. On 7th April, 1842, Causton married Frances Louisa, eldest daughter of T. T. Tatham, esquire, of Highgate. Charles Causton, who succeeded, conveyed Old Hall to Andrew Wark, esquire, of Bartholomew Close in 1870. Alderman Cotton had occupied the house prior to that date. Mr. Wark died in 1883 and his widow, Margaret Cuthbertson Wark, on 10th April, 1911.

IX—THE SITE OF ASHURST HOUSE, AND THE MONUMENTS IN ST. MICHAEL'S CHURCH

GENERAL NOTE.

The church of St. Michael was built in 1832 from the designs of Lewis Vulliamy on the site of a fine 17th-century house built by Sir William Ashurst, Lord Mayor of London, as his Highgate residence. The best representation of the house is an engraving of *circa* 1720 (Plate 41), and its character agrees with the date of 1675, when Sir William acquired the site of the Banqueting House of Arundel House. An interesting architectural problem is raised by earlier views of this site. In the first place we may dismiss an engraving in the Heal Collection (St. Pancras Public Library, Chester Road) which shows a building entitled " Ashurst House," together with a shield of what purports to be the Ashurst arms. This engraving, in spite of its title, is quite clearly of Abingdon Town Hall, a not dissimilar building in its roof and general proportions. The architect of the Town Hall is unknown, and the mistake of the engraver might be explained if the designs for both buildings came from the same architect's portfolio. There are two early 19th-century drawings of the house (Plates 42 *a* and *b*) which confirm the details in the earlier engraving of the " Seat of Sir William Ashurst."

Ashurst

The predecessor of Ashurst House is shown in the bird's-eye view of William Blake's Ladies' Hospital at Highgate (Plate 39) about 1688, and it is curious that while it has marked differences from the later house, it yet shows much the same proportions and is similarly roofed. It seems possible that this house of William Blake's was his adaptation of the original Banqueting House of the Earls of Arundel, a subject already discussed (p. 50) in connection with the remarkable early drawing of Arundel House formerly in the Gardner Collection (Plate 36*a*).

The view of the Ladies' Hospital also shows an elaborate courtyard with cloisters and a large flanking building (marked C, C and D) to the east of the " Petitioner's own House " (marked EE, the predecessor of Ashurst House), which if they had been built, would have occupied the site of Old Hall and No. 16, South Grove. A more elaborate version of the scheme, with the addition of a large three-storeyed institution to the south was engraved and is reproduced on Plate 40. It is clear that this engraving is from an architect's drawing, and the quality and distinction of the design shows him to have been someone of eminence.

The building of St. Michael's Church followed the judgment given by the Court of Chancery in 1826, which restored the status of Highgate School Chapel which had hitherto been considered as the Chapel of Ease for both Highgate and Hornsey (see Introduction, p. 4). Many inhabitants of Highgate had been buried at the school chapel, and the following monuments were removed here at the building of the new church, two of them being beneath the south gallery; two more in a room in the tower, and the last on the west wall above the gallery. The first memorial to be erected in the church was that to the poet Coleridge, who was buried in a vault in the old chapel. Beneath the church are some foundations which in all probability belonged to Ashurst House. It may perhaps be added that in addition to a fragment already referred to on page 97 a doorway bearing the Ashurst arms is preserved at No. 42, High Street, on the Hornsey side of the border. The dedication to St. Michael is the same as that of the Hermitage that used to occupy the site of Highgate School Chapel.

SIR EDWARD GOULD. . . .

Under the gallery on the south side of the church.

An inscribed tablet framed in festoons of drapery with cords, tassels and two pairs of winged cherubs' heads. Above the inscription is an achievement of arms with mantling and crest.

Arms   *Party saltirewise or and azure a lion likewise parted and counter-coloured, for GOULD, with in pretence Azure a cheveron between three wolves' heads razed or, for GOWER (referring to Elizabeth Gower his first wife), impaling Argent a cheveron sable between three oak leaves vert with three bezants on the cheveron, for MONOUX,* (referring to Frances Monoux his second wife).

Crest   *A demilion azure bezanty* (but the bezants seem to have been omitted).

Near this Marble lyes the Body of
Sir EDWARD GOULD Kn.t
(one of ẙ Governours of this Chapel)
who departed this life the 26.th day of Septem.r [1728]
Aged 80 years
His firſt wife was ELIZABETH GOWER Daughter of
RICHARD GOWER of HIGHGATE in ẙ County of Midd.ſx Gen.t

his ſecond wife was FRANCES MONOUX, Daughter of
Sir HUMPHRY MONOUX of WOOTTON
in ẙ County of BEDFORD Barᵗ
He left a large real Eſtate after the Death of his
Widow FRANCES to EDWARD GOULD and
WILLIAM GOULD, the Surviving Sons of EDWARD GOULD
his Nephew; He alſo left to this Chapel a Legacy
of ĵŏo; and left Several Legacies to
his Nephews & Nieces, & Several
Charitable Legacies.
This Monument is Set
up by his Widow

SAMUEL FORSTER, 1752
MARY FORSTER, 1744

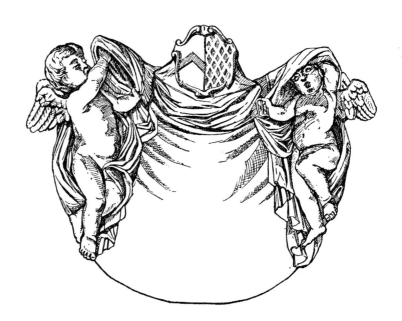

On the south wall of St. Michael's Church under the gallery adjoining
the foregoing.

An inscribed tablet in the form of drapery displayed by two full-length
figures of cherubs. Above is a shield of arms nearly obliterated shewing a
cheveron but no other charges impaling a fretty coat.

56

Near this Place
the Bodies of SAMUEL FORSTER Esqre
and of MARY his wife
are buried in their own Vault.
He died on the 25th day of April 1752
in the 65th year of his Age:
She died on the 14th day of June 1744
in the 65th year of her Age.
In their lives they were lovely, & in their Deaths
they were not divided. May their Ashes rest in Peace,
untill they arise to a bliffull Immortality
thro' our Lord and Saviour Jefus Chrift!

MR FORSTER, one of the worthy Governors of the
Free Grammar School of this Town, bequeathed
to them by his last Will three hundred pounds,
to be laid out at their Difcretion for the Increase
of the Pensions of the poor Widows in the
Almshouses here.

REBECCA PAUNCEFORT, 1719.

This monument, which was originally in the Grammar School chapel, was placed in the room in the tower of the church of St. Michael. It became dangerous and had to be taken down, only the two portions bearing the inscriptions remaining in the tower, the flanking columns being removed to the crypt.

On the smaller slab,

M.S.E.
REBECCA EDWARDI PAUNCEFORT
de HIGHGATE Armigeri Uxor:
Eademq7 Filia Natu Maxima
D: SAMUELIS MOYER, de PITSY HALL
in Comitatu ESSEXIÆ Baronetti.
Exceffit Secundo Die Novembris,
Ætatis XLII,
Salutis MDCCXIX, Anno.

On the larger slab,

Mulier, dum Vita fuppetebat
Dictis, Factifque juxta,
Prudentiâ Virili.
Erga Deum Pietate,
Beneficentia in Egentes

Prope Singulari
Sic Vita erat Sanctæ Religionis
Officiis infervire et tenuioribus
Quam plurimum prodeffe
Aft Ægritudinis humanæ,
Funerifque præmaturi,
Eheu! non ideo Exfors.
Quippe adverfa Valetudine
Conflictabatur diu
Quam tamen gravefcentem indies
Egregie toleravit.
Morbiq7 Sævâ Vi evicta tandem
Compofito Animo, Summifoq7
Etiam in Extremis egit.
Ingens ademptæ Defiderium
Conjugi manet Defolato,
Omnibufq7, quæ in Vitâ
Videntur effe, Blandimentis.
Uxore cum Placenti,
Unà Viduato.
Mærens hunc Lapidem Sacravit
Propter repofto Cineri:
Ipfe quoque, Quandocunque
Diem expleverit Supremum,
Ibidem Tumulandus:
Non in Morte Deferturus
In Vitâ unicè Dilectam.

JOHN SCHOPPENS, 1720.
MARY SCHOPPENS, 1718.

Architecturally the most imposing of the memorials removed from the old School Chapel, it is now placed upon the west wall of St. Michael's Church above the gallery (Plate 43). The inscription tablet, which is semicircular-headed, is surmounted by a tent-like canopy. Surrounding it is an elaborate architectural frame composed of two fluted columns with composite capitals supporting an entablature which forms a semicircular arch. Above the arch is an achievement of arms and on each side a fluted vase. The columns are flanked by carved scroll ornament on the wall face and the whole rests on a moulded shelf over moulded and carved console brackets. On the apron, which terminates in a winged cherub's head, is a cartouche also bearing a shield of arms.

Arms   *Quarterly: 1 and 4, Gules three running deer argent; 2 and 3, Azure three axes or.*

Crest   *An arm in armour, the hand holding a broken object* (perhaps an arrow). On the apron a shield of the first quarter of the above arms with a scutcheon in pretence (nearly illegible).

58

M.S.
Near this place lieth the Body of
JOHN SCHOPPENS
late Merchant of LONDON & Inhabitant of this Hamlet
who after an induftrious Life paff'd with Integrity
& Honour & clof'd at laft by a tedious Illnefs born
with Patience & Resignation.
died in ẙ 71ſt year of his Age ẙ 22ᵈ of June A.D. 1720
having furviv'd about a Year & Six Months
the lofs of his Dear Wife
MARY
The Daughter of WILLIAM GIBBES Citizen & alfo
Merchant of LONDON a lofs irreparable to all to whomfoever
fhe was related, as a Wife, a Matron, a Miftrefs or a Friend.
Being faithful in the Difcharge of every Duty of Life,
& so holding herself in a conftant ftedfastness for Death,
She was feiz'd but not furpriz'd, by a fudden one on ẙ
28ᵗʰ of December A.D. 1718, in ẙ 55ᵗʰ year of Her Age:
having that Morning receiv'd ẙ Holy Communion here,
in perfect health.
They both lie in a decent Vault, a little eaftward from hence
which (JOHN) their Eldeft Son purchaf'd
to preferve the Remains of his Family.
by whom alfo this Monument was erected
to the Memory of his Parents.

JOHN EDWARDS, 1769.

This tablet, now in the room in the tower, possesses two inscriptions, the lower one being on a rectangular stone which projects boldly in front of a moulded background in the form of a sarcophagus. The upper one is circular and is linked by carved ribands to a vertical recessed pier, diminishing upwards, with a crowning cornice supporting a large urn with flames. The circular panel is flanked by weeping cherubs. The lower part of the tablet has a deep cove beneath the centre on a fluted and foliated corbel and scallop shells as pendants at the sides.

Near this Place
are deposited the Remains of
JOHN EDWARDS of Highgate *Esqʳ*
only surviving Son of the
undernam'd THOMAS EDWARDS *Esqʳ*
and JANE his Wife who died Decemᵇʳ 18ᵗʰ,
1769 Aged 82 Years

The many Virtues, by Which He was
deservedly distinguish'd through a long
and happy Life have given to Posterity
an Example worthy Imitation
in the Character of this truly
benevolent and upright Man.

Subtùs
In loco Sepulchrali Joannis Schoppens Armigeri
Mortalitatis fuæ exuvias depofuit
Josephus Edwards
Secundo genitus Thomæ Edwards
Nuper de Civitate Bristol Armigeri
et Janæ Uxoris ejus
Dignus Parentum filius
Quem in ipfo virilis ætatis flore correptum
Febris Continua ab hâc valle Miferiarum

Ad meliorem tranftulit vitam
Ea ibi accepturum præmia
Cum judicabit Christus et vivos et mortuos
Quæ tam bene merueruunt
Sincera erga Deum ufq7 a pueritiâ pietas
Ergà Parentes obedientia
Erga fratres et forores amor plufquam fraternus
Erga clientes fides integerrima
Erga omnes deniq7 ut uno complectar verbo
Candor et benevolentia.
Obijt Cœlebs 22do die Julij An^o. Dom. 1728vo. Ætatis Suæ 43^{tio}

Note. *The above are all exact transcripts from the originals.*

Historical Notes.

In 1674 Francis Blake of Highgate (father of William Blake) conveyed the westernmost section of the Arundel estate to Andrew Campion, clerk, and Anne his wife. It was described as a messuage called the Banqueting House, with orchards, gardens, etc., enclosed with a brick wall, then or late in the occupation of Francis Blake and formerly the inheritance of William Payne, esquire, abutting north on Highgate Green, east on the garden of Francis Blake then in the occupation of Thomas Johnson, south on a field belonging to Francis Blake, and west on a field in the occupation of John Ives. The frontage thus extended from the site of Old Hall (the residence of Thomas Johnson) to Bromwich Walk, including Ashurst House (site of St. Michael's), Voel and South Grove House. John Ives owned what was afterwards Cutbush's Nursery on the west side of Bromwich Walk (Nos. 45, 46 and 47, West Hill).

1675-82. Andrew Campion conveyed the Banqueting House to William Blake of London, vintner, in 1675, and settled on himself at the same time a newly erected house in his own occupation. This new house was South Grove House (Section X), built on land previously attached to the Banqueting House, an alteration indicated by the fact that the copyhold quit rent was at the same time apportioned at 3d. In 1681 William Blake conveyed the original house to his son, Daniel Blake, citizen and vintner of London, by whom it was conveyed in the following year to William Ashurst. It was the residence of William Blake (see p. 52), nephew of William, the vintner, whose efforts at founding an extensive charity at Highgate are described on p. 52.

1682-1725.   William Ashurst of Paternoster Row and Highgate, mercer of London, was a son of Henry Ashurst of London, merchant tailor (d. 1680) by Judith his wife, daughter of William Reresby of London, gentleman, and grandson of Henry Ashurst of Lancashire. He married Elizabeth, daughter of Robert Thompson of London, by whom he had a numerous family. He was knighted on 29th October, 1687, was Lord Mayor 1694-4, M.P. for the City 1689-90, 1695-1702 and 1705-10. He was elected a Governor of the Grammar School on 23rd June, 1697. Ashurst died on 12th January, 1719-20, and his widow, Dame Elizabeth Ashurst, on 14th March, 1724, when their grandson, William Pritchard Ashurst, esquire, of Monken Hadley, succeeded. He was the son of Henry Ashurst, Town Clerk of London, who died in 1705. In 1725 he conveyed the estate to John Edwards of London, merchant, Charles Shales, esquire, being then mentioned as the occupier, succeeding Sir William Ashurst. Charles Shales (a member of a firm who were goldsmiths[80] to William and Mary, Anne, George I and George II), was elected a Governor of the Grammar School on 1st November, 1728. His wife, Anne, daughter of Thomas Barrington, esquire, died on 17th November, 1729, and he died on 5th October, 1734.

1725-69.   John Edwards married the daughter of John Schoppens, a Dutchman who was naturalised by Act of Parliament in 30 Charles II. Schoppens was buried in Highgate Chapel and his monumental inscription was removed to St. Michael's Church, where it remains (see above, p. 58). John Edwards was elected a Governor of the Grammar School in place of Charles Shales on 7th November, 1734, and died on 18th December, 1769, bequeathing to the Governors of the School £300 for the better support of the almswomen. He also directed that the legacy of £150 left by his brother-in-law John Schoppens (son of the John Schoppens mentioned above) should be paid over to them. John, son of John Edwards, born in 1716, died on 17th March, 1747, of a quinsy contracted by catching a cold at Lord Lovat's trial. He left three daughters, Sarah, born on 2nd February, 1741, and Frances (by his first wife Sarah Holford, whom he married in February, 1740), and Mary (by his second wife, Ann Manship), who married Jacob Preston of Beeston St. Lawrence, Norfolk. The last mentioned became the owner of Nos. 1-6, The Grove (Pemberton Row), and her mother married at Gray's Inn Chapel[81] on 5th June, 1753, Thomas Allen Greenhalgh, who had changed his name from Allen. Their son, Thomas Allen of Henrietta Street, Cavendish Square, was lord of the manor of Bibsworth, in Finchley.

1769-1830.   Sarah, the eldest daughter of John Edwards, married Thomas Cave of Marylebone, son of Sir Thomas Cave, baronet, on 7th August, 1778. They had an only daughter, Sarah, who married Henry Otway of Stanford Hall in the counties of Northants. and Leicester, who changed his name to Henry Otway Cave. Frances Edwards married John Fremantle, by whom she had four sons and two daughters. Thomas Cave was elected a Governor of the Grammar School on 13th January, 1770, and died on 30th May, 1780, aged 43. His father collected material for the *History of the County of Leicester* and was Chairman of the Committee for printing Bridges' *History of Northampton*. The tenant of the house following John Edwards was Thomas Walker, esquire, Accountant-General of Chancery, who was elected a Governor of the Grammar School on 2nd October, 1796. He died on 29th January, 1802. Dame Sarah Cave seems to have lived at the house in 1804-5, followed by Sir Alan Chambré, 1806-11. Sir Alan Chambré was a judge, described by Lord Brougham as being " among the first ornaments of his profession, as amongst the most honest, and amiable of men." He was the eldest son of Walter Chambré, of Halhead Hall, Kendal, barrister, by his wife Mary, daughter of Jacob Morland of Capplethwaite Hall, Westmorland, and was born at Kendal on 4th October, 1739. In 1767 he went the northern circuit, of which he soon became one of the leaders, and in 1796 was appointed Recorder of Lancaster. In 1799 he was appointed a Baron of the Exchequer, and was translated in the following year to the Court of Common Pleas, where he remained until his retirement in 1815. He died at the Crown Inn, Harrogate,

20th September, 1823, in his 84th year, and was buried in Kendal Parish Church. He was unmarried. In 1812 (21st March) an advertisement appeared in the newspapers as follows : " Grove House, Highgate.—To be Let and entered upon at Lady-Day, all that elegant Mansion, known by the name of Grove House, Highgate, now in the occupation of Sir Alan Chambré. It is situated on the summit of the hill, boldly commanding a view of the Metropolis, with the Surrey, Kentish and Essex Hills, and the meanderings of the River Thames as far as the Nore, together with that beautiful and variegated country through Middlesex and Herts, to the North, and the surrounding rich domains. A servant will shew the premises, . . ." Dr. Daniel Dowling took the house about this time and kept a school there, apparently until it was demolished.

In 1830 Sarah Otway Cave, widow of Henry Otway Cave, and her eldest son, Robert Otway Cave, with the Right Hon. William Henry Fremantle of Stanhope Street, Mayfair, only surviving son of Frances Fremantle, widow, deceased (the sister of Dame Sarah Cave), sold the house to H.M. Commissioners for Building New Churches, who thereupon erected the present St. Michael's Church.

In conclusion it may be noted that the section of South Grove between the Angel and St. Michael's Church was at one time known as " Pembrook Row," as may be seen by referring to the map of 1804 reproduced on Plate I. The explanation of this name has not so far revealed itself.

X—VOEL (NO. 18, SOUTH GROVE) AND SOUTH GROVE HOUSE (NO. 19, SOUTH GROVE)

GROUND LANDLORDS, LEASEHOLDERS, ETC.

Both these houses were originally copyhold of the Manor of Cantlowes, but were enfranchised. No. 18 is in the ownership and occupation of the Misses Owen. No. 19 is now demolished.

GENERAL DESCRIPTIONS AND DATE OF STRUCTURE.

No. 18, South Grove.

This house was no doubt built in the 17th century but was refronted both towards the road and the garden in the 18th. Its present plan (Plate 44)

is not unlike that adopted for some of the later houses round Highgate Green, but it may represent a rearrangement when the Georgian improvements were made. It has a hall which takes up the middle of the house from front to back and contains a well staircase, the upper part of which is original. Each side of the hall is a large room; that to the right (south-west) being the kitchen. The latter is the only panelled room in the house, although there are fragments of cornices, etc., elsewhere. The garden side is largely obscured by modern additions.

The front (Plates 44 and 45) is of stock brick with brick bands, the ground floor being rendered in cement. It is as remarkable for the fewness of its windows as its neighbour, No. 19, had been for their number. The door has a charming hood with carved console brackets, and leads to the lower level of the hall by two descending steps. The panelling of the kitchen (already referred to) is of the Georgian period, and the most interesting internal feature is the upper part of the staircase (Plates 46 and 47). This ascends round a well in the style of the latter part of the 17th century with turned balusters, 3 inches square, standing upon a close string. It is illustrated by a measured drawing (Plate 47).

THE VILLAGE OF HIGHGATE

CONDITION OF REPAIR.
Good.

HISTORICAL NOTES.

This house is first mentioned on the court rolls in the year 1713, when Sir Francis Blake and Elizabeth his wife conveyed to Joseph Saunders "a messuage in Highgate in the tenure of John Ripper, and the Walke." This "Walke" was "Paradise Walk," consisting of the strip of common in front of this and the adjoining houses. The name survived until the middle of last century. The owners were as follows:

1713-23.	Joseph Saunders (from Sir Francis Blake).
1723-59.	Mary, daughter of Joseph Saunders. From 1726 onwards she was the wife of Robert Waddilove, a lawyer, who was deputy steward of the Manor of Cantlowes from 1723 until 1731 and thereafter steward.
1759-86.	Thomas Bromwich of Ludgate Hill, paper merchant (from Robert Waddilove of Bartlett's Buildings and Mary his wife).
1787-1812.	Henry Isherwood of Ludgate Hill, nephew-in-law of Thomas Bromwich (under the will of Mr. Bromwich), and Elizabeth Bromwich, the widow. The tenant at this time was Mr. Hodgson.
1812-37.	Robert Isherwood, only son of Henry Isherwood. In 1813 he had licence to lease the house to John Tatham, esquire, for 10 years. He died on 14th July, 1837. Mr. Tatham appears to have lived there until 1820.
1837-57.	Anna Maria Chester, only child of Robert Isherwood, and wife of Henry Chester, whom she married in 1837.
1857	Jane Bloxam, Louisa Bloxam and Emily Bloxam, spinsters (by purchase from the Chester Trustees).

No. 19, South Grove.

This house, or rather the northerly portion of it, may have dated from the latter part of the 17th century but it appears to have been extended towards the road in the 18th when a new front was constructed. All the outbuildings and other additions on the south were modern, but structures of some sort are indicated between the main block, and the right of way, later known as "Bromwich Walk," on the 1746 edition of Rocque's *Survey.*

The original plan (Plate 44) of the main block was practically the same as that of Voel (No. 18), which adjoined it on the east; namely a hall with staircase in the middle and a room on either side, but in South Grove House the entrance faced north-east and was therefore overshadowed by the western wall of Voel.

The space between the houses was originally open, but was later filled in by one-storey structures forming a hall and lobby and a small library. The main front of the house thus faced north-west towards South Grove and the wall of the façade was actually narrower than the rest of the house, the connecting angles being treated as "splays" with windows in them on each floor. The ground-floor rooms on the front were unimportant. They contained four windows overlooking South Grove in addition to the ones in each splay. The fireplaces were in the wall adjoining Voel. A large curved bay had been added to the garden front, almost entirely eliminating the old wall. On the upper floors the arrangement of rooms was similar to that below.

64

SOUTH GROVE HOUSE

The elevation to South Grove was built of stock brick with red brick quoins and window dressings (Plate 48). The windows, except the two centre ones on the first and second floors, were square-headed with rubbed red-brick flat arched heads. The space occupied by the two centre windows of the ground floor was filled on the second floor by a semicircular-headed sash flanked by two smaller rectangular sashes, forming one group. On the second floor a similar triple arrangement was included under one arch. There was a moulded brick cornice and parapet, the floor levels being marked by one brick and one stone band. In the north-east wall were vestiges of four circular brick panels, two on each of the upper floors, flanking the single windows above the original entrance.

The house was pulled down towards the end of 1934 and the garden is now covered by a large block of flats.

HISTORICAL NOTES.

The site of this house was included in the original Arundel House estate and formed part of the premises conveyed in 1674 by Francis Blake to Andrew Campion (see Section IX).

When Andrew Campion died at Totteridge on 24th January, 1678, his widow, Anne Campion, took under his will[82] a messuage lately built, but then empty. Their son Cornelius was baptised at Highgate on 22nd December, 1674. The subsequent owners were as follows:

1678-80.   Anne Campion, widow of Andrew Campion, who afterwards married John Franklyn of Whetstone.

65

E

THE VILLAGE OF HIGHGATE

1680-7.   George Evett, citizen and cutler of London (from John and Anne Franklyn).

1687-1700.   John Evett, with his brother, George, and mother, Mary Evett, widow of George
                    Evett. In 1700 she appears as the wife of John Smith of London, gentleman, her
                    third husband.

1700-20.   William Campion of St. Bride's (from John Evett, who became 21 years old at that
                    time). On 17th December, 1705, Susanna, daughter of Mr. William Campion of
                    St. Pancras and Susanna his wife, was baptised at Highgate.

1720-4.   The Rev. Henry Sacheverell (from William Campion). He came to Highgate
                    at the age of 48, ten years after the trial before the House of Lords which resulted in
his being suspended three years from preaching because he had violently preached against the
principles of the Revolution Settlement and the Act of Toleration. In 1713 Queen Anne presented
him to the living of St. Andrew's, Holborn, and the House of Commons asked him to preach to
them and thanked him. He died in this house on 5th June, 1724.

1724-39.   Mary, widow of the Rev. Henry Sacheverell (under his will). She afterwards married
                    Charles Chambers, gentleman, and died on 6th September, 1739, aged 75.[25]

1739-42.   Charles Chambers (after the death of his wife). He died on 20th May, 1749, aged 88.[25]

1742-59.   Thomas Morris, apothecary (from Charles Chambers).

1759-88.   Thomas Bromwich of Ludgate Hill, paper merchant. At the time of his admission the
                    previous owner is mentioned as Mrs. Duncalf. He was elected a Governor of the
Grammar School on 17th February, 1770. His death was announced in *The Gentleman's Magazine*
28th July, 1787, where he is described as having "acquired a genteel fortune on Ludgate Hill by his
ingenuity in manufacturing paperhangings in imitation of Stucco work." Between South Grove
House and No. 45, West Hill, there was once a footpath running to the bottom of Swain's Lane
southward across the Holly Lodge estate, which bore the name Bromwich Walk. In November, 1904,
it was closed to the public by order of the Quarter Sessions. It was enclosed on either side by brick
walls so high that it was impossible for the tallest person to look over : these walls were built by Mr.
Thomas Coutts of Holly Lodge, after he had vainly tried to get the path closed. Mr. Lloyd, in his
History of Highgate, says that the upper end of the walk originally came out nearer St. Michael's
Church, but was altered by Mr. Bromwich when he enlarged his house.[83] (See key plan, page 6.)

1787-96.   Elizabeth Bromwich, widow of Thomas Bromwich. *The Gentleman's Magazine*
                    for 1789 gives the following announcement of her marriage : " Sept. 13. At St.
Pancras' Church, Mrs. Bromwich, of Highgate, aged near 80, to her coachman, James Wheeler,
a stout young man, aged about 25. She was the widow of the late Mr. B., paper machee manufacturer,
on Ludgate Hill, who opposed Mr. Wilkes in the Aldermanship of Farringdon Without. She possessed
near £1,000 per annum. Her children, some time since, offered Mr. W. £500 if he would quit her
service, and afterwards £400 a year, both of which he refused, conceiving the whole property
better than a part, which the lady generously gave him on condition of taking her person into the
bargain. This is the fourth time the above lady has been married."

1796-1812.   In accordance with the will of Thomas Bromwich, Henry Isherwood became the
                    owner on the death of Mrs. Bromwich. He died 25th January, 1812.

1812-37.   Robert Isherwood, son of Henry Isherwood. He was elected a Governor of the
                    Grammar School on 21st February, 1802, and died on 14th July, 1837. His daughter,
Elizabeth, married William Bloxam, esquire, of Fairseat, and died on 5th December, 1826,
aged 58. A tablet in St. Michael's Church was " erected by her sorrowing children, in testimony
of their affection and gratitude for the best of Parents."

1837-57.   Anna Maria Chester, only daughter of Robert Isherwood and wife of Harry Chester,
                    whose father, Sir Robert Chester, lived at Old Hall. Mr. Chester was Permanent
Secretary to the Committee of the Privy Council on Education (the forerunner of the Board of
Education) and took a practical interest in promoting education in the village of Highgate, by
founding the Highgate Literary and Scientific Institution, of which he was the first President, as
well as by actively promoting the building of the Highgate National Schools in North Road. He
was elected a Governor of the Grammar School on 27th July, 1842, and resigned on 23rd June,
1860. He died at Rutland Gate on 16th October, 1868.

1857-   Angela Georgina Burdett Coutts (from the Chester Trustees).

66

XI—NOS. 45 AND 46, WEST HILL (SITE OF THE WHITE HART)

GROUND LANDLORD, LEASEHOLDERS, ETC.

The house was originally copyhold of the Manor of Cantlowes, but has been enfranchised.

The occupiers are, No. 45, Mrs. Bonser.

No. 46, Miss Parker.

GENERAL DESCRIPTION AND DATE OF STRUCTURE.

Nos. 45 and 46, West Hill were originally one house, and although they contain no features of special architectural importance the lower part of the external walls is of brickwork of early character. The bricks are very narrow and are laid in English bond. The house can easily be identified on the map of 1804, where it is marked as " Mr. Bowstreed's Nursery," which later passed into the hands of Messrs. William Cutbush & Sons.

HISTORICAL NOTES.

These three houses occupy the site of an inn which is first mentioned as the White Hart, in 1664. The ownership can be traced as far back as 1493, when John Leche died and John, his son, succeeded to a croft and garden at Dancope Hill and some 40 acres of land. When the latter died in 1509 the estate passed to his three married daughters, Eleanor, wife of John Pylborough, vintner of London, Margery, wife of Edward Wylle, gentleman, and Katherine, wife of Richard Hawkes, gentleman. In 1523 Edward Wylle's widow married Richard Harriong. In 1533 Margaret Whetnall, widow, died seised of this property (she may have been this same Margery married a third time), leaving a daughter, Elizabeth, wife of Thomas Harlakyndon, and two grandsons, sons of Bridgit Bellyngham, another daughter. There was a Thomas Harlakendon, Lent Reader of Gray's Inn in 1525. After 1533 there is a gap in the records until 1599, when Anne Widmore, widow, came into possession of these houses as well as of land between Swain's Lane and High Street (see p. 24). When her son, Nicholas, succeeded in 1635 the property was described as a tenement called Dampoipe Hill, with barn and orchard. A heriot was due on his mother's death consisting of the best beast on the land. In 1659 William Roberts of Willesden acquired the property from Nicholas Widmore, and sold it in 1663 to Peter Sambrooke, apothecary of London, by whom it was conveyed soon afterwards to John Short, draper, of London, being then described as a messuage and field of four acres in the occupation of Roger Andrews, victualler. At the same time (January, 1664) Mr. Short obtained a strip of the waste in front of the house 56 feet long and 4½ feet wide. He died in 1666,[84] leaving four sons, John aged 15, William aged 11, Daniel aged 9, and Samuel aged 4, in the keeping of their mother, Elizabeth. William Short died at the age of 15 and John Short when 37 years of age, leaving the other two brothers, Samuel and Daniel Short. Samuel Short was a lawyer, being described as of the Inner Temple in 1694, in which year he conveyed his half-share to his brother, Daniel Short, who was a merchant of London. He sold the house and land to Henry Ashurst, esquire, in 1703. In addition to the White Hart with the four-acre field behind, Ashurst bought from Short a house called the Cow and Hare, a meadow called Renkish Hill, and several other fields amounting to 58 acres, late occupied by John Ives and then by Thomas Hart, all of which came to Daniel Short from his father, who had bought them from Sir William Roberts in 1662.

From 1703 to 1770 the Ashurst family owned this estate, which was bought from William Pritchard Ashurst in 1770 by Thomas Bromwich, paper merchant, of South Grove House (see p. 66). Mr. Bromwich's estate was identical with that of Sir William Roberts in 1662 and can be accurately identified from a plan of the property made in 1776.[85] It came to Robert Isherwood, esquire, in 1812, and the greater part was sold by him in 1815 to Harriot Coutts, wife of Thomas

Coutts, the banker. It consisted of all the land between Swain's Lane and West Hill (except the Cow and Hare) northward as far as the land of Dame Sarah Cave, whose land is now the Highgate Cemetery behind St. Michael's Church. The White Hart and what had then become Bowstread's Nursery passed on the death of Robert Isherwood to his only daughter, Mrs. Chester, and was sold by the Chester Trustees in 1856 to the Baroness Burdett Coutts, daughter of Sir Francis Burdett and granddaughter of Thomas Coutts.

The Cow and Hare was the farm-house of a 50-acre farm, leased together with the White Hart and four acres by Mrs. Elizabeth Ashurst in 1722 to Thomas Phillips, innholder of Highgate, for 21 years at £112 per annum,[86] which two leases were assigned by the executors of William Baker (see p. 73) to William Duffield, gardener of Highgate, in 1733. The Cow and Hare was mentioned as being new erected in 1770, when Mr. Greenwood farmed the land. It was this farm that Mrs. Coutts bought in 1815 from Mr. Isherwood. The Cow and Hare itself was leased by Mr. Isherwood in 1827 to Giles Redmayne, esquire, for 11 years, and when that lease expired in 1838 was conveyed by Mr. Harry Chester and his wife to Richard Barnett, esquire, who died on 15th December, 1851, aged 72. On the site his sister, Anne Barnett (who died on 1st July, 1868, aged 85), erected at her sole charge the church of St. Anne, Brookfield, Highgate Rise, in his memory.[25] In 1780 Mr. Bromwich had licence to lease the White Hart and five acres to William Bowstread. In 1822 it was occupied by Mr. Cutbush, and the firm of William Cutbush and Son remained there about 100 years, their place of business being the present No. 47, which then had a door opening straight on to the road in the northern part, while the southern part (under the gabled roof) was a shop. The frontage southward of the house was occupied by a greenhouse, with wooden railings in front, and an entrance in the middle. The shop was closed in 1918 but the nursery gardens were in the old kitchen gardens of Kenwood for some years. They are now at Barnet.

XII—NO. 48, WEST HILL AND HOLLYSIDE, NO. 49, WEST HILL

GROUND LANDLORD, LEASEHOLDERS, ETC.

The house was originally copyhold of the Manor of Cantlowes but was enfranchised in 1870 and is now in the ownership of Mrs. Cloutman. The occupier is Admiral Sir H. E. Purey-Cust.

GENERAL DESCRIPTION.

Nos. 48 and 49, West Hill were originally one house and occupy part of the site of a property at one time in the hands of the Cholmeley family and possibly of Sir Roger himself. The greater portion of the old house is now numbered 49 and is known as Hollyside. The plan is a half-H facing west towards West Hill with very slight projections on the opposite front. It is noticeable for the two massive chimney-stacks which probably survive from a much earlier house. Most of the internal features to-day date from the latter part of the 18th century and only one room on the first floor retains its original panelling intact. In one or two others a portion still remains. The room to the north of the present hall, now used as a drawing room, is lined with some excellent early 18th-century panelling, but this was brought here from some other house in London, as is also the case with the charming late 18th-century marble fireplace in the room above this on the first floor.

HISTORICAL NOTES.

These houses, together with No. 50, occupy the site of a house which William Cholmeley conveyed to Sir James Harrington in 1656, then described as a messuage, garden, yard, stable and hayloft, and 20 feet adjoining to the west side of the stable, 35 feet in length towards Kentish Town, with the barn thereon and one pole of ground. At the same time it was found that the brick wall and coachhouse, 10 poles 4 feet in length, before the north side of the house and garden, stood on a strip of the waste half a pole wide, and also that a high paling $4\frac{1}{2}$ poles 7 feet in length similarly enclosed a strip of the waste. If the length of these two strips be added it will be found that the total frontage thus brought forward on the waste amounted to some 265 feet, which is, in fact, the length of frontage now occupied by these houses. Sir James must have lived at Highgate some years before he bought the house, since he had a son, Henry, baptised at Highgate Chapel in 1640, and a daughter, Martha, in 1642, and he had a lease of the house which he assigned to his sister, Lucy Harrington, in 1653. His father, Sir Edward Harrington of Swakeleys, had died in October, 1652. In 1647, 1653 and 1654, three of his daughters were buried at Swakeleys.[87] He sat as one of the judges of King Charles I, and fled from England at the Restoration. In the account of his property attached to a letter which he sent to his wife in 1661, he included " A House at Highgate in Middlesex, mortgaged and forfeited for £400 debt." The schedule of his debts shows that he owed £400 to Mistress Lucy Harrington and £500 to Serjeant Fountayne. In 1663 he conveyed the house to John Fountayne, esquire, serjeant-at-law, the husband of his other sister Theodocia. This surrender was in lieu of payment of £400 to Fountayne as a nominee of Lucy Harrington. Mr. and Mrs. Fountayne appear to have lived there, as it is subsequently described as " late in the tenure of John Fountayne." It was acquired from him in January, 1664, by Francis Blake, gentleman, the father of William Blake of " The Ladys Hospital " fame and of Sir Francis Blake. In 1672 the house was conveyed by Francis Blake to his son, William Blake, from whom it went in 1678 to his brother, Francis (afterwards Sir Francis) Blake. In 1685 Francis Blake had two daughters, Susanna and Katherine, baptised at Highgate. In 1709 Sir Francis Blake and Elizabeth, his wife, conveyed the house to Robert " Osbolston " of Kensington, esquire, whose name appears in John Harris's View of Ashurst House (Plate 41), which gives a good view of the house from the south. Three years later, in 1712, he also

69

bought of Thomas Kemp and Mary his wife a messuage and two fields called Danskett Hill and Horsepasture, containing 13 acres. This estate was the site of Holly Terrace (which lay to the south-west) (see Plate 2), and the northern portion of the Holly Lodge estate which extended to the foot of West Hill. Quarter-Master Major Thomas Kemp was a "monyer" of the Tower, that is, an officer employed at the Royal Mint. He married Mary Noble of London, who was buried in the church of St. Peter-in-the-Tower in 1725.[88] Major Kemp had obtained the estate in 1706 from the sons of William Bluck of Monken Hadley, to whom it had been conveyed in 1690 by Mrs. Thomasina Jones, widow of Francis Jones and daughter of William Cholmeley.

Cooke of Hackney

Robert Osbaldeston, gentleman, of Kensington, in his will proved on 2nd March, 1715-6,[89] bequeathed the whole property to Dame Elizabeth Child "for more ample jointure." She was the widow of Sir Josiah Child, bart., son of Josiah Child of Wanstead, Essex, by his second wife, Mary, widow of Thomas Stone, merchant of London. Sir Josiah Child was born about 1668 and married, at the age of 22, Elizabeth Cooke, spinster, aged 16, daughter of Sir Thomas Cooke of Hackney, the marriage licence being dated 27th February, 1691.[90] He died without issue on 20th January, 1704, at Hackney, and Dame Elizabeth was buried at Hackney on 26th January, 1741. Her husband's half-brother, Sir Richard Child, afterwards Earl Tylney, built Wanstead House. She left the estate to her godson and nephew, John Cooke (son of her brother, John Cooke), who was then under age. Dame Elizabeth Child apparently lived in the house, which was leased by Mrs. Abigail Cooke in 1742, acting on behalf of her son. The latter, who was then known as John Cooke of Hatton Garden, esquire, died in 1807, leaving four sons, John Cooke of Maltby (Yorks.), Sunderland Cooke of Stowborough, the Rev. George Cooke of Sprotborough, and Henry Cooke of Bedford Square, and afterwards of the Steam Mills, Westminster Bridge Road.

Continuing the story of the Hollyside estate, we find that the house, formerly the residence of Francis Blake, Sir Francis Blake, his son, Robert Osbaldeston, esquire, and Dame Elizabeth Child, was in 1809 held on lease by John Graham, upholsterer of St. Martin's-in-the-Fields, and Martha his wife, their two children being Alexander Graham of St. Martin's, and Ann Graham. Before that date the occupier had been Mrs. Mary Markham, who was paying rates in 1779.[42] Two more houses had been erected by John Tate. When the property was leased from the Cooke family in 1821[91] by John Hillman, ironmonger, of Foster Lane, Cheapside, five houses stood on the site, viz. the present No. 49 (Hollyside), the residence of Admiral Sir H. E. Purey-Cust, with Mr. Pratt's house adjoining it on the north, and Mrs. Slade's house the next on the south, while a pair of semi-detached houses, one occupied by Mr. Richard Gurney, stood southward. By the roadside immediately southward of the last-mentioned houses, stood stables and coachhouses occupied by Mr. Mottley. In 1803 the houses were occupied by Robert Webster, Mr. Graham, John Brooks, Mrs. Mary Mitchell and James Milne. Robert Webster remained until 1817,[42] his executors held his house in 1818, in 1819 it was empty and Samuel Pratt followed from 1820. John Graham remained until 1819 and his house was empty until 1824, when Mr. John Hillman occupied it. Edward Ambrose followed Mr. Brooks in 1805, and Thomas Bramley in 1811, Arthur Slade in 1812-24, and Henry Cooke from 1825. In 1831 only two names appear, William Hillman and Henry Cooke.

The other portion (Holly Terrace) of the Cooke estate, with the house formerly occupied by Thomas Kemp, was leased in 1722[92] by Dame Elizabeth Child for 41 years to William Bridges, esquire, of Highgate. It was described as a messuage, garden and parcel of waste and 2 roods 2½ perches, part of Horsepasture, abutting north on the garden pale of the messuage, containing from east to west 240 feet, abutting east on the said garden pale 80 feet, south on the field from east to west 265 feet, and west on the high road 90 feet. The house stood in the middle of what is now Holly Terrace. William Bridges, who was elected a Governor of the Grammar School on 3rd March, 1724-5, was a brother of John Bridges, F.R.S., Cashier of Excise, who collected materials for the *History of Northamptonshire*, and died on 16th March, 1723-4. They were sons of John Bridges of Barton Segrave (who died on 5th January, 1713, aged 71) and Elizabeth, his wife, sister of Sir William Trumball, knight, Secretary of State. William Bridges, who was appointed secretary to the Commissioners of Stamps on 7th November, 1727, married Martha Hart of Brill, Bucks., who predeceased him. He died on 5th January, 1740-1, being then resident at Lambeth, Surrey. He had previously lived at Hornsey.[93] On the north side of West Hill opposite this house was a garden lying between No. 36, Highgate Lodge, and No. 37, West Hill Lodge, which then and for a long time afterwards went with the house. The tenant shown on the map of 1804 was Dr.

Crombie, whose land, including the garden opposite, covered 14 acres. He seems to have first paid rates about the year 1797 and was gone in 1806.

George Smart of Tinker's Acre, Lambeth (the site of the County Hall), a builder whose activities extended into many parts of London, " developed " the Holly Terrace estate for the Cooke family. A lease was granted of No. 3, in 1806, for 99 years, and of No. 5 in the same year, followed by leases of No. 2 in 1810 for 95 years, No. 4 in 1811, and of the remaining houses in 1819 for 86 years, thus the leases were all terminable in the year 1905.

Holly Lodge itself, which afterwards attained world-wide fame as the residence of the Baroness Burdett Coutts, lay farther south and was leased from 24th June, 1809, for 48 years, " by direction of George Smart and of Sir Henry Tempest of Hope End, Hereford, Bart.," to Harriot Mellon of St. Paul's, Covent Garden, spinster, when it was described as " a capital messuage lately erected."[94] In passing it may be noted that Miss Mellon is stated to have met Sir Henry Tempest and his wife at the house of Mr. Graham the magistrate, and manager of Drury Lane Theatre, in 1798, having been introduced to him by R. B. Sheridan, when she was playing at the theatre. " Sir Henry Tempest had just built part of the villa at Holly Lodge ; and, as they frequently had the merry actress staying there, it may be supposed what delight she experienced in leaving close, dark Little Russell Street, for the pure, dry air, and rural walks of Highgate."[95] In 1815, when he was 80 years of age and she was 38, Miss Mellon married Thomas Coutts the banker. He died on 24th February, 1822, leaving an immense fortune to his widow. On 16th June, 1827, Mrs. Coutts married William Aubrey de Vere, 9th Duke of St. Albans. She died on 6th August, 1837. She devised the great fortune derived from Mr. Coutts to his granddaughter, Angela Georgina, daughter of Sir Francis Burdett and Sophia, his wife, youngest daughter of Thomas Coutts by his first wife, Susan (Starkie). She assumed the name of Burdett-Coutts and was gazetted Baroness Burdett-Coutts of Highgate and Brookfield, on 26th May, 1871. Although Miss Burdett-Coutts (as she was then) held Holly Lodge on lease, it was not until 1870 that the copyhold was conveyed to her from the Hillman trustees. When John Cooke and his brothers conveyed it to John Hillman in 1824 it was described as land on the south-east side of the road from Kentish Town to Highgate (West Hill) and 16 messuages, 11 whereof are in Holly Terrace and four more above, and one below in the occupation of Mrs. Coutts, and 13 acres of land, and garden ground on the top of the hill on the north-west side of the road in the occupation of Mr. Agar. The garden ground last mentioned was that previously referred to, next to Highgate Lodge. Mr. Hillman died in 1832,[96] leaving a widow, Jane Hillman, three sons and four daughters.

Lady Burdett-Coutts

XIII—WITANHURST (SITE OF PARKFIELD) NOW NO. 41, WEST HILL AND THE SITE OF THE FOX AND CROWN

GROUND LANDLORD.

The property was originally copyhold of the Manor of Cantlowes but has been enfranchised and is now in the ownership of Sir Arthur Crosfield, who resides at Witanhurst.

GENERAL DESCRIPTION.

Parkfield was a good early 18th-century house which probably incorporated and certainly occupied the site of a much older building. It had a picturesque range of stabling and was situated in a position adjoining Dorchester House to the west. A view is given on Plate 50a, but the house was pulled down towards the end of last century by Mr. Walter Scrimgeour, who, however, incorporated part of it in the new work. Since that date it has been reconstructed on a large scale by Sir Arthur Crosfield, Baronet, who has also incorporated a small fragment of the front, that used to face West Hill, into the lower portion of the walls of his billiard-room.

The Fox and Crown Inn (Plate 49) stood back from the road on the north-west side of West Hill just below Parkfield. It lay behind an ample courtyard and apparently dated from the late 18th century, although an inn occupied the site from the beginning of that century. It was pulled down by Mr. Walter Scrimgeour, who built a range of stabling on the site.

HISTORICAL NOTES.

Parkfield, now incorporated in Witanhurst, stood on the site of a house which Peter Sambrooke, apothecary of London, and Sara his wife, conveyed to Simon Baxter, draper of London, in 1665. Its earlier history is obscure, but it was included in the Warner estate (see Section XIV, The Grove) acquired by Sir Robert Payne, and was sold by his mortgagees to Sambrooke in 1663.* Baxter apparently lived here until 1666, when he took out a licence to lease the property which was assessed at 11 hearths for the Hearth Tax. In 1685 it was conveyed by Simon Baxter and Sarah, his wife, to John Hinde, esquire, of Highgate, a goldsmith of London, who had acquired Lauderdale House some five years before. According to Hilton Price's *Handbook of Bankers*, John Hinde's name appears in 1663 in Alderman Backwell's ledgers as having an account with him, and in 1677 the *Little London Directory* shows that John Hinde and Thomas Carwood were keeping running cashes over against the Exchange on Cornhill. This may be the John Hinde of Highgate. He was declared bankrupt on 7th November, 1686, having previously mortgaged the house to Anne Gower, the daughter of Richard Gower (of Bisham House). She became the wife of William Rutland, junior, merchant of London, and they seem to have resided here after 1687, in which year she foreclosed and took possession. In 1696 Mr. and Mrs. Rutland conveyed it to John Hart, citizen and merchant of London. With Frederick Hertough he carried on the business of "scarlett dyers" in Clerkenwell, but became bankrupt in 1706,[97] and the trustee in bankruptcy sold the house in 1708 to Richard Bealing, esquire, of Highgate.

Behind the house was a four-acre field which was probably rented by the occupiers of the house until it was bought by Richard Bealing in 1714 from Francis Pemberton, son of Sir Francis.

* Peter Sambrooke also acquired from the Draper family the estate known in later times as Kentish Town House, south of Swain's Lane, facing west to Highgate Road opposite Parliament Hill Fields.

This field, called Robinson's close or Baxter's field, is interesting because it was the property of the Cholmeley family. When Sir Francis Pemberton bought Dorchester House he also acquired this field from Mrs. Thomasina Jones, the last of the Cholmeleys (see pedigree in Appendix). As stated elsewhere (see p. 5) Jasper Cholmeley's Highgate property was mostly derived from Sir Roger Cholmeley, and that this was the case with Robinson's close is shown by a case recorded on the Sessions Roll of Middlesex for 5th December, 1563,[98] when the jury found a true bill that at Highgate, in the parish of St. Pancras, John Crofton, a tailor of London, had stolen a linen shirt belonging to Roger Cholmeley in the custody of William Robinson, one of the Queen's servants, and two linen shirts of William Robinson himself. It may seem somewhat odd to trace the ownership of land through a stolen shirt, but the inference is irresistible that we have here the man whose name became attached to the field in question, now part of the grounds of Witanhurst, southward of the site of Dorchester House. Since the houses in the Grove (Pemberton Row) are built in a terrace with no space between for a horse and cart to reach the gardens behind, the tenants were accustomed to go across this field to their back gardens. When the houses on the one hand and the field on the other passed into separate ownership their rights in this respect were safeguarded by an agreement made between John Schoppens and Richard Bealing in 1716, renewing an agreement made in 1713 between Bealing and Pemberton, whereby Richard Bealing agreed he should not stop or obstruct any of the drains lying in the field belonging to any of the houses, but should permit the respective occupiers for the time being, their servants and workmen at seasonable times, to repair the same, and not to plant trees or erect buildings or set stacks of hay or wood in the field on that part adjoining the back gardens of the houses or do anything that might obstruct or hinder the view, and that Robert Doughty, merchant, and Major Hart, or the tenants of those houses for the time being, might carry dung to their gardens through the close as formerly, during the four months from November to February.

Richard Bealing was buried at Highgate on 19th October, 1724, and his son, Marmaduke Bealing, succeeded to "an ancient messuage and garden" in Highgate, and one acre of land near the messuage heretofore of Sir Francis Pemberton, and four acres heretofore of Francis Pemberton, a parcel of waste with a barn and stable thereon and a parcel of waste lying before the house late of Richard Bealing. Marmaduke Bealing was also buried at Highgate on 18th April, 1726, leaving a widow, Anne Bealing, who sold the estate two years later. The house heretofore belonging to William Rutland, and Baxter's field, went to John World of St. Clement's Danes, while Richard Baker, plumber, of Holborn, had "part of the land where heretofore stood the capital messuage of Henry, late Marquis of Dorchester, containing one acre, abutting north and east on the garden and a passage leading to the house of John Schoppens, esquire, west on the passage leading to the house of —— Hill, gentleman, and south on the waste and High Road, and on part whereof late was built a messuage in the possession of Richard Baker, and a parcel of land late waste lying before the last mentioned called the Walk."

Before continuing the story of the house on the site of Parkfield we will trace the subsequent owners of this acre of land definitely stated to be the site of Dorchester House; the earlier history of the house itself will be found in Section XIV. Richard Baker died on 12th December, 1732, leaving a widow, Adreana Baker, and a daughter, Elizabeth, wife of William Pearce, brewer, of Highgate, and of St. Giles-in-the-Fields. Besides owning this house Richard Baker had several leases of farms[99] in Highgate which his daughter and her husband in 1733 assigned to James Cotton, citizen and haberdasher of London, viz. from Dame Elizabeth Ashurst (i) the Cow and Hare and 50 acres, (ii) the White Hart and four acres, and from the Sons of the Clergy (iii) four fields containing 26 acres, lying between Millfield Lane and West Hill. Thomas Phillips of the Cow and Hare was tenant of (i) and (iii). Mr. and Mrs. Pearce had licence to lease in 1735. Nothing more appears on the rolls about it until 1784, when their grandson, William Pearce of Abingdon Street, Westminster, esquire, came into possession. He left the property in his will (1792) to his mother, Mary Pearce, and his aunt, Elizabeth Jennings, and the latter bequeathed it to Mary Cooper, Mary Ann Gibbs and Ann Poole (1816). In 1818 they, with John Pearce, heir of William Pearce, conveyed it to Charles Augustus Hoare of Queen's Square, esquire, who leased it in the next year to Miss Mary Elizabeth Summersum, for 21 years. She had previously occupied No. 5, The Grove. Charles Augustus Hoare died on 5th November, 1862, bequeathing his estate to Rear-Admiral J. J. F. Newell, who died on 24th December, 1862, bequeathing it in turn to his brother, Henry Edmund

Newell, then living at Gibraltar. On the death of the last named on 27th February, 1873, it went to his sister Augusta, wife of Captain Robert Bradshaw, R.N., of No. 3, Lansdowne West, Bath, the occupier then being the Rev. William Douglas Bodkin. It was bought in 1874 from Captain Bradshaw by Peter William Bodkin, esquire, of Merton Lane, who conveyed it a few months later to his son, the Rev. W. D. Bodkin, who married Miss Catherine Elizabeth Rawlins in 1875. It was then known as " Grove Bank " (Plate 50b).*

The main portion of Mrs. Bealing's estate was sold to John World in 1728. In 1736 it was bought from the executors of John World by William Congreve, esquire, whose wife was Catherine, daughter of Thomas Niccoll, the owner of the Grove House estate (see p. 93), and he conveyed it in 1774 to John Crutchfield, esquire. It remained in the ownership of this family for a hundred years, viz. 1761-76, William Crutchfield, nephew of John Crutchfield; 1776-1820, John Crutchfield, esquire, son of William; 1820-7, Ann Crutchfield, widow of John Crutchfield, who leased the estate to John Routh for 21 years in 1821; 1827-43, John Crutchfield Sharpe of Market Deeping, Lincolnshire (under the will of John Crutchfield). The occupier in 1836 was George Harrison, esquire. It was purchased in 1843 from John Crutchfield Sharpe by Allen Williams Block, esquire, and sold by his son in 1889 to Walter Scrimgeour, esquire, of No. 5, The Grove, Highgate.[100] The house was then called Parkfield. The conveyance included also The Limes in Fitzroy Park, the Fox and Crown, Sutton Cottage adjoining, and also three cottages at the north end of the yard at the back of No. 1, The Grove. Mr. Scrimgeour made many alterations in the property, rebuilt Parkfield and pulled down the Fox and Crown. In 1892 he bought Grove Bank (on the site of Dorchester House) from the Rev. W. D. Bodkin. It was then leased to the Rev. Joseph Fayrer, the previous occupant having been the Rev. John Bradley Dyne, D.D., Headmaster of Highgate Grammar School. Dr. Dyne was appointed in 1838, when there were only 18 scholars; in ten years the number had increased to 102, and in thirty years to 167. He retired in 1874, having transformed what had been a small village school into an important public school.[56] Grove Bank was sold by Mr. Scrimgeour in 1898 to Miss Rebecca Lacey of the adjoining No. 1, The Grove, who kept a school for girls. It was pulled down about 1933.

The Fox and Crown inn, absorbed by Mr. Scrimgeour into the Parkfield estate, occupied part of a piece of common enclosed in 1663 and granted to Isaac Odam, an adjoining plot to the south-west having been granted to Elizabeth White, widow, whose daughter, Elizabeth, was married to Isaac's son, Anthony Odam. The widowed mother and her married daughter lived in adjoining cottages on this site, described in the 17th century as " near the Claypits." Southward again of Mrs. White's cottage Philip Butterfeild had built a house on the common and enclosed six poles with hedge and ditch. Thus we have on the Hearth Tax roll for 1665, Butterfeild 2 hearths, Skillett 2 hearths, Widow White 6 hearths and Odam 2 hearths—four houses, of which Mrs. White's was by far the largest. In 1674 the four had increased to seven, viz. William Butterfeild 2, John Tayler 2, Empty 4, Widow White 2, Widow Burden 2, Richard Flinders 2, Anthony Odam 3, and William Lewis 5. Isaac Odam had died in 1671 and was succeeded by his three sons, John, Thomas and Anthony Odam, who divided up 13 poles of the land between John Tayler, labourer, and Frances his wife, daughter of Isaac Odam, William Kirke, labourer, and Margaret his wife, another daughter, Anthony Odam and Elizabeth his wife, while the remainder went to Richard Flinders, basket maker, except a part which Isaac Odam himself had surrendered in 1670 to William Burden, *alias* Crosse, labourer, and Obedience his wife, another daughter of Isaac Odam. These cottages, with perhaps two exceptions, are not individually of importance, and it is only necessary to note that for two centuries and more a varying number of houses stood on what was originally a wide strip of common at the top of West Hill in front of Robinson's Field, belonging formerly to the Cholmeleys, and that they were finally demolished by Mr. Scrimgeour, who brought forward his boundary to the present frontage of Witanhurst.

The two exceptions referred to above are the Fox and Crown alehouse, which lay back

---

* Grove Bank was a boarding-house for boys attending the Cholmeley School, Highgate. The Rev. W. D. Bodkin, M.A., was for many years a master at the School. His father, Mr. William Peter Bodkin, J.P., D.L., Middlesex, lived at West Hill Place, Highgate, from 1874 to 1900, and took up his residence there on the death of his father, Sir William Henry Bodkin, Assistant Judge of Middlesex 1859-73, and Recorder of Dover 1832-72.

from the road, and the house on West Hill at the southern corner of the passage leading up to the inn, called Sutton Cottage, in 1889. The inn itself, after the death of Isaac Odam, was sold to Richard Flinders, basketmaker (died 1704), and then went to Robert Bulkley and his wife Frances, niece of R. Flinders (1704-15), being for the first time referred to as the Fox and Crown in 1704. Frances Bulkley conveyed it in 1715 to James Crompton, carpenter, who mortgaged it in 1730, when the tenant bore the apposite name Mathias Tipler. In 1753 it was bought by John Southcote, esquire, from Francis Gillow, brewer, the tenant then being George Frost. In 1801, when John Southcote's two widowed sisters-in-law sold it to Augusta Frances Drummond of Finchley, the tenant was Ann Cartland. Mrs. Drummond (died 1832) left it to her son, who leased it in 1833 to John Turner. His tenancy became memorable in local annals by an incident narrated in the following extract from the *Estates Gazette* of 21st May, 1904: "The death on Saturday of Mr. James William Turner, of Highgate, recalls a thrilling incident in the life of Queen Victoria. His father kept the Fox and Crown, a quaint little tavern, which until then had been known as the Fox under the Hill. On July 6, 1837, Her Majesty and her mother were being driven down the hill in a carriage drawn by four horses ridden by postillions, when the horses became restive and plunged violently. Being without a drag chain, the carriage pressed upon the horses, which greatly increased their fright. At this juncture Mr. Turner sprang forward, and in the most intrepid manner, succeeded in blocking the wheels of the vehicle. Her Majesty, who was naturally much alarmed, alighted from the carriage and sought refuge in the tavern. The horses were quieted and a drag chain having been secured, the journey to Kensington was resumed. In addition to a handsome present, Mr. Turner was granted a licence to mount the Royal Arms outside his house. Underneath was placed the inscription :—' This coat of arms is a grant from Queen Victoria for services rendered to Her Majesty while in danger travelling down this hill.' This board has now been placed in the Highgate Literary and Scientific Institution." In 1835 the inn was bought by Douglas Charles Gardiner from Mr. Drummond and was sold by his son to Allen Williams Block, thereafter remaining in the same ownership as Parkfield. Mr. Scrimgeour placed an inscription relating to it on the stables he built on the site.

Sutton Cottage replaced two cottages occupied by John Taylor and Frances, his wife, (daughter of Isaac Odam), which were conveyed in 1707 to Robert Rogers, draper, of St. Clement's Danes, who died on 8th October, 1710. His sons conveyed them to William Bridges, esquire, of Highgate, afterwards of Barton Segrave, Northamptonshire. When the latter conveyed the estate in 1736 to William Waines, gentleman, of Whitby, the two cottages had been replaced by a house occupied by the Rev. Edward Yardley, B.D., who had been appointed Minister (preacher) of Highgate Chapel on 5th November, 1731, in place of Lewis Atterbury, LL.D., Rector of Hornsey, deceased. The Rev. Edward Yardley, who was collated Archdeacon of Cardigan on 26th May, 1739, died on 26th December, 1769, and was buried at Highgate. In 1746 the house passed, on the death of William Waines, to his nephew, William Waines of Beverley, who conveyed it in 1747 to John Gregory, timber merchant, of Holborn, from whom it passed in 1764 to Henry Woodfall of Islington, esquire, being then in the occupation of a Mr. Greenwood. In literary circles Mr. Woodfall would be more generally recognised by his description of citizen and stationer of London. His widow, Mary Woodfall, immediately sold the house to John Jaques of Highgate, in Hornsey, butcher. Henry Woodfall made his will on 13th December, 1768, and added a codicil dated 15th February, 1769.[101] It was proved 17th March, 1769. He bequeathed the business of printing the *Public Advertiser* to his son, Henry Sampson Woodfall. The *Letters of Junius*, which occupy so important a position in English literature and political history, 70 in number, were published in the *Public Advertiser* between the 21st January, 1769, and the 21st January, 1772, and were reprinted two months later by Henry Sampson Woodfall. He was prosecuted for printing and publishing one of the letters on 16th December, 1769, but was acquitted on a technical point. Mr. Greenwood's successor was a Miss Harvey, and in 1778 the occupier was William Owen, butcher, of Cannon Street, who bought the house in 1787 from John Jaques. The subsequent owners were James Richardson, esquire, of New Inn (1800-4), Robert Wells (1804-9), Richard Hollings, pork butcher, of Blackman Street (1809-31), James Hollings, son of Richard (1831-5), Douglas Charles Gardiner (1835-61). The occupier after James Richardson was Edward Gutteridge, who was followed by Thomas Chapman and then by A. Fenner. Allen Williams Block bought it in 1862 from the son of Mr. Gardiner, when the tenant was James Hill.

75

THE VILLAGE OF HIGHGATE

It will be observed from the older maps that a footpath formerly ran along the front of Grove Bank next to No. 1, The Grove, leading to a yard running northward at the west end of that house up to three cottages which lay behind No. 1. All this was altered by Mr. Scrimgeour and Mr. Bodkin. The cottages were swept away, and by an order of Quarter Sessions on 7th July, 1890, the highway in front of Grove Bank was closed, thus enabling the present frontage to be formed.

XIV—NOS. 1 TO 6, THE GROVE
(SITE OF DORCHESTER HOUSE GARDEN)

GROUND LANDLORDS, LEASEHOLDERS, ETC.

All these houses were originally copyhold of the Manor of Cantlowes but were enfranchised and are now in the following ownerships and occupations:

No. 1. Mr. and Lady Marjorie Stirling.
No. 3. Mr. J. B. Priestley.
No. 4. Mrs. Webster.
No. 5. Mr. Matthew Watt Drysdale.
No. 6. Miss King and Miss Sells.

GENERAL DESCRIPTION AND DATE OF STRUCTURE.

In the early days of the 19th century the houses now numbered 1 to 6, The Grove, together with two adjoining ones that used to overlook the top of West Hill, must have formed an architectural group as representative as any in London of the work of the late 17th and early 18th centuries. To-day, however, so many alterations and additions have been made to the original structures that it is no longer easy to realise their original beauty, although many details of interest still remain. When Mr. C. H. James, F.R.I.B.A., was recently entrusted with the reconstruction of No. 5, a careful inspection of the house revealed the fact that so much of the early structure had been cut away or otherwise interfered with that the only course left was to replan and rebuild it altogether. Thus it comes about that No. 5, while it displays a plan that differs entirely from the other five, yet possesses an elevation dating from the 20th century which represents the house as it would have appeared before a large square bay window had been added to it in the 19th. To that extent it has been brought into closer consistency with the general character of the row.

The date when the first six houses were erected can be approximately determined from two sources: (i) the court rolls of the Manor, which are fully quoted in the historical notes that follow; (ii) the curious MS. plan (*circa* 1688) drawn and annotated by William Blake (Plate 39) which contains the information that he had erected the six houses on the garden of Dorchester House and that the rent obtained from them was intended to form part of the endowment of the Charity School that he had founded and opened in that house (see also p. 90). A description with a plan of Dorchester House is also given in the historical notes.

From a comparison of the above sources of information we can be fairly certain that these six houses were completed by 1688. While it is not easy to form a very definite idea of their exact external appearance no such difficulty exists in the case of their plan. They were erected as three pairs of semi-detached family residences, each pair presumably being alike. An interesting sketch elevation bearing William Blake's initials and entitled

THE VILLAGE OF HIGHGATE

" The Ladies' School at Highgate " reproduced on Plate 51 from *The Gentleman's Magazine* (July, 1800) suggests that it was really a draft for the new houses in The Grove. The initials " H. C." also attached to the plan are those of Henry Cornish, a trustee of the estate. The illustration was the frontispiece to Blake's booklet *Silver Drops*. Blake's more ambitious scheme for his School for Ladies will be found described on p. 90.

On Plate 53 will be found complete plans and elevations of the houses as they were in 1932. Each house contained three rooms on the ground floor and a hall with a space for the staircase, which was planned against the side external wall between the hall and the smaller room on the garden front. A feature of the plan was the massive chimney-stacks, in some cases starting from the ground floor. Four angle fireplaces, two to each house, formed a diagonal block in the centre of each pair, while the north and south elevations consisted largely of a pair of great stacks with the staircase lights between them. A view of the south elevation of No. 5 taken some years ago shows how these stacks originally projected boldly from the walls, but the spaces between them and the stairs appear to have been utilised sometimes by erecting framing flush with the external face of the stacks and covered with beaded weather-boarding. A portion remains to-day only in the case of No. 4.

Each house consisted of a basement, ground and first floors with attic, and the elevations from the beginning must have shown four openings on each of the principal floors. On the ground level the second opening from the north or south was usually the front door leading into the hall. A plain brick string course marked the position of the first floor and a moulded cornice with grouped modillions extended right across the fronts of each pair of houses just above the first-floor windows, the attic above being lighted usually by four, but occasionally by two, dormer windows.

Each pair of houses had two parallel roofs running right through from north to south terminating in twin gables between each group of chimney-stacks. The rooms were apparently finished internally with typical late 17th- or early 18th-century panelling (large panels above a dado) with the moulded cornices of the period. In one case (pp. 84, 85) examples of early wallpaper have been found beneath the old panels. The angle fireplaces in the principal rooms were presumably all treated on similar lines with bolection moulded surrounds and two oblong panels above and narrow ones at either side. One of these typical surrounds can be seen to-day in the back attic at the top of the staircase in No. 4. The staircases show some variation in design, but in certain cases they may represent later insertions. The architectural features as they are to-day will be referred to in the description of the individual houses that follows.

There were two other 18th-century houses immediately to the south and west of No. 1, The Grove, and overlooking the top of West Hill, which were removed without any records being obtained. They were of a little later date than those in The Grove since they occupied the site on which Dorchester House actually stood, and they differed from them in that they were detached instead of being semi-detached. Their history will be found on

78

p. 73. With their disappearance the transformation of the scene on the summit of West Hill was complete. A view of the one known as " Grove Bank " is reproduced in Plate 50.

Nos. 1 and 2, The Grove were converted into a single residence in 1930-1 by the then owner, Sir Neville Pearson (Messrs. Paget & Seely, architects), certain Victorian features both internal and external were removed and the principal elevations regained their original appearance with some important exceptions (Plate 54). The very characteristic north elevation was condemned as unsafe and taken down together with its chimney-stacks. At the same time the entrance to No. 1 was removed and replaced by a window while the overdoor was taken from No. 2 which became the principal entrance to the house. In order further to emphasise the alteration the fine wrought-iron gate (Plate 55) which belonged to No. 1 was repaired and re-erected with its brick piers opposite the centre of the main front. The gate to No. 2, which was similar to those of Nos. 3 and 4, was removed and not replaced. The projecting building at the south end was rebuilt to form a garage and servants' hall while a loggia was added at the northern end.

Pearson Bart.

The plan of No. 1 was transformed, the hall becoming a pantry and larder and the dining room a kitchen. The two rooms on the garden front were combined to form a new dining room and a door was opened in the party wall to provide access to a similar drawing room in the adjoining house.

In No. 2 the original arrangement was more nearly retained but the partition between the hall and the staircase has been removed and a new handrail, balusters and strings have been designed to match the old work. The twisted balusters, which are of substantial design, stand upon a continuous string both in the case of this staircase and of that in No. 1. The room on the ground floor adjoining the entrance hall contains a late 18th-century fireplace of Coade stone. On the first floor the planning is repeated, the two rooms on the garden front being again thrown into one. All the rooms are panelled but the original panelling was only found in the smaller room on the ground floor and the larger room on the first floor, where it had been covered with canvas and paper. This panelling appeared at first to consist of plain squares but when the canvas was removed it was discovered that the panels had originally been bolection moulded but the mouldings had been carefully removed and re-nailed on to the back of the panels to keep them in position. On the half landing of the staircase in No. 2 an original window remains, constructed of oak with early stout glazing bars. The attic floors have been entirely remodelled.

The original plan of No. 3 may still be traced through the alterations and additions which have been made in it from time to time. The wing to the south seen on Plate 53 was originally built in the latter part of the 19th century during the ownership of the late Mr. Charles Church, who may also have added the second floor to the main structure, but the cornice which now crowns this portion has only recently been placed there and the wing rebuilt by the present owner, Mr. J. B. Priestley. A room is preserved at the back on the second floor, which was occupied by the poet, Samuel Taylor

THE VILLAGE OF HIGHGATE

Coleridge, who died here in 1834, during the tenancy or ownership of the Gillmans.

Mr. Charles Church had already extended the original staircase from the half landing between the ground and first floors into his new wing and this portion was again entirely reconstructed and given new balusters to match the old by Messrs. Paget & Seely for Mr. Priestley. They also made the original entrance hall into a room and converted the old dining room adjoining it into the hall by moving the front entrance doorway. Other alterations included the moving of the panelling forward in the principal rooms and on the ground and first floors in order to make cupboard space, while the double room on the ground floor garden front was lined with entirely new panelling generally in keeping with the old. In making these changes some old fireplaces which had been blocked up at various times were revealed. The smaller front bedroom on the first floor was a particularly fine example of a panelled room of the period.

No. 4, The Grove, has been selected for complete illustration in this volume (Plates 57-61) because, of the houses as they are at present, it is the one that is the fairest guide to the appearance of the row in its earlier state. It must be remembered, however, that changes may have taken place from time to time in the arrangement of doors, windows, panelling and fittings, of which no record has come down to us. On the ground floor (except that the partition between the two rooms on the garden front has been in part removed) the original plan remains intact.

The house is entered by a doorway in the second opening from the north into a hall surrounded to-day with plain, square deal painted panelling (three panels high without any dado mouldings), and separated from the staircase by a solid partition. The principal feature is the opening to the staircase hall which is set slightly forward from the rest of the partition. The opening is semicircular-headed with a long narrow key block round which break the lower members of a wooden cornice of early 18th-century character which traverses the opening, but of which the upper member only is carried round the rest of the hall. On the left of the front entrance is a six-panelled door with beaded panels slightly raised in the centre. The window opening is not fitted with a window seat but the original shutters and casings in two heights remain. The fireplace has a marble surround of 18th-century character. Between the chimney back and the staircase partition is a recess or cupboard corresponding with a similar one on the floor above, while beneath the stairs is another cupboard to which access is now gained from the hall, but which was formerly only accessible through a hinged panel on the basement flight.

The room on the left of the hall is lined with late 17th- or early 18th-century beaded and painted deal panelling with moulded dado rail. There is a characteristic moulded cornice similar to the fragment in the hall. The fireplace is modernised, but the original arrangement of the panelling around and above it remains—two oblong panels over the opening flanked by two long narrow ones. The door leading into the room facing the garden

80

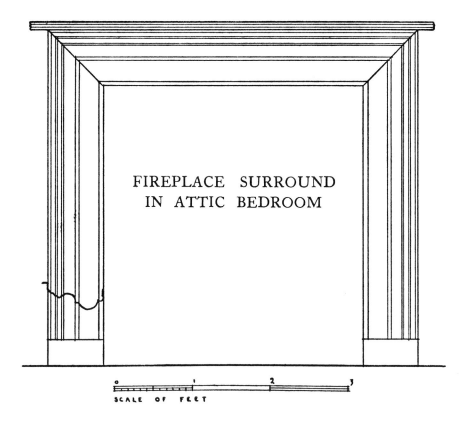

FIREPLACE SURROUND
IN ATTIC BEDROOM

SCALE OF FEET

is of the same type as the one from the hall and so are the doors on the first floor. The two rooms facing the garden are combined and panelled throughout with plain square deal painted panels, with slightly more elaborate architraves to the doors. The usual cornice has been removed in the larger room, but the original arrangement of panels remains over the fireplace.

The staircase is of the early type; solid newels, plain and square, with the moulded handrail breaking round but no base mould. The strings are continuous and the balusters spiral of substantial design, eight to each flight, with a short one where the handrail is mitred back on to the main carriage or string. Two of these newel posts have their original circular moulded pendants. On the ground floor opposite the basement flight (which is enclosed in a solid partition) is a door leading into the larger room on the garden front which obviates the necessity of its becoming a passage room. This door seems to be of early design. Only this portion of the walls of the staircase well is panelled to its full height. Up the flights the dado alone remains. On the half landing the original sash window with its heavy glazing bars has been removed and an opening cut through to one side to some steps down to a modern wing. Beside these some old panels have been re-used.

All the first-floor rooms except the smaller one facing the garden, which is covered with canvas above the dado, have panelling similar to that

81

F

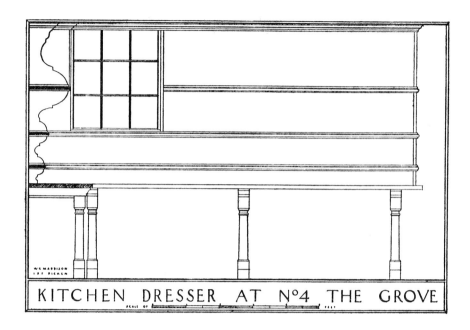

KITCHEN DRESSER AT Nº4 THE GROVE

on the ground floor, sometimes beaded but more generally plain. The doors also are precisely similar in style. The north front room has been divided into two and in the larger room facing the garden the long narrow panel to the left of the fireplace bears the marks of a hinge.

On the attic floor two of the doors on the outside appear to be plain square four-panelled but on the inside they are six-panelled bolection moulded. In the smaller room overlooking the garden there is a fine heavy bolection moulding around the fireplace opening of the type one might reasonably have expected to find in some of the principal living rooms.

The basement contains some features of interest; the back door is boarded, ledged on one side, and studded with nails. The other internal doors consist of three broad planks with long strap hinges with ornamental points, ledged on one side and with two narrow panels on the other. The kitchen is fitted on two sides with a dresser apparently contemporary with the date of the house; the lower shelf is supported on seven turned baluster legs, each with a delicate moulded cap. The upper shelves are stout, moulded on the edges and stopped against elaborately shaped ends. There is a small cupboard of contemporary date at the ceiling level. In the cellars are the original partitions, with their upper portions constructed in lattice work for light and ventilation. No upper storey having been added, the main front towards the Grove retains its eaves, cornice, and general early character and original grouping of the openings. The front door is of unusual height. The entrance gates are formed with square wooden posts with moulded caps supporting curved iron brackets carrying the lamp fitting.

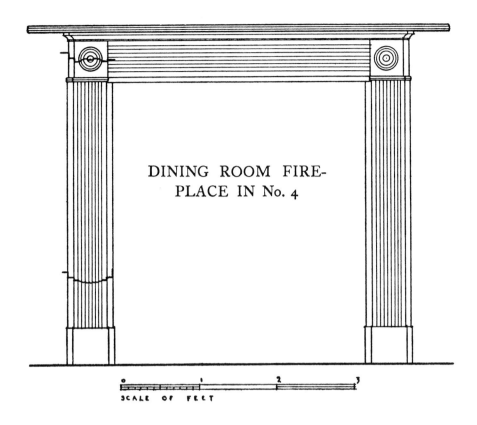

DINING ROOM FIRE-
PLACE IN No. 4

SCALE OF FEET

No. 5, The Grove, had until recently an early Georgian appearance owing to the addition of a second storey, and a narrow projecting wing on its south side (Plate 62). The windows on the first floor had been altered, and, with the new verge above, had arched brick heads. A brick band marked the top of the first and also of the second floor, and a plain brick parapet hid the roof. The wing had a projecting cornice at second-floor level. The back of the house had also been completely altered, but it presented a most picturesque appearance (Plate 63).

The whole structure has now been rebuilt by Mr. C. H. James, F.R.I.B.A., the general appearance of the front to the Grove alone being retained, although the spacing of the windows is slightly different and the details of the Regency porch have been varied. The old plan, before the rebuilding, is shown on Plate 53, and the various changes, additions and modifications which had occurred can be seen therein. The principal staircase was of fine design and dated from the early 18th century (Plates 64 and 65). It led from the ground to the first floor only and had a cut string with carved brackets, three spiral balusters to each step and beautiful fluted columns for newels. The balustrading has been preserved and is adapted to the new house. When this staircase was inserted the original stair on both floors was removed, and a second stair to serve the top floor was designed in the

18th-century south wing. The panelled walls of the principal stair can be seen in the photograph (Plate 65). Beyond this a few pieces of door furniture and a couple of later fireplaces were all that remained of interest.

The most important fact, however, concerning this house was the discovery on the removal of some of the painted deal panelling of four beautiful examples of early 18th-century wall-papers beneath it. It would seem, therefore, that the panelling was of a later date. We are indebted to Francis W. Reader for the following notes on the papers and to the Victoria and Albert Museum, where they are now preserved, for the photographs which are reproduced on Plates 66 to 69.

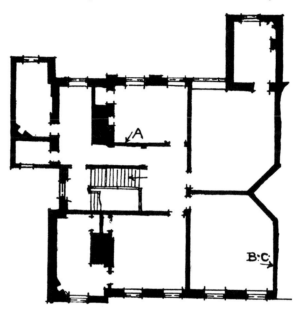

These papers were all found in rooms on the upper floor, and behind 18th-century panelling, but the activities of the house-breaker were well advanced before they came to the notice of the architect, Mr. C. H. James, F.R.I.B.A., who fortunately appreciated their importance, and sent portions to the Victoria and Albert Museum.

The positions of three of the papers were noted, and are indicated on the plan.

Unfortunately the panelling which covered them was of such simple construction that it had no characteristics that would enable it to be closely dated. The house was built about 1685, and in one instance only were two of the papers superimposed. It may be fairly assumed, therefore, that the walls were panelled early in the 18th century, and that the papers were of the last years of the 17th or the first years of the 18th century.

Other features which confirm this period are, the small size of the sheets of paper, and the absence of excise stamps. This latter would indicate that the papers must have been made before 1712, when the first tax was imposed.

The exact size of the sheets was not ascertained, but it was noticed that they were small square pieces and not continuous rolls. The patterns, also, were engraved on square wood blocks, and not on cylinders.

Example A has a geometrical pattern of interlacing quatre-foils and ovals containing conventional flowers and foliage, the design having been cut out on a wood block leaving the background as the printing surface, the printing being simply black on a white paper. Patterns printed in black ink on white paper have been found as early as the 16th century, and this method was continued throughout the 17th century and gradually came into more general use. In the early 18th century, black and white papers became obsolete owing to the advent of coloured inks and tinted papers.

Although the design of this example is graceful and delicate, its general effect must have been gloomy and depressing as a wall covering.

Example B is much more advanced both in its design and its engraving. It is a rich brocade pattern of bold flowers and foliage, which flow in beautiful curves, and is in the style of the Italian textiles of the 15th and 16th centuries. The engraving is a reverse process of that of example A, as in this it is the background which is cut away, leaving the pattern as the printing surface, except only for the details of the flowers and leaves, the pattern generally is printed on the white background of the paper. In its present state it appears as if printed in a mottled grey, or poor, attenuated black ink. In the reproduction the contrast has been somewhat forced, and is stronger than in the original. It is difficult to imagine that this condition represents the finished article. It seems probable that it was originally a flock paper from which the flock has been washed off, leaving the impression of the adhesive medium, some kind of varnish in which was sufficient pigment to enable the printer to judge the accuracy of his work.

Overlying this paper was example C, of which only a small fragment was preserved, but this is of great interest. Originally it was a printed paper, most of the pattern of which had been cleaned off, which in many of the early stainings would not have been a matter of great difficulty. In places traces of the printing remain and can be seen in the reproduction, the pattern having apparently been produced from an engraved copper plate. Finally it was stencilled with a simple " all-over " brush-work pattern in brown.

The treatment of wall-paper in this way affords striking evidence that in the early days of the industry, wall-papers must have been expensive, and that handwork with the stencil could compete successfully with the printed article. A few years ago an instance occurred at Aylesbury of a decoration stencilled directly on the plaster, which had been prepared only with a buff-colour limewash as a background, and on which an effective pattern was stencilled in black, white and brown. The period was probably late 18th century.*

Example D differs from the others in being a coloured paper of three printings, black, red and blue. The position of this paper was not noted, but it is known to have been the only paper on the wall it occupied, and was, like the others, behind 18th-century panelling. It may be thought that a paper of this sort must be later in date than those previously described, as the colours are in good distemper inks. Little is known as to how early colour printing was practised. Coloured papers appear to have been produced in the 17th century, but usually a printed black basis was hand-painted or stencilled. At the close of the 17th and early in the 18th century, the demand for coloured papers was greatly stimulated by Chinese hangings, which then became fashionable, and were extensively imitated by English producers.

* *Arch. Jour.*, Vol. LXXXIX, Plate XVII.

THE VILLAGE OF HIGHGATE

It is not generally considered that colour-printed papers had got beyond the experimental stage, until about the middle of the 18th century. It would not be safe, perhaps, to claim the same antiquity for this example as for the others, as we do not know how long the wall on which it was found may have been left uncovered. On the other hand, it bore no excise stamp, so far as could be seen, but the portion of this paper submitted to the Museum was not large enough to make this point certain. The printing, however, was from flat wood blocks, the border lines of which can be seen on two sides of the red block. That the method of printing was primitive, is shown by the imperfect register, to which not a little of the charm of this paper is due. The grey tone which has come by age over the white background helps to soften what in its original condition may have been a somewhat crude decoration. The design, which is of a Chinese character, consists of a series of sprays of flowers, so arranged as to have the effect of an all-over pattern. The sprays all start from curious and varied forms which are probably conventional representations of the ground from which the flowers grow.

Mr. C. O. Masters, judging from the photograph, suggests that the black only was printed and that the two colours were added by means of the stencil. Should this be the correct explanation, any difficulty as to the date would be removed and this paper brought within the same period as the others.

The discovery of these examples of early wall-papers at The Grove is of importance in throwing some light on an obscure period of the wall-paper industry.

No. 6, The Grove, would at first sight appear to have undergone considerable modifications internally, but there are several points of interest that have some bearing on the story of this group of houses. It is evident that this was the last of the six erected by William Blake and it may have been occupied by the widow of Judge Pemberton, who owned the estate after Blake. Its northern garden wall is that which terminated the two enclosed gardens of Dorchester House (see Plate 39), and the great circular bastion at the north-west corner of the terrace garden to-day must be one of those referred to in several conveyances entered in the court rolls of the Manor of Cantlowes, while the ornamental niches in the same wall near to its junction with the Grove may also belong to the Dorchester House period. The bastion is of considerable size and is planned in three curves, a semicircle flanked by two quarter-circles. The garden of No. 7 is also made-up ground, but the terrace wall continues westwards at right angles to the base line of the bastion.

The difference in level between the Grove roadway and the gardens in the rear is most marked and is no doubt the result of the levelling of the Dorchester House gardens, which apparently left an elevated terrace along their east side, which may to-day be represented by the forecourts of Nos. 1-6, The Grove. The date of this groundwork is probably about 1600. William Blake's plan is the only record of the layout of the gardens which formed these

86

two enclosures. Some scheme may have preceded these, since it is known that a considerable length of waste along the east side of this garden was enclosed by Sir Robert Payne, a predecessor of the Marquis of Dorchester. The west boundary wall of the Grove gardens is of considerable antiquity with four centred arches and recesses, one with a rough pediment above it, and there is a drop of about 10 feet between the upper and lower gardens behind the Grove houses. This terrace work is continued both to the north and the west to include the whole of the garden of No. 7, The Grove, which is called " The Great Garden " on the map of 1804 reproduced on Plate 1.

The plan of No. 6 is similar to that of the rest except for the later insertion of a chimney built into the partition between the two rooms on the garden front. As in the other houses the basement forms the ground storey on the garden side, due to the change in level referred to above. New kitchen offices have been added on the north, and the lower ground floor is disused. The partition between the hall and staircase on the ground floor was replaced by an open screen arcade in recent times.

In the decorations of the house it is noticeable that no 18th-century panelling appears to remain and possibly it never was panelled at all. William Blake may even have been unable to complete the building since we know he was in financial difficulties. The doors on the first floor have curved heads which suggest completion by another hand. The staircase, too, is of later date (early 18th century) and is similar to that inserted in No. 5, but in this case it serves all floors (see measured drawing on Plate 70). The elevation to the Grove retains its roof and main cornice and the attic is lighted by two dormers with semicircular heads which share the character of the features already noticed.

Nos. 7 to 12, The Grove, are modern houses on the site of the mansion built by Sir Francis Pemberton and afterwards owned by the Fitzroy family, Lords of Southampton. Its history is detailed below.

CONDITION OF REPAIR.
Good.

HISTORICAL NOTES.
The houses now numbered 1 to 12, The Grove, occupy the frontage of an estate that belonged, at the beginning of the 17th century, to the eminent family of Warner, several members of which held prominent positions in the City during a century and a half. The mansion house belonging to John Warner was called the Blewhouse, and had previously been occupied by Sir Edward Cleeve and afterwards by John Panton, esquire. The land appears to have measured some 38 acres, extending on the west to an ancient farm called " Sherricks," which stood in a triangular space south of Hampstead Lane between Ken Wood and Warner's land. In 1610 John Warner leased to Richard Lyllie of Kentish Town, bricklayer (builder), two acres on the north of his house (part of a five-acre field called Broomfield), on which Lyllie immediately built a house. See below, Nos. 7-12, The Grove.

John Warner was the son of John Warner, eldest son of Mark Warner, by his second wife, Elizabeth, daughter of Philip Meredith of London, gentleman, and great-grandson of Robert Warner of Stroud Green, citizen and draper of London, second son of Alderman John Warner, grocer (d. 1511).[102] On the death of John Warner in 1619, his son, John Warner, esquire, succeeded, the widow, Avys Warner, being admitted to her third for dower. They conveyed the

Warner

estate in the following year to Robert Payne, son of William Payne of Barton Stacey, Hants. (*see* Section VIII, p. 50). It was then described as a messuage called the Blewhouse with one acre of land attached, five acres of land formerly a field called Broomfield, now divided into several parts, and a messuage on part of Broomfield lately built by Richard Lyllie, a cottage occupied by Anne Daie, widow, and 32 acres held by Robert Sprignell.*

The site of the Blewhouse can be identified with that of Dorchester House, standing on the triangle of ground between No. 1, The Grove, and the house of Sir Arthur Crosfield called "Witanhurst," now No. 41, West Hill. Its exact position is described in Section XIII, p. 73. Its site is now occupied by a tennis court. The garden extended from the north front of Dorchester House and occupied the area on which Nos. 1 to 6 were afterwards erected. Henry Pierrepont, first Marquess of Dorchester, is mentioned as early as the year 1650 in a lease from Payne to Thomas Collett, which refers to the "ways hitherto used in or through Broomfield or Gravel Field now let by Sir Robert Payne to Henry, Marquess of Dorchester," and it was probably about that time that he came to Highgate, succeeding Henry Savage, esquire, as tenant of the Blewhouse, while Thomas Collett, by the lease referred to, came into possession of the house built by Richard Lyllie, etc., to the north (see p. 92).

Sir Robert Payne mortgaged the estate to Robert Holt, citizen of London, on 8th February, 1653-4, and the mortgage was never redeemed. Sarah, the only child of Robert Holt, succeeded him in 1657 and she married, on 7th April, 1658, at Hackney, William Roberts of Willesden, esquire, son of Sir William Roberts by Eleanor his wife, daughter of Robert Aty of Kilburn Priory.[103] Sarah Roberts and her husband became mortgagees in possession in 1657; in 1660 they held "a messuage called the Blewhouse late in the occupation of Henry Savage, gentleman," which in May, 1661, was included in the property mortgaged by them to Richard Gower, citizen and grocer of London, described as "a messuage in the occupation of the assigns of Henry Savage, gentleman, deceased." The last named is mentioned in 1656 as occupying the house, and at the time of his death, in 1662, he appears to have owned the property. His son, Paul Savage, goldsmith, with his wife, Mary, and his mother, Katherine, then conveyed it to the Marquess. It may be assumed that there was a conveyance from Roberts to Savage, which has not been found.

Pierrepont, Marquis of Dorchester

A coroner's inquest was held on 13th January, 1659-60, concerning the death of William Barnes in Dorchester House, when it was found that he, with Thomas Collins, "being in a certain hall in the house of Henry, Earle of Kingston situate at Highgate. . . . Thomas Collins having a fowling piece under his right arm, charged with small shot and gunpowder, took the same into his hand with the intention of laying it up under the mantle tree of the hall and, pulling the muzzle forwards in laying it up, it went off and wounded William Barnes in the left side, whereof he died instantly."[104] The Marquess of Dorchester had received his title from King Charles I on 25th March, 1645-6, for his services against the Cromwellians in the Civil War. It will be noticed that in the coroner's inquest of 1660 he is referred to by his hereditary title of Earl of Kingston. He had made his peace with the Commonwealth Government and possibly found it advisable not to assume the higher title. He was the eldest son of Robert Pierrepont, first Earl of Kingston, and was born in 1606. On 11th January, 1641-2, he was created Baron Pierrepont. He was a learned man and, according to Walpole, studied ten or twelve hours a day for many years. He had a considerable knowledge of both law and medicine, and he was admitted a Bencher of Gray's Inn and a member of the College of Physicians. He was a little man with a very violent temper. His activities as an amateur doctor excited the ridicule of his opponents. His daughter, Ann, married at Highgate on 15th July, 1658, John, Lord Roos, who was afterwards first Duke of Rutland. This marriage was dissolved by Act of Parliament in 1666 and her issue bastardised. Lord Dorchester was admitted a member of the Royal Society on 20th May, 1663. His second wife, whom he married in September, 1652, was Katherine, third daughter of James Stanley, seventh Earl of Derby. Dorchester died at his house in Charterhouse Yard, London, on 8th December, 1680, leaving by his first wife, Cecilia, daughter of Paul, Viscount Bayning (d. 18th September, 1639), a daughter, Grace, who was four years old when her mother died, and who died unmarried in the parish of St. Anne's, Soho, on 25th March, 1703. The divorcée, Anne, died before her father.[55]

In a list of tenants recorded on the court rolls in 1664, the Marquess of Dorchester appears

* For Robert Sprignell see *Cromwell House*, by Dr. Phillip Norman (London Survey Committee).

88

as tenant of a messuage and 5 acres 3 roods 11 perches of land. The actual site of the house has long been in doubt, several writers thinking that it faced the roadway now called The Grove, occupying approximately the combined sites of Nos. 3 and 4. Actually, the house, which was long and narrow, stood at right angles to the direction of the modern Grove to which the long walled garden was consequently parallel. Further information about the mansion came to light with the identification of the plan (Plate 51*b*) of a house at " Higate " in the Thorpe collection in the Soane Museum in Lincoln's Inn Fields. A comparison with existing views established the fact that it was undoubtedly The Blew House or Dorchester House, to use the name by which it is more generally known. Some account of the Thorpes (there were two, father and son) is given by Mr. Arthur T. Bolton in a paper read before the Architectural Association on 27th November, 1911, since reprinted by the author. In this paper Mr. Bolton quotes the only printed reference to these two architects, made by Peacham in the *Gentleman's Exercise*, first edition, 1612.*

We cannot tell whether the Highgate plan is by the elder or the younger Thorpe, but it is certainly of the highest interest on account of its unusual character. Its normal features are the central passage with its screen after the medieval manner, between it and the hall, communicating with a porch at either end and with the kitchen and offices to the left. The latter section includes a large parlour and other lodgings of unusual size. The striking feature of the residential part is a parlour beyond the hall, which it exceeds very much in size. This parlour is furnished with two bay windows—one, a large circular bay in the end wall—and two small retiring rooms. An elaborate double staircase is placed between the outer wall and the hall chimney, and appears to lead both from the screens passage and the great parlour.

That this plan represents the house pretty faithfully is borne out by the remarkable sketch of the exterior in William Blake's " Delineation of the Ladyes Hospitall at High-gate " (Plate 39). There the bay window and porches are shown and the angle-pilasters or buttresses are seen rising the full three storeys. There is no scale on Thorpe's plan, but Blake tells us that in his proposed reconstruction for the accommodation of " Mayden " children, he could obtain a hall 130 feet long, which is probably the internal length of the house.

It stood at the very summit of " West Hill " facing nearly south and looking right over London. The long garden coincided exactly with the upper gardens of the six Grove houses. Some niches still remain in the garden wall of No. 6, where can also be seen a " round " similar to that referred to in the entry in the court roll for 1st May, 1656, when it was found that " the wall on the east side of the messuage (described previously as in the occupation of Henry, Marquess of Dorchester) from four feet beyond the garden gate northward to the Round upon the south corner, containing six poles in length, and the said round and the wall from the said Round westward containing 11 poles 1 foot in length and all the elm trees within the two courts (except the great elm wherein is the dog's kennel) stands upon the waste and within the said wall from four feet beyond the garden gate aforesaid to the round in the south corner aforesaid is enclosed in breadth one foot, the said wall and enclosure being done by Sir Robert Paine, knight." The remarkable terrace supported by a massive retaining wall forming the gardens of the houses in the Grove is referred to on p. 86. Doorways in this wall lead into brick-vaulted cellars designed as four centred arches of distinctly Tudor character and therefore likely to have been in existence when Thorpe built or altered the Great House.

On the death of the Marquess of Dorchester, his daughter, Grace, conveyed the estate to Hugh Willoughby of Barton Stacey, esquire (doubtless a trustee), who surrendered it in 1682 to Edward Hildeyard of the Inner Temple, esquire, and Henry Burman, citizen and salter of London. From the prints issued by William Blake (Plates 39 and 40) we learn that he owned Dorchester House, as well as two other houses in South Grove. Dorchester House is so called by him and no difficulty arises in its identification, although his name does not occur in the court rolls in any conveyance of the house. Simultaneously with the conveyance to Hildeyard and Burman, William Blake was admitted to a parcel of the waste by the wall of his capital messuage late in the tenure of Henry,

---

* " John Thorpe of the Parish of St Martin in the Fields, my especial friend, an excellent geometrician and surveiour, whom the rather I remember because he is not only learned and ingenuous himselfe but a furtherer and favourer of all excellency whatsoever, of whom our age findeth too few. And lastly the afore-named Master John Thorpe, his sonne, to whom I can in words never bee sufficiently thankefull."

Marquess of Dorchester, 17½ poles by 2 poles at the south end and another parcel of waste 46 poles by 1½ poles to be used as a common walk and not enclosed. When Francis Pemberton was admitted to this waste in 1691 the piece 17½ poles by 2 poles was described as lying before the wall of divers messuages lately built there, where heretofore stood the capital messuage of the Marquess of Dorchester. We may therefore conclude that the conveyance from Hugh Willoughby to Edward Hildeyard and Henry Burman in 1682 was really a conveyance to William Blake. He intended to use Dorchester House as a Charity School for girls, and the building appears to have been actually occupied in this fashion. The notes appended by Blake to his bird's-eye view state that the grounds (10 acres), might be cut up into plots for the erection of houses where wealthy citizens of London might lodge in the summer. He says there were " six tenements now built " (the present Nos. 1-6, The Grove), and room for 10 or 12 more with gardens. Having mortgaged his property, alienated his family, and been locked up in the Fleet for two years for debt, he appealed to six London parishes to send children there to board and to buy or build houses on the estate, apparently to provide a revenue for the support of the School. " If Sir Francis Pemberton, Francis Blake, my brother, and Mr. William Ashurst, draper, who are the mortgagees would yet comply all might go immediately forward, with some £100 annual advantage to the Town of Highgate." In January, 1683, we find the Vestry of St. Clement's Danes promising to send to the Hospital 20 parish children when it should be ready, and to pay £6 yearly per head for their board, lodging and education, both in sickness and in health. At the same time the Vestry of St. Giles-in-the-Fields appointed a committee to report on Blake's proposals, and if they found them satisfactory, to agree to place 20 parish children there at £6 p.a. each.[105] It is not impossible that his difficulty in maintaining a revenue large enough to support his Hospital arose from dwindling support from the wealthy ladies on whom he evidently depended. Blake's six houses were built between the years 1682 and 1685. The Vestry Books of St. Giles for 1687 contain a record that £10 was granted towards the release of William Blake, a prisoner in the Fleet, in recognition of his having at some time provided several suits of clothes for poor children in that parish. Thereafter he disappears from the records and we cannot say when or where he died. There is insufficient material to pronounce a judgment regarding his financial abilities, but his own writings afford ample evidence that he struggled nobly to befriend the poor children of London, at that time one of the most pitiably oppressed and neglected classes of the community. In a list of the " worthies " of Highgate he would stand second to none.

In 1683 Hildeyard and Burman surrendered the property to Charles Bishop and Oliver Smith, trustees for Sir Francis Pemberton. These bare facts obviously fail to tell the complete story but, since William Blake commented bitterly on the conduct of his mortgagees, amongst whom he included Pemberton, we can pretty well guess that underlying these records is the fact that the unfortunate philanthropist, unable to repay the mortgages, was obliged to let Dorchester House go to Sir Francis Pemberton.

The exact year when Sir Francis Pemberton pulled down Dorchester House does not appear, but it was standing in 1688 and had disappeared when the trustees were admitted under his will in 1699.

From the time of their erection in the garden of Dorchester House the owners of Nos. 1-6, The Grove, were as follows.

1688-97.   Sir Francis Pemberton, who lived at Grove House on the site of Fitzroy Park (see below p. 93).

1697-1714.   Lady Ann Pemberton, widow of Sir Francis, and her sons.

1714-28.   John Schoppens (from Lady Ann Pemberton and her sons). He was elected a Governor of the Grammar School on 1st August, 1726. There is an entry in the Register of Highgate Chapel, under date 4th August, 1701, of the baptism of Hannah, daughter of Mr. John and Mrs. Mary " Scopins " of St. Pancras, merchant. He died on 1st July, 1728, aged 40, and was buried at Highgate. He left £150 to the Governors of the School to keep his tomb in repair, and when not wanted for that purpose to be disposed of at their discretion. This £150 was given to his brother-in-law, John Edwards, upon trust to buy land at Highgate and to apply the rent in repairing his monument and the wall adjoining, the surplus rent to belong to the said John Edwards and his sister, and after the death of the survivor of them, the same was given to the Governors. The inscription on his monument now in the tower of St. Michael's Church is given on p. 58.

1728-36.   Mary, the wife of John Edwards, sister of John Schoppens (under his will). She was buried at Highgate on 5th November, 1736.

1736-69.   John Edwards, formerly the husband of Mary. He was elected a Governor of the Grammar School on 7th November, 1734, and died on 18th December, 1769, aged 82 (see p. 59).

1769-82.   Mary Edwards, spinster, daughter of John Edwards by his second wife, Ann Manship.

This John Edwards was the son of the John Edwards mentioned above, and predeceased his father. Under the provisions of an Act of Parliament for confirming a partition between John Edwards, esquire, and others of several estates devised by the will of John Schoppens, Mary Edwards became entitled as from 24th June, 1769, to " dwelling houses fronting the Grove of the east aspect in Highgate, called Pemberton Row."* These houses are described as in the tenures of :

George Johnson	at £42 per annum
Samuel Tatton	at £40 ,,
Thomas Palmer	at £40 ,,
Edward Yardley	at £20 ,,
Mark Smithson	at £40 ,,
Walter Gibbons	at £43 ,,
Alexander Hunter	at £10 ,,
John Wakelin	at £6 ,,

Mary Edwards also became entitled to three fields and a grove in the tenure of the Hon. Charles Yorke at £20 per annum.

1782-97.   Charles, 1st Lord Southampton, purchased the property from Jacob Preston, of Beeston St. Lawrence, Norfolk, and Mary his wife, formerly Mary Edwards.

1797-1808.   Ann, Dowager Baroness Southampton, widow of Charles the 1st Baron. She was a daughter of Admiral Sir Peter Warren, K.B.

1808-31.   Lieut.-General Charles Fitzroy, second son of the above. He married 21st September, 1816, Eliza (née Barlow), widow of Clavering Savage, esquire, and died 18th October, 1831.

1831-51.   The Hon. Eliza Fitzroy, widow of General Charles Fitzroy.

1851-62.   The Rev. Frederick Thomas William Coke Fitzroy (under the will of Mrs. Eliza Fitzroy). He died 20th February, 1862.

In 1863 the houses were sold, mostly to the individual lessees. The following particulars of the lessees and occupiers, which is not exhaustive, have been gathered from different sources.

No. 1.   Walter Gibbons, 1769; William Blamire, 1775; Edward Wallbank; — Martin; Henrietta Gibbon, 1792; Thomas Rae Swain of Newgate Street, wine merchant, 1793; Anne Swaine, 1812; William Taylor Abud, of Clerkenwell, refiner, 1817; Henry Diggery Warter, 1847; Henry Lake, who was elected a governor of the Grammar School on 9th February, 1859, and died 3rd April, 1863; Mary Lake, who died 28th January, 1870, and was followed by her son, Benjamin Greene Lake, solicitor, of No. 10, New Square, Lincoln's Inn; Miss Rebecca Lacey, Sir Neville Pearson, Mr. and Lady Marjorie Stirling.

No. 2.   Mark Smithson, 1769; John Hurford, 1779; Edward Bulkley, 1794; — Procer, 1801; William Prosser, 1812; and later by H. S. Benbow Price.

No. 3.   Edward Yardley, 1769; Richard Banks, 1776; William Johnson, 1794; Mrs. Ann Divett, 1795; H. Dew, 1801; Thomas Dew, 1804; Edward Dew, 1812; Nathaniel Harden, 1817; Dr. James Gillman, 1824. In 1816, when the poet Coleridge came to live with him, he was at No. 14, South Grove (see p. 45). Coleridge died in 1834, and Dr. Gillman in 1839. Peter Brendon, 1847; Dr. Charles Blatherwick; Henry Goodenough Smith, 1863; Charles Church; J. B. Priestley.

No. 4.   Thomas Palmer, 1769; Margaret Woodfield, 1787; Mary Woodfield, 1794; Thomas Hayne, 1804; Richard Nixon, 1808; William Henry Saltwell, 1847; Thomas Blanford, Mrs. Webster.

* The houses in The Grove were at this time called Pemberton Row and in the map of 1804 this was described as Quality Walk.

No. 5.   Samuel Tatton, 1769; John Sherer, 1775; — Mason; Mrs. Phillips, 1794;
        Sarah Phillips, spinster, 1806; Miss Summersum, 1817; George Kinderley, 1820;
Henry Nisbet; James Beaumont of No. 19, Lincoln's Inn Fields; Arthur Ranken Ford, who died
on 22nd January, 1933, at Guildford, in his 85th year, retired from Highgate in 1920. He was
born at No. 5 in 1848, the son of William Ford, who afterwards moved to Brookfield, Millfield
Lane; Roger Gaskell, M. W. Drysdale.

No. 6.   George Johnson, 1769; Thomas Chetham; Rhoda and Sara Armstrong, 1795;
        Mrs. Armstrong, 1797; empty, 1806; Thomas Jones, 1807; Louisa Jones, widow;
Francis Smith, 1847, " a great lover of trees—all the younger trees in the Grove and its approaches
he stated were planted by him personally,"[56] he died 7th February, 1880; Edward Fry, barrister,
1863,[106] afterwards the right hon. Sir Edward Fry, Lord Justice of Appeal. A. Pye Smith; J. J. Joass,
Miss King and Miss Sells.

Nos. 7 to 12, *The Grove* (Site of Grove House).

Collett

The land mentioned on p. 87 as having been leased by John Warner to Richard Lyllie
in 1610, and conveyed with Dorchester House by his son in 1620 to Robert Payne, was leased by
Sir Robert Payne to Thomas Collett of the Middle Temple on 14th January, 1650-1, as "a messuage
heretofore in the possession of Robert Gore and late in the tenure of Richard Pierceson and now in
the possession of Sir Robert Payne, near the Green in Highgate, and a close of one acre behind the
said messuage and another messuage adjoining the aforesaid messuage now in the possession of
Richard Ashman, bricklayer, and another close adjoining the west end of the above-mentioned
close and adjoining to ground called Sherricks now in the tenure of Nathaniel Seddings, being one
acre (except such ways heretofore used to or from the same premises in or through Broomefeild or
Gravel Feild now let by Sir Robert Payne to Henry, Lord Marquess of Dorchester."

The first-mentioned messuage was, no doubt, the " messuage upon Broomfeild " mentioned
in 1619 as " lately built by Richard Lyllie," while Ashman's house was a cottage. When Mr.
Collett took this lease he also had from Sir Robert a licence to build and make walks, orchards and
gardens, and to take away the room or shed adjoining the first-mentioned messuage heretofore in
the tenure of Robert Gore and to take down the tenement in the occupation of Richard Ashman,
and to cut down trees. He also brought forward his fence two feet before the east side of these two
messuages, towards the Green, for a distance of 7½ poles, an encroachment which was " presented "
at the manor court held on 1st May, 1656.

At the Heralds' Visitation in 1664 Thomas Collett signed his pedigree, showing that he
was the son of John Collett of London, merchant, by Susan, daughter of Nicholas Farrar of London,
merchant, and that his wife was Martha, daughter of James Sherington of London, merchant. He
had four brothers and seven sisters. In the record of his admission[107] to the Middle Temple on
4th June, 1619, he was described as the son of John Collett of Bourne, Cambridgeshire, and he
took the place of a Mr. Farrer in the chamber of Mr. Charles Cockes, a " master of the Utter Bar,"
in Essex Court. Many years afterwards Mr. John Cocks, a barrister, was expelled (29th November,
1652) from the Inn for opprobrious language and laying of violent hands upon Thomas Collett,
esquire, a Master of the Bench. In the following June Mr. Collett offered to surrender his part of the
chamber to Mr. Cocks for a reasonable consideration, and the offending barrister was restored " upon
his humble submission to Mr. Collett and his respectful behaviour towards the other Masters of the
Bench. John Collett, his son and heir, was admitted to the Inn on 12th January, 1651-2. The
Marquis of Dorchester was for many years lord of the Manor of Cantlowes and employed Thomas
Collett as his steward. Collett presided regularly at the manor courts. He held his last court on
10th November, 1674, shortly before his death, which took place in the beginning of the following
year. He presided at the court when his own encroachment on the waste was presented in 1656.
He was elected a Governor of the Grammar School on 24th February, 1658-9.

In 1662 Thomas Collett was granted licence to make, at his own cost, a causey from the
Chapel of Highgate on part of the waste before the dwelling-house which he occupied on the east,
containing from east to west, viz., from the king's highway to a quickset hedge before the courtyard
of the house 16½ poles, and from north to south one pole, and to plant 24 trees in and on both sides
of the said causey, " which premises are not only an ornament to the Village of Highgate but a
convenience to the Lord's tenants and people going to the Chapel." This was the old chapel

belonging to the Grammar School opposite the Gatehouse, habitually used by the inhabitants of Highgate as a Chapel of Ease until the judgment of Lord Eldon put a stop to the practice in 1826. Although Mr. Collett's interest in the amenities of the village may have been genuine enough he did not go unrewarded, since he and his son were allowed at the same time to enclose a considerable portion of the common between his house and the causey, apparently the land now occupied by the Metropolitan Water Board's reservoir.

This estate was included in the mortgage of 8th February, 1653-4, by Sir Robert Payne to Robert Holt, and therefore, like Dorchester House, came into the hands of the latter's daughter, Sarah, the wife of Sir William Roberts. In December, 1662, Sir William and his wife executed a release to John Collett of the Middle Temple, esquire, son of Thomas Collett, of the premises, which were described as two messuages, etc., and two closes of two acres, one converted to an orchard and garden in the occupation of Thomas Collett. John Collett mortgaged it in 1667 to John Mapletoft of London, gentleman, when his father is mentioned as the late occupier. Martha, the wife of Thomas Collett, was buried at Highgate on 5th September, 1667. In 1678 John Mapletoft of London, M.D. (who had been admitted on the forfeited conditional surrender in 1675), conveyed the estate to Samuel Blackwell of Watford, esquire, whose daughter had married Sir Robert Payne's only son (see p. 52). Dr. Mapletoft (1631-1721) physician and divine, M.D., 1667, practised medicine in London with Thomas Sydenham and became intimate with John Locke; he was Professor of Physic at Gresham College 1675-9, and Vicar of St. Laurence, Jewry, 1686 to 1721, when he died, aged 84.[108]

Pemberton

In 1678 Samuel Blackwell conveyed these two houses to Francis Pemberton, one of the most celebrated of the inhabitants of Highgate. His father was Ralph Pemberton, twice mayor of St. Albans, where Francis was born in July, 1624. He was 54 years of age when he acquired his Highgate property. He was called to the Bar in 1654 and married, in 1667, Anne, daughter of Sir Jeremy Whichcote of Hendon Hall. He received the honour of knighthood on 6th October, 1675, was appointed a Justice in the Court of King's Bench on 3rd April, 1679, and Chief Justice of the Court of Common Pleas in 1682, when he was also made a Privy Councillor. His daughter, Jane, married Edward Gould in 1701, thereby becoming the mistress of Bisham House in the High Street. Sir Francis is said to have been a profound lawyer, much versed in records, yet of indifferent mind and, for his age, indifferent honest. Sir Francis Pemberton pulled down the two houses and built himself a " capital messuage " on the site, converting the land to a garden and orchard. The house is clearly marked on the St. Pancras map of 1804 (Plate 1), and on Rocque's survey of ten miles round London of 1741-5. On the plan of 1804 will be seen a large garden adjoining No. 6, The Grove, and extending about as far as the modern private roadway, Fitzroy Park. The map also suggests an avenue of trees leading up to an important house, and the " great garden " is so named. Rocque's survey of 1746 indicates a similar arrangement and there is little doubt that the mansion houses shown in 1746 and in 1804 indicate the residence of Sir Francis Pemberton, which was later called Grove House. The house is also shown on the plan of Highgate given in Prickett's *History*. Although not a very reliable author for ancient history Frederick Prickett was a capable surveyor, a native of the village, and practised his profession there. Sir Francis Pemberton was buried at Highgate Chapel on 15th June, 1699.

In 1706 the trustees of Dame Ann Pemberton sold the house to Thomas Nicoll, citizen and merchant of London, and Catherine his wife.[109] She was the daughter of John Niccoll, Alderman of the Ward of Farringdon Within, 1670, Master of the Leathersellers' Company, 1670-1, Treasurer of St. Bartholomew's Hospital, 1681-1703, who died in May, 1703. John Niccoll of Colney Hatch was his brother-in-law. Catherine, only child of Thomas Niccoll and Catherine his wife, married William Congreve, esquire, who lived on the site of Witanhurst. Thomas Niccoll died in the November following his purchase, and his widow, Catherine (who was buried 9th August, 1734), conveyed the property to Jacob Mendez Da Costa of London, merchant, in 1733. On his death, his son, Isaac Mendez Da Costa, sold it, in 1757, to John Edwards, esquire.

John Edwards (see p. 61) on 6th January, 1768, was granted licence to lease Gravel Field, Broomfield and Home Steer, and the ground called Highgate Green in the possession of Benjamin Colborn and quarter-acre, part of a field late in the tenure of Elizabeth Mendes and a capital messuage, all in the occupation of Charles Yorke. The Right Hon. Charles Yorke, second son of Philip, Earl of Hardwick, was born on 30th December, 1722, and married as his second wife,

Yorke

THE VILLAGE OF HIGHGATE

Agnetta, daughter of Henry Johnson, esquire, of Berkhamsted, on 30th December, 1762.[55] As he was elected a Governor of the Grammar School on 14th January of that year he must have been a resident at Highgate before his second marriage. In this year he also became Attorney-General. John H. Lloyd in his *History of Highgate* remarks that " it is a matter of regret that this house has not so far been traced." With our identification of Grove House Mr. Lloyd's problem has been solved. Mr. Yorke's last days were tragic. On 17th January, 1770, King George III held a levée at St. James's at which Mr. Yorke was present, and he was persuaded by the king to accept the office of Lord Chancellor. On 20th January, four days later, he died of fever caused by the extreme nervous tension and mental suffering he had undergone. It appears that his acceptance of office in the Grafton administration was directly contrary to the pledge which he had given to his party, and Lord Campbell writes of him that " he was overpowered by the royal blandishments and a momentary mistake as to the duty of a good subject ; but he was struck with deep remorse, and his love for honest fame was demonstrated by his being unable to survive the loss of it."

Fitzroy, Lord Southampton

On the death of John Edwards in 1769 this house went to his granddaughter Mary Edwards, by whose trustee it was conveyed in 1782 to Lieut.-General Charles Fitzroy, 1st Lord Southampton (1764-97). It was then described as a messuage heretofore in the occupation of Catherine Niccoll, afterwards of the Hon. Charles Yorke and " now of Stephen Buckingham." In the Act for Watching and Lighting the Hamlet of Highgate (1775) is mentioned " the house in the Grove occupied by Stephen Beckingham, esquire, and the houses in the lane leading by the side of the Grove towards the door of the stable yard of the said Stephen Beckingham, esquire." In 1808 the property is described as the " site of Grove House long since pulled down and other improvements made on the site, 8 acres of meadow annexed to Fitzroy Farm and three lower gardens behind or westward of the houses in Pemberton Row, two of which gardens are occupied with two of such houses and the other garden is annexed to the grounds of Fitzroy Farm."

Lord Southampton from 1832 onwards granted leases for 99 years of plots of the land, on which houses were built.

XV—NOS. *52, 53* AND *54,* SOUTH GROVE

GROUND LANDLORDS AND LEASEHOLDERS.

These houses were originally copyhold of the Manor of Cantlowes but have been enfranchised and are now in the following ownerships and occupations.

No. *52* belongs to Mr. M. A. Wetherell, and is in the occupation of Mr. Leslie W. Johnson.

No. *53* is in the ownership and occupation of Mrs. Dickinson.

No. *54* is in the ownership and occupation of Mr. L. H. LeVay.

GENERAL DESCRIPTION AND DATE OF STRUCTURE.

No. 52, South Grove.

The plan of the front portion of this house is of a type which will be found repeated in several cases in South Grove (Plate 72). It consists of a narrow central entrance hall or passage containing the staircase with one large room on either side of it. The kitchen quarters of No. *52* are grouped at the back and contain several old features. The little apartment leading out of the present dining room on the east side and next to the gatehouse has been added subsequently to the erection of the centre portion of the house, but it was certainly built before the close of the 18th century. It appears in a sketch attached to a deed of 1813 referred to below. The chimneys are planned at either end of the main block, which is the usual arrangement in the village. The first-floor plan corresponds with the ground plan and there are attics in the roof. There is a lead cistern in the back quarters with the initials W. W. and the date 1789.

The elevation towards South Grove (Plates 71 and 72) is finely designed and of a rather more pretentious character than that of some of the other houses in the neighbourhood. The central entrance with its six-panelled door is flanked by a pair of Doric pilasters carrying a pediment. The ground-floor windows on either side have flush frames and are set below arches of rubbed red brick over which is a string course formed by a projecting brick band. All the first-floor windows are square-headed under flat red-brick arches, except the central one, which is set in a slightly recessed semicircular arch which breaks the line of the main eaves cornice. The latter is well moulded and has modillions. The centre projects to carry a fine pediment over the three central windows. A plain brick parapet now rises above the cornice and stops against the sloping backs of the pediment. There are three flat-topped dormers in the roof.

In the Court Rolls for the year 1813 there is a rather elementary sketch attached to an entry recording an application for varying a right of way that originally passed in front of the house. Though the drawing is naïve in character the elevations of Nos. *52, 53* and *54,* South Grove, are quite recognisable. The pedimented head to the entrance doorway of No. *52* is clearly shown, but the main cornice and pediment appear to be omitted and there is a side door in place of the ground-floor window in the eastern annexe, which has a small gable instead of the present treatment. It is

95

doubtful how much weight should be given to this evidence. The same drawing gives us the date of the lay-out of the garden in front and to the side of the house. Further information about the right of way will follow in the account of No. 53. The wrought-iron railings with cast vases and the gate with its graceful pilasters no doubt date from this period.

Attached to the side or end of the house within the garden is a charming porch or pedimented roof supported on a pair of wooden columns and corresponding pilasters against the wall. This porch affords access to the sitting room and to the kitchen quarters by two separate doors at right angles to one another. Both are glazed with stout glazing bars, but the one to the kitchen is boarded on the inside.

In the view of this porch (Plate 73) the rear portion of the house, which is of three storeys, can be seen; and to the left the low projecting scullery, which has a moulded eaves cornice and pantiled roof.

Amongst the principal features surviving in the interior is the staircase, which has a cut string with carved brackets and two balusters to each tread (Plates 75 to 77). The balusters to the basement stair are of a slightly different pattern. The twin newels are in the form of dwarf Doric columns. In the sitting room west of the entrance is an interesting chimney piece with a boldly carved panel and pediment. In the kitchen is a dresser which appears to have been shortened. It has shaped sides which support the shelves. There is also a fitted cupboard with panelled doors and fluted pilasters behind them, shaped shelving, and some early panelling, no doubt moved from other positions. Preserved in the garden porch is a piece of carving, with the date 1682, which came from Ashurst House.

CONDITION OF REPAIR.
Mainly good.

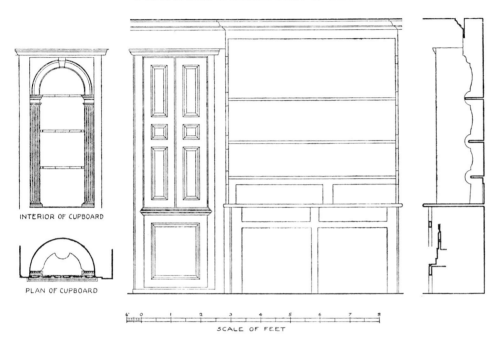

Nº 52 SOUTH GROVE, HIGHGATE,
CUPBOARD & DRESSER IN KITCHEN

INTERIOR OF CUPBOARD

PLAN OF CUPBOARD

SCALE OF FEET

Nos. 53 and 54, South Grove.
These two houses (which, with No. 52, were at one time in the same ownership) were no doubt erected in 1729, the date marked on the lead rain-water head on the front. The initials $\begin{smallmatrix} & D & \\ I & & E \end{smallmatrix}$ represent Joseph Davis and Eleanor his wife (Plate 79*b*).

The plan of No. 53 (the eastern house) was affected by the existence of the old right of way from South Grove to Hampstead Lane, which was varied in 1813 and was finally closed in the year 1919, at which time the land in front was also enclosed, having formerly been part of the waste of the Manor of Cantlowes. No. 53 has long been a school. The wash-houses projecting to the north (Plate 79*a*) and the school room on the eastern side of the right of way appear on the parish plan of 1804. The former originally consisted of a weather-boarded structure which has since been rebuilt in brick. The school was taken over by Dr. A. E. C. Dickinson in 1885, who had both houses and connected them by cutting doorways through at the different floor levels.

G

THE VILLAGE OF HIGHGATE

The entrance doorway to No. 53 leads into an oblong hall with a semicircular niche centrally placed on the opposite wall. Adjoining is an opening leading into a smaller staircase hall with flights leading to the upper floors and the basement. There is a secondary stair also of interest at the opposite end of the house adjoining the right of way. The back room is quite effective and gives little evidence of the rather unusual planning of the fireplace and recesses. On the first and second floors the arrangement of the principal rooms is a repetition of those below. The attic storey was not added till 1858.

No. 54 is a smaller house though somewhat similar in plan. The entrance, however, is not in its original position. In the sketch attached to the application of 1813 already referred to, the entrance door is shown in the position occupied by the westernmost window of the front room and not as now in a side annexe. It should be noted, however, that some form of annexe certainly existed in 1813, but for what purpose is not clear.

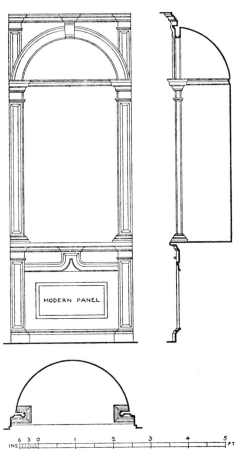

N° 53 SOUTH GROVE, HIGHGATE, NICHE IN HALL

MODERN PANEL

The front and back elevations of both houses are of stock brick with slightly projecting bands to mark the floor levels, the dividing line between the two houses being emphasised by an original rain-water pipe. On each floor is a recess corresponding with the window openings which have flat arched heads of red brick with similar dressings. There are five of these on each floor to No. 53, and three to No. 54, the centre windows of each house (on the first and second floors) being emphasised by a bracket ornament cut on the surface of the arches. None of the original sash bars remain. The back elevation shows more change, and the variation in the arrangement of its windows, due to the position of the stairs, can be seen in Plate 79a.

The entrance to No. 53 has a fine porch with a pair of slender wooden columns on pedestals and corresponding panelled pilasters against the wall face. The columns carry an entablature and pediment. The six-panelled door is set within an arched opening with pilasters and a fanlight over (Plate 82).

98

The entrance door of No. 54 is also panelled and is set within two unusually narrow fluted pilasters with Corinthian capitals, over which are carved brackets supporting a moulded hood. The architrave of the frame curves upwards to the centre of the frieze. The fanlight is glazed in vertical divisions with slender metal bars.

The interior of No. 53 is almost certainly panelled throughout though every room has been canvased and papered with the exception of the entrance hall. In the basement are several ledged and moulded battened doors having a variety of hinges. There is also an early 18th-century dresser of simple design with shaped ends to the shelving. Its back is made up with Jacobean panelling.

The entrance hall is panelled in the 18th-century manner. The niche, semicircular in plan, opposite to the entrance door is flanked by a pair of panelled pilasters and has a semicircular arched head with key block, an additional pair of smaller pilasters framing the upper part (Plate 81 and p. 98).

The principal staircase has continuous strings and spiral balusters; the newel posts are also spiral of good design, and the moulded hand-rail butts against the newel of the ascending flight without a ramp. The dado panelling on the staircase walls follows the line of the balustrading.

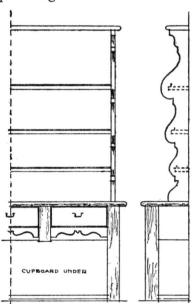

CUPBOARD UNDER

The secondary stair is also of interest and being fitted into a series of rather irregular spaces affords considerable variety in design. On the lower flights the balusters, partly spiral and partly turned and moulded, are grouped three to each step. The newel posts are turned shafts with delicately moulded caps and bases, and the hand-rail follows round as a capping. Above the first floor the stair reverts to the continuous string.

The doors generally are six-panel and original.

In No. 54 the chief feature is the stair, which is severely simple with continuous moulded strings, plain turned balusters, square newels and hand-rail without ramps (Plates 83 and 84). The walls have a panelled dado corresponding to the balustrade. The panelling to the ground-floor rooms is modern in part, and only in the case of the second-floor front room does the panelling remain intact, in the others it is partially concealed. A good 18th-century dresser has been moved from the basement to the modern kitchen.

CONDITION OF REPAIR.
    Fair.

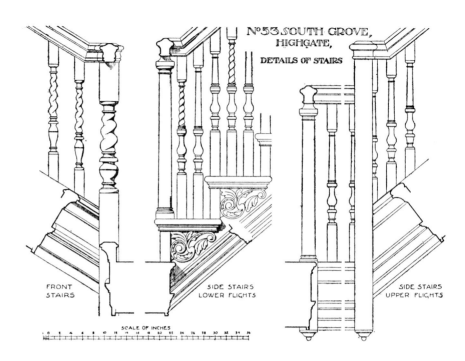

No 53 SOUTH GROVE, HIGHGATE, DETAILS OF STAIRS

FRONT STAIRS

SIDE STAIRS LOWER FLIGHTS

SIDE STAIRS UPPER FLIGHTS

SCALE OF INCHES

HISTORICAL NOTES.

These houses stand on land enclosed from Highgate Green in the middle of the 17th century. The land attached to them extends across the parish boundary northwards into Hornsey, a boundary which is of historical importance, because it was also the boundary of the Bishop of London's Park of Harringay, of which the portion from North Road and North Hill westward was called the Great Park, distinguishing it from Hornsey Little Park eastward of that thoroughfare. A road must always have run from the Gatehouse to the Spaniards (these two houses representing entrances to the Park where tolls were levied), but the present road was made at the end of the 18th century, when the old road, following the parish boundary, was diverted.

In 1659 William Crosse acquired from the widow and son of Robert Harrison, gardener, a cottage then lately divided into two tenements on the waste, and a garden containing from east to west 58 feet, and from north to south 25 feet adjoining the cottage on the east side (the messuage of Edward Baker being upon the west side and the messuage of Anthony Turner upon the east side). Before dealing with the estate of William Crosse we will trace the " messuage of Anthony Turner," now represented by No. 52, South Grove. In 1656 it was found that Anthony Turner had erected two messuages and enclosed the waste. Remembering that Thomas Collett, the steward of the manor, lived within a stone's throw of this house, and that he in this same year presided at the manor court that " found " the encroachments of himself, Mr. Turner, and his neighbours, it is evident that the formal presentment in court was no more than the first step in giving a legal title to the land, following a prearranged bargain with the lord of the manor (and possibly the Vestry). We are witnessing here a process that went on for centuries as population increased, and with that increased population the demand for dwelling places. The next step was in 1663 when Mr. Turner was granted another piece of the waste measuring from east to west 88½ feet, and from north to south 29½ feet. From him it passed successively to his daughter, Judith Barnes, widow (1680), her daughter, Dorothy Clenell, wife of Alexander Clenell (1690), and the children of Dorothy Clenell (1736), it being sold by the last-mentioned owners in 1750 to Benjamin Colborne, apothecary. So far all those mentioned appear to have dwelt in the house, which evidently took the place of the two houses previously there. In 1771 Mr. Colborne took out a licence to lease " a messuage near the Gatehouse " to William Wetherall, apothecary, for 21 years. From the year

1750 the house has remained the home of medical men, Mr. Wetherall being the first of several generations of that name. Mr. Colborne went away to live at Bath and sold the house to Mr. Wetherall in 1788. In 1813 a considerable alteration was made in front of the house, as shown on the sketch reproduced on p. 96. In his petition for permission to divert the footpath, Mr. Wetherall stated he was the owner of a house adjoining the Gatehouse, and of two other houses in the respective occupations of Lewis Beauvais and William Barron towards the west (the present Nos. 53 and 54, South Grove). There was a footpath from the Gatehouse to a house of Lord Southampton, then lately occupied by Edward Simeon, esquire, at the corner of Hampstead Lane, running immediately in front of his house and the other two, but used only by persons resorting to the premises of Lord Southampton and the others mentioned. It lay lower than the adjoining gardens, and in wet weather was in a very bad state, scarcely passable and consequently requiring continual repair. Being a private road the parish had refused to repair it, and this expense had consequently fallen on him. He submitted that it would be a great convenience to himself and the adjoining occupiers and no sort of inconvenience to the public if he were permitted to throw the existing footpath into his garden and instead thereof to make and keep in repair a path or footway to run parallel with the trees described in the sketch as shown by the dotted lines. This was agreed to at a court held at the Angel on 21st April, 1813. It was arranged that Lord Southampton should enclose part of the piece of ground formerly in the occupation of John Sanders and, in return, agree to the making of the present open space in front of the house, giving up his rights therein.

The house still remains in the hands of William Wetherall's descendants, having descended to his son William Roundell Wetherall, surgeon (1814), and Nathaniel Thomas Wetherall (1832), son of the last named. It was leased from the Misses Wetherall in 1898 by Dr. F. H. Crowdy, surgeon, who lived there until his death in 1926.

The two houses Nos. 53 and 54, South Grove, first came into one ownership in 1714, when Joseph Davis, junior, draper, of Aldgate, who then owned a cottage formerly occupied by Robert Blockley, and two tenements, a messuage, etc. (the first mentioned being on the land mentioned above as belonging to Edward Baker to the west of William Crosse's house in 1659, and the second being the premises previously of William Crosse, between the houses of Baker and Turner), also acquired a house occupied by Ralph Thompson, formerly belonging to Edward Baker. Taking the house of Edward Baker first, we find that in 1656 he had built two houses and enclosed part of the waste, and two years later was granted a piece of the waste measuring 99 feet by 49½ feet. This he leased to Christopher Keemer, gentleman, of Highgate, in 1658, and obtained a further piece of the common in 1663 containing 115 feet on the north, 128 feet on the south, 62 feet west, and 33 feet east. Christopher Keemer acquired the whole from Edward Baker in 1663, and conveyed one of the houses in 1680 to Moses Cooke, cordwainer, of St. Giles-in-the-Fields. The premises were described as a messuage late erected at Highgate, heretofore in the occupation of John Gannock, now of Anne Traherne, widow, and a parcel of waste on which the said messuage was erected. Moses Cooke conveyed them to Joseph Davis in 1714, the occupier then being Ralph Thompson. The other house of Mr. Keemer went, at his death (1696), to his daughter, Elizabeth, wife of Robert Blockley of Highgate, yeoman, and from them in 1700 to Moses Cooke of Holborn, spurrier, who conveyed it to Joseph Davis in 1703.

William Crosse, infant son of William Crosse, deceased, was granted in 1664 a further piece of the common containing from east to west 68 feet and from north to south 27 feet, which was conveyed in 1679 by William Crosse of St. Martin's-in-the-Fields, ironmonger, to John Saunders, gardener, of Fryern Barnet, and Elizabeth his wife, with a cottage thereon. There was also another enclosure four poles square, made by Robert Harrison, which he conveyed to John Collett in 1660, who conveyed it to Pemberton in 1676. The latter conveyed it to Joseph Palmer in 1677. It was conveyed by Palmer to Saunders in 1679. John Sanders or Saunders in 1690 conveyed to John Hardrett, citizen and barber surgeon of London, a parcel of waste on Highgate Green four poles square, heretofore enclosed by William Harryson, and a parcel of the waste containing from east to west 4 poles 2 feet, and from north to south 27 feet and a cottage thereon lately erected. This also was acquired by Joseph Davis from John Hardrett in 1706, and the initials of himself and his wife Eleanor appear on a rain-water head in front. When Mr. Davis died his widow succeeded under his will (1732) to a cottage of Robert Blockley, a messuage late of John Sanders and a messuage formerly of Ralph Thompson. These were conveyed in 1750 by Peter

Storer, acting as executor of Eleanor Davis, to Benjamin Colborne, and remained in the same ownership as No. 52 until 1843. In 1771 Benjamin Colborne took out a licence to lease these houses for 21 years. In 1813 William Wetherall had licence to lease No. 53 to Louis Beauvais for 21 years, and No. 54 to William Barron for 21 years. In 1801 the occupiers were Ann Burwood and Ann Pointer. Ann Burwood was followed by J. A. Wardell in 1804-6 ; James Kearsley, 1807-9 ; and William Barron in 1810. In 1817 Michael Grayhurst was there. He was succeeded by his widow, apparently in 1843. Ann Pointer at No. 53 (the school) was succeeded by Francis Tweedel in 1805-6, after which it stood empty for two years until the advent of Louis Beauvais in 1809. In 1817 the occupier was John Bassi, who remained until 1824. In 1831 James Fenner appears.[42]

In 1842 Nathaniel Thomas Wetherall, surgeon, of Highgate, and Louisa Mary, his wife, sold to Charles Dix of No. 135, Windmill Street, Gravesend, gentleman, and Charles James Fenner of Park House, Hampton Wick, schoolmaster, two houses, one in the occupation of Mrs. Grayhurst and the other of Zachariah Fenner, schoolmaster, and two stables occupied by Mrs. Grayhurst, and a building partly occupied by Zachariah Fenner as a school room and partly by Nathaniel Thomas Wetherall as a coachhouse and stable, and separated from the house occupied by Zachariah Fenner by a narrow passage leading from the Grove to Hampstead Lane, but connected with Fenner's house by a way or gallery built over the passage. This passage, which used to be open to the public, was closed in 1919. The house continued to be occupied as Grove House School until December, 1930.

XVI—THE GATEHOUSE TAVERN

GROUND LANDLORD.

The proprietor is Mr. A. M. Shuter.

GENERAL DESCRIPTION AND DATE OF STRUCTURE.

Although the greater portion of this building stands within the boundary of the parish of Hornsey, just sufficient is within St. Pancras to enable the story to be given here. It has little architectural interest, but it is important because of its connection with the name of the hamlet. The old tavern has been entirely modernised, but a view taken about 40 years ago (Plate 85*a*) shows a Georgian building of two periods, the northern portion being the earlier. The arch of the gateway adjoined the latter and there was until recently an old stair (Plate 86) from which the passage over the gate was approached.

The parish boundary stones can be seen in the external view, the upper one bearing the date 1791.

CONDITION OF REPAIR.

Newly constructed.

HISTORICAL NOTES.

Probably this site has been occupied by a building as long as any in Highgate, since the Gatehouse was one of the three entrances to the Bishop of London's Park of "Haringeye" or Hornsey, the two other gates being at the Spaniards, and at Newgate by East Finchley Railway Station. For the use of the road across their Park from Highgate to Finchley (where it debouched on to Finchley Common), the Bishops exacted tolls at the Gatehouse, the collection of which was leased by them for a fixed yearly amount. Thus in the year 1408-9 Henry Smith, "farmer of the tolls of the Park," paid 30s. on 1st March, and 60s. by the hands of John Ellis on 16th July.[110] Again in 1420-1, William Payable paid 66s. 8d. for the farm of the tolls that year. In 1638-9, John Bette, who then leased the tolls, paid £6 13s. 4d. Generally the tolls were leased with the pasturage of the Park, as in the lease of 20th May, 1541, of the herbage, pannage, and pasturage of the "Greate Parke of Haringhey alias Harnesey" with "a messuage and tenement with the appurtenances at Hyegate some tyme an hermitage." The hermitage appears to have stood adjacent to the Chapel which occupied the site of the present Chapel of Highgate School.

On 23rd May, 1503, the Vicar of St. Pancras and his parishioners were beating the bounds when they came into conflict with "Thomas Walterkyn, heremyte of St. Michel besides Highgate, in the parisshe of Harnesey," possibly owing to some uncertainty, real or pretended, as to the parish boundary. According to the hermit, when he was in the garden with his servant they came into his house, broke down the paling of his orchard and garden, hit him over the arm with a bill, and would have murdered him if he had not escaped to the steeple of the hermitage, where he remained until they had gone. He also alleged that they stole two altar cloths, a surplice and "grayle," i.e. a book of antiphons. The Vicar replied that they were going in procession as usual about their parish when the hermit would not allow them to pass, although courteously asked to do so. The hermit was in his garden, armed with a great club, and having with him two others also armed with clubs, they suddenly struck at William Chadwick, of St. Pancras, yeoman, over the pale. They broke some of the pales and then the St. Pancras people pulled down some more to make room to pass and so departed peaceably. The Vicar then went on to say that so far from the "grayle" having been stolen by them, the hermit, who was a man of ill conversation and rule, had pawned the book and other stuff to one John Phelippe, who was ready to testify the same. The hermit rejoined that the Vicar

London Bishopric

103

and his parishioners were guilty of the riot, that the hermitage was in Hornsey and not in St. Pancras, although divers persons had been accustomed to enter the chapel to hear divine service at convenient times. He denied the Vicar's allegation of being a man of misrule or that he had pledged any stuff belonging to the hermitage. It is likely that the Vicar had a grudge against the hermit because his Highgate parishioners found it more convenient to attend mass at the chapel and make their offerings there than to travel all the way to old St. Pancras Church. There is no record of the verdict of the Court of Star Chamber (who tried the case), and it is hardly possible to determine the rights and wrongs of the matter, but the St. Pancras people must have been wrong in going through the hermitage, since that lay entirely in Hornsey.[111]

The present Gatehouse Tavern stands partly in Hornsey and partly in St. Pancras, the part in St. Pancras having been added by encroachment on Highgate Green. In 1670 Edward Cutler, gentleman, who then owned the Gatehouse, obtained " a parcel of the waste at Highgate, adjoining to the Gatehouse, containing from east to west from the highway from Highgate to Islington (High Street) 30 feet and from north to south 12 feet." On his death in 1680 his brother, Henry Cutler, gentleman, of London, obtained the property, and he conveyed it in 1682 to Elizabeth Marshall, widow, of Highgate, who obtained a grant in 1682 of a parcel of waste at the Gatehouse, containing from north to south at the east end 26 feet, abutting north on the manor of Hornsey, east on the king's way to the Gatehouse, and containing from north to south on the west, 36 feet abutting on Hornsey, from east to west on the south 46 feet, abutting west on the house of widow Barnes, and north on the manor of Hornsey. The " Widow Barnes " was Judith Barnes, living at the house now No. 52, South Grove (see p. 100). Elizabeth Marshall married Thomas Simonds, who was ordered at the Middlesex Sessions in July, 1690, to pay 1s. 6d. *per annum* assessed upon him for the relief of the poor of St. Pancras for that part of the Gatehouse at Highgate which is in the parish of St. Pancras, and in his possession.[112]

Until about the year 1790 the road from the Gatehouse to the Spaniards followed the parish boundary, as was natural, because that boundary was formerly the line of the paling enclosing the Park. Between the Gatehouse and The Grove the road formed the northern boundary of Highgate Green until houses were built there in the 17th century. Hampstead Lane was substituted to the north of the old road, at the instance of Lord Mansfield and Lord Southampton when they were developing the Ken Wood and Fitzroy Park estates. Highgate Green may be visualised in its earliest state as a triangular space lying before the entrance to Haringey Park, having a large pond on the site of Pond Square, the base of the triangle being approximately South Grove and the other sides the High Street and the Grove. The Gatehouse stood at the apex of the triangle, the Angel and the Flask at the ends of the base.

XVII—NOS. 39 TO 67, HIGH STREET (AND SITE OF THE OLD FORGE)

GROUND LANDLORD, ETC.

These houses were all originally copyhold of the Manor of Cantlowes but have now been enfranchised.

GENERAL DESCRIPTION.

The houses between Pond Square and the High Street are all numbered in the latter; all except one seem to have been rebuilt, but a few years ago their backs presented a most picturesque appearance towards the Square. Nos. 39 and 41 occupy the site of the old forge—an extremely picturesque structure of which a view is given on Plate 87a.

HISTORICAL NOTES.

From the Angel to the Gatehouse the eastern side of Highgate Green was formerly open to the road. At the beginning of the 17th century the edge of the common bore the attractive name of "The Bank before the Elms," suggesting a row of elm trees between the pond and the road. Successive enclosures provided sites for the existing houses and shops, of which the earliest was built in the reign of James I. In 1619 Robert Atkinson was granted for 21 years a cottage which he had lately built in a place called the Bank before the Elms, in which he lived. To-day Nos. 47, 49 and 51, High Street, stand on this site. Atkinson in 1621 leased the cottage for 20 years to John Hudson, who added to it a building made of timber. In 1648 it was owned by John Flood or Lloyd, "cordwainer," and in 1672 by his son John Lloyd, labourer, with his wife, Frances, and son, John. John Flood conveyed it in 1680 to John Graves, barber, and in 1689 it was conveyed by Graves to Edward Townsend, brewer, of Highgate, whose house stood on the site of the House of Mercy (formerly Park House) at the top of North Hill. Probably this indicates the date of its conversion to an inn, though it is not unlikely that the occupiers before then had sold ale in addition to their other means of livelihood, as is still the case in many a village to-day. In 1694 Townsend conveyed the house to Edmund Mullins, yeoman, of Tottenham, who bequeathed it in 1720 to his kinsman Thomas Clark of Tottenham, a child of 3½ at that date. It was then described as the King's Head, late in the occupation of Mrs. Warner, deceased.

At the age of 21, Thomas Clark, then a periwig maker, conveyed it to Edward Smith, victualler, of Tottenham, as "the King's Head, now called the Carpenters' Arms, in the occupation of William Thorne, victualler." His rent was £16 a year. Probably Thorne was the last to occupy the premises as an inn, since it was described in 1785 as a cottage, etc., heretofore in the occupation of Robert Upton, "wheeler," which for some years past had been converted into two tenements in the occupation of John Hillyard, poulterer, and Henry Atwell, painter. They were both succeeded by their widows, who were the tenants when Benjamin Mitchell, farrier, acquired the property in 1799. He owned several houses in Highgate and lived at No. 51, North Hill. Two houses were added by him to the pre-existing two. He died on 26th March, 1816, as appears from a notice in *The Times* of 5th May, 1834, to his creditors. His daughter and her husband, Abraham Bennett, conveyed the four houses to George Moore in 1851, and he to George Watson in 1865. Mr. Watson died on 22nd July, 1866, and left them to his wife and second son, Robert Watson, schoolmaster, who lived at No. 98, North Road. The property was then known as No. 5, York Place, with a cottage at the rear, leased to William Rawlins; No. 6, York Place, occupied by Hannah Walters; and No. 7, York Place, occupied by James Attkins, pork butcher.

The site of Nos. 39-45 seems to have been the next piece of land to be enclosed. For many years the most attractive feature on this side of the High Street was the old forge which stood at the corner of South Grove facing the Angel Inn (p. 28), and was eventually removed in 1896, being replaced by a printing works. The earliest reference to this site is in 1664, when Thomas Sconce or Conce, blacksmith, was granted "a parcel of the waste in the Bank before the Elms," on which he built a house, and dying on 7th November, 1674, left his property to his wife. When she died the shop, stable, and forge went to their son, Thomas Sconce, and the adjoining house, in which they had lived, to the other son, Henry Sconce. The only child of Thomas Sconce was a girl, Anne, who was four years old when he died, in 1685, and 13 years old when her mother died. At that time, 1694, the forge was in the hands of John Hix. At the age of 18, when she was the wife of John Allen of London, surgeon, she conveyed it to William Jewkes, draper, of St. Clement's Danes, the tenant being William Poulson, blacksmith, and the dimension from north to south being recorded as 40 feet. This agrees with the frontage of the present Nos. 39, 39a and 41. The subsequent owners are hardly of sufficient interest to record here, but the tenants mentioned are John Bostock (1733) and John Dodd in 1782, 1808 and again in 1845, probably not the same individual. From 1854 until the end of the century it was owned by the Broadbent family. The house adjoining the forge and blacksmith's house passed at the death of Henry Sconce in 1692 to his brother Lawrence, the occupiers then being Ann Hatton, junior, widow, and William Jones, spurrier. Laurence Sconce, labourer, conveyed it to John Orton, bricklayer, in 1692. The Orton family lived on the site of Ridgemont Terrace, Nos. 1-11, North Road, in a house on the north side of the Mitre.[22] John Orton died on 14th October, 1716, and his daughter, Mary, wife of Thomas Woolford of Pangbourne, Berks., pattern maker, sold the property to Robert Harrison, bricklayer, in the following year. By that time the number of houses had increased to three and there were four in 1728, as shown in the settlement on the marriage of Harrison and Penelope Turlington, dated 2nd December, 1728, where they are described as being in " Middle Row."[113] They remained in the possession of his family until 1807.

The next enclosure was in 1685, when Elizabeth Brogden was granted a piece of the waste northward of the house occupied by John Graves, barber, which house, as we have seen, occupied the site of the present Nos. 47-51, High Street. Eventually Mrs. Brogden's land came into the hands of Charles Lyne, at whose death in 1825 the occupiers were Love, Sones and Attkins. To-day Mr. Attkins, a descendant, owns and occupies Nos. 55 and 57. The adjoining No. 59 is on the northern extremity of the plot granted to Elizabeth Brogden.

On the site of No. 61, facing the end of Southwood Lane, used to stand the Cage or " lock-up " and the Watch House. The Cage stood on the site of No. 59 until the year 1811, when Charles Lyne in a petition to the lord of the manor stated that he owned " a small tenement in the occupation of a man of the name of Pickles situate at Highgate on the west side of the High Road . . . extending backwards towards the Ponds there; that there is a small bit of unenclosed and useless ground lying at the north end of Pickles's house between the same and a little erection there called the Cage and which piece of unenclosed ground is already the property of your Petitioner "; and " that there is also a dwarf building adjoining the Cage on the north which is called the Watch House and used as such." He urged that it would be no sort of detriment to the public if he were permitted to remove the Cage at his own expense to the other and north side of the Watch House and that this would be a great accommodation to him, for such removal would open a space between Pickles's house and the Watch House which, in addition to the unenclosed plot mentioned, would be sufficient to contain another small tenement. " So far from inconveniencing anybody (it would) add strength to the road and that side of the Ponds and be ornamental to the neighbourhood." The result was that Mr. Lyne built a cottage on the site, now No. 59. The frontage of the Watch House was 17 feet and the depth 14 feet 6 inches. The Cage thus removed from the south to the north was 8 feet 6 inches wide in front and 12 feet deep.

Adjoining the Cage northwards was a plot 11 feet 10 inches wide and 21 feet deep, granted to Robert Colson in 1828, now No. 63. Between this and the passage to Pond Square was a plot granted in 1811 (enlarged in 1813) to the parish of Hornsey " for the purpose of erecting thereon an engine house " which the parish leased to Robert Colson in 1814 for 35 years on condition that he spent £200 in erecting a building. This is now No. 65. The ground north of the passage was enclosed in 1828.

XVIII—NOS. 46–51, SOUTH GROVE

GROUND LANDLORD, ETC.

These houses were originally copyhold of the Manor of Cantlowes but have been enfranchised.

GENERAL DESCRIPTION.

To the north of the Ponds lie a few houses numbered in South Grove, most of which have been rebuilt, but two early ones still remain. The one numbered 46 is a cottage, but No. 47 is a more considerable structure with a Mansard roof. The sash window frames are of mid-18th-century character, but set four and a half inches back from the face of the brickwork. Similar frames on the back elevation are flush with the face of the wall, and it is likely that the house has been refronted towards South Grove. The entrance doorway is flanked by a pair of pilasters carrying an architrave with a blocked cornice and pediment.

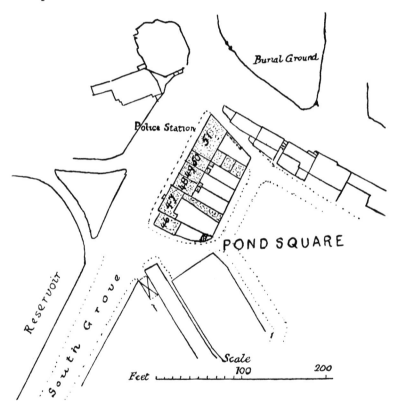

HISTORICAL NOTES.

This row of houses occupies a piece of the " waste land " which John Leech of Highgate, wheelwright, obtained licence to enclose in the year 1692, when it was described as a parcel of the waste on Highgate Hill near the Gatehouse, abutting on the king's way to the Gatehouse against the Bowling Green south, and east on the said road near the Pond, containing 46 yards on the north and west and 30 yards on the south and east, as staked out with four small stakes before this grant. It is uncertain where John Leech was living at this time, but he lived in Hornsey from 1695 onwards in a cottage in North Road. This was afterwards divided into three cottages, later the Red Lion and Sun, now Nos. 21, 23 and 25, North Road.[22]

In 1693 John Leech conveyed his land on Highgate Hill to the Hon. Francis Pemberton, serjeant-at-law, the owner of Dorchester House and Pemberton Row. The sons of the latter conveyed it to William Congreve of Hornsey in 1721, and he sold it in 1739 to Thomas Reynolds of Highgate, carpenter, when it was stated that a messuage had been lately erected thereon. Reynolds' sons (under age) succeeded on his death in 1745 and conveyed the property in 1774 to Edward Hilliard the younger of New Inn, gentleman. The occupier was then said to be Robert Batt, carpenter, the previous tenant being William Hartwell, carpenter. James Reynolds, one of the sons of Thomas, was a carver and gilder living in Clerkenwell. He emigrated to Philadelphia before he and his brother, Thomas, sold this estate in 1774.

The property descended in the Hilliard family until the year 1884, by which time six houses had been erected on it, *viz.* Nos. 1 to 6, Grove Place, one of them being the Highgate District Police Station and Justice Room. In that year the Rev. John Edward Hilliard, Rector of Cowley, Middlesex, conveyed the estate, then described as Nos. 46 to 51, South Grove, to John Wingrove Smith of No. 4, Park Street, Grosvenor Square, gentleman.

XIX—NOS. 1 TO 6, POND SQUARE

GROUND LANDLORD.

These houses were originally copyhold of the Manor of Cantlowes but have been enfranchised.

GENERAL DESCRIPTION AND DATE OF STRUCTURE.

The houses numbered in Pond Square form a group to the west of the site of the Ponds, and the southernmost house is named Rock House from an occupant of the late 19th century. In a sketch of 1845 from the George Potter Collection, now in the British Museum (Plate 87*b*), it is named Harcourt House.

Its principal and entrance front is towards the south and it is remarkable for the two large bay windows which project from the first floor (Plate 90). These are both of canted form with three sash windows of equal size, one filling each face and have white aprons contrasting well with the brick background. Their boldness gives great character to the design, which is considerably helped by a delightful doorcase of Doric three-quarter columns, carrying sections of entablature with triglyphs and the sloping cornices of a pediment. Beneath the bays are two sash windows, one each side of the door (the western now hidden); between them one window and above them three in the second storey. A simple wood railing guards the area to the basement and returns upon the east front, which forms a plain rectangle, lighted on the ground floor by a shallow bay window and by single sashes on first and second floor.

THE VILLAGE OF HIGHGATE

The remainder of the row of houses which started from the south with Rock House (No. 6) constitute the picturesque group shown in the photograph on Plate 88*a*. Since then Nos. 1 and 2 have been partly reconstructed, but Nos. 3, 4 and 5 remain in their original form. The two latter have the broad-framed sashes of the first half of the 18th century ; the walls are built of red bricks mixed with dark headers, and the roofs are tiled (see Plate 88*b*). The houses form a symmetrical pair with their doors, protected by simple hoods on brackets, at each end of the building. The rooms are lighted by one sash to each house on the ground floor, two on the first, and a double dormer in the roof. Recessed panels mark the centre of the pair on both floors, and projecting string courses occur above and below the first-floor windows. The flues are grouped in one stack at the rear and the front gardens are fenced with a simple iron railing and gate. The back elevation has been partly rebuilt and one early window remains.

HISTORICAL NOTES.

The group of houses, Nos. 1 to 6, Pond Square, and No. 45, South Grove, stand on a piece of ground which appears to have been enclosed from Highgate Green in 1692, by Christopher Ryles. It was then described as " a parcel of the waste on Highgate Hill at the north and east of the Bowling Green, near the Pond, as now enclosed with a hedge." A cottage there is mentioned in 1739. Robert Morgan of Highgate, bricklayer, acquired the land in 1750 from the heirs of John Croute, tailor, to whom it had been conveyed in 1739 by Mary Johnson, widow, the daughter of Christopher Ryles. The site of No. 6, Rock House, emerges from a tangle of records in the year 1777, when Anne Morgan, daughter of Robert Morgan, sold to David Jones of Kentish Town (who owned the Mother Red Cap) " a parcel of land formerly waste on which a messuage hath lately been erected heretofore in the possession of — Wells." The house, then untenanted, was on ground where a stable had stood, formerly in the possession of Robert Morgan. The successive owners after the death of Mrs. Ann Jones, widow, were Mary Ann Durling, wife of John Durling, farmer, of Brentwood (under the will of David Jones), Mary Durling (only child of Mary Ann Durling), 1819-23, John Vaux, widower of Mary Ann Vaux (*née* Durling), 1823-9, John Lowden and his executors, 1829-41, John Matthias Clark, 1841-78, Mary Ann Clark (daughter of John Matthias Clark, who married Henry Munday Clark), 1878-9. Mrs. Clark died on 16th June, 1879, leaving seven sons, two under age.

For many years before 1820 the tenant of Rock House was Mrs. Deborah Ellison, daughter of Richard Shillingford, carpenter, wife and then widow of John Ellison, mariner, who lived at Pennington Street, St. George the Martyr, in 1787. The tenant before Mrs. Ellison was Elizabeth Brownsworth, and after 1820 Thomas Brocksopp. The tenant from whom the house was named appears to be recorded on a monument in Highgate Cemetery[25] to " Mary, wife of John Dennis Rock, of Highgate." She died 2nd June, 1846, in the 42nd year of her age. In a publication called *Mons Sacer* for July 1846, Vol. I, No. 1, we find recorded " Deaths,—18th June at Highgate, at the house of her son in law, Mr. J. D. Rock, Mary, relict of the late Mr. Frederick Roope of London."

The adjoining houses, Nos. 1-5, Pond Square, and No. 45, South Grove, occupy land that belonged to Richard Shillingford, carpenter, from 1760 to 1785. The house in which he lived was on the site of Nos. 2 and 3, while the yard and garden attached to his house formed the site on which were afterwards erected No. 1 and also No. 45, South Grove, adjoining the back of No. 2. He bequeathed to his eldest son, Richard, property in Holloway and to his younger son, John, the house in which he lived, which was occupied after his death in 1785 by his married daughter, Susanna, wife of Robert Colpus, bricklayer. The name of Colpus as occupier last appears in 1817, and his widow's in 1818.[42] The two houses adjoining Shillingford's own dwelling house, Nos. 4 and 5, went to his two daughters, Mrs. Susanna Colpus and Mrs. Deborah Ellison, the first-named becoming sole owner from 1787, when Mrs. Ellison surrendered hers to her sister. Their brother John Shillingford lived in No. 1 next door to Mrs. Colpus.

110

XX—THE FLASK TAVERN (NO. 26, SOUTH GROVE)

GROUND LANDLORD AND LEASEHOLDER.

This house was originally copyhold of the Manor of Cantlowes but has been enfranchised.

GENERAL DESCRIPTION AND DATE OF STRUCTURE.

The Flask Tavern, which was the scene of many sittings of the Manor Court, appears by name in the court rolls as early as 1716. The present buildings consist of a house of three storeys facing south-west of 18th-century date, and a smaller structure shown in the parish plan of 1804 as an outbuilding and since refronted to form a two-storey extension to the tavern. Above the window that lights the bar in this smaller building is an oval tablet with the initials W. C. for William Carpenter, and the date 1767.

The bar window forms an attractive feature. It is three sash lights wide and flanked by a pair of long narrow reeded pilasters with diagonal panels in place of the ordinary capitals. Over the window runs a small architrave mould and above it a deep frieze or fascia. Above this again is a bold projecting cornice, of which the soffit is decorated with reed ornament.

CONDITION OF REPAIR.

Good.

HISTORICAL NOTES.

The Flask Inn is not referred to by that name on the court rolls before the year 1716, but it is safe to assume that it stood there at least as early as 1663 when William Royles was granted two pieces of the waste which, by the description and measurements given, seem to fit the area now occupied by the inn and adjacent property. After the death of William Royles, his widow and three sons and two daughters, in 1682, conveyed to William Blake, citizen and vintner of London, a messuage, garden and several pieces of land on the Green, together with the bowling green, the whole of which comprised the area now bounded on two sides by South Grove, and by Pond Square on the other side. The area of the bowling green was three-quarters of an acre, covering all the site mentioned, except the Flask with Nos. 23 to 32 at the south-west end, and Nos. 37 to 44, South Grove at the north-west.

The bowling green appears on the rolls in 1672 when the lord of the manor, with the consent of the homage, granted to ten local property-owners " a parcel of the waste on Highgate Hill called the Bowling Green, lying on the south and west of the Great Pond there, which has been used for a Bowling Green beyond the memory of man, containing three roods and now enclosed with hedges and ditches and planted with trees." No doubt the landlord of the Flask acted as " groundman " of the bowling green, and this interesting record shows the intention to protect this part of the Green for the use of the public, much as a cricket field might be provided at the present time. In a lease dated 6th May, 1736,[114] of the land on which now stand Nos. 37 to 44, is mentioned ground enclosed on the west side of a piece of ground lately a bowling green and " the place where the stairs lately went up out of it into the said bowling green." From this we learn that the bowling green was raised above the level of the roads and that its use as such had ceased in 1736.

That the trustees ever met as a body is not probable and what control they exercised is not known, but their names are noteworthy and imposing, viz. John, Duke of Lauderdale, Henry, Marquis of Dorchester, George Pryor, esquire (who lived in " Andrew Marvell's Cottage "), Elisha Coysh, M.D. (of Swain's Lane), Francis Blake, esquire, William Blake his son, Richard Gower, gentleman (of Bisham House), Simon Baxter, gentleman (who lived on the site of Witanhurst),

THE VILLAGE OF HIGHGATE

Peter Sambrook, gentleman (who lived on the site of Holly Village), and William Cholmeley. Fresh trustees were never appointed although the conditions attaching to the grant of 1672 are consistently recited until as late of 1807. After the death of the surviving trustee, Simon Baxter, in 1714, the lord granted it in 1718 to Edmund Rolfe of King's Lynn, who died in 1725, bequeathing to his daughter Elizabeth, wife of Thomas Phillips, vintner, the Flask and the bowling green adjoining. In 1730 she was granted licence to dig there and carry away gravel, sand, clay and soil for seven years, " provided that in two years' time she level it and reconvert to a Bowling Green so that she permit the inhabitants of Highgate to walk there and play bowls." Only eight years afterwards occurs the casual reference to " ground lately a bowling green " mentioned before, so that the restriction was not taken very seriously.

It must be recognised that the legal record of ownership on the court rolls does not always disclose all we should like to know about property and its owners. The steps by which the ownership of the Flask went from William Blake in 1682 to Edmund Rolfe in 1716 are given below, but the transactions underlying the record are obscure. In 1682 William Blake surrendered conditionally to Susanna Carpenter of Abbots Langley, and she foreclosed in the following year. In 1684 she conveyed the property to James Hooper of the Middle Temple, and he, in 1685, to Mary Blake, spinster, of London. A few months later Mary Blake and Daniel Blake of St. Paul's, Covent Garden, woollen draper, conveyed it to John Brooke of London, esquire. Brooke's sons were admitted in 1689, after his death, and surrendered in 1692 to Mary Hooper, spinster, of London. She had two married sisters and a brother, Edward Hooper of Hurn Court, Christchurch, Hants. Mary Hooper bequeathed this estate to her sisters, Phillipa, the wife of John Martyn, and Mrs. Amy Nutley. They kept the portion now occupied by the houses in South Grove numbered 37 to 44, and sold the Flask and Bowling Green in 1716 to Edmund Rolfe of Thavies Inn, gentleman. Charles Lacey of Hornsey, citizen and cordwainer of London, acquired the property in 1737 from the four daughters of Mrs. Elizabeth Phillips, the daughter of Mr. Rolfe. Mr. Lacey lived in Colney Hatch Lane, and as he took out a licence to lease his Hornsey property in this year, being thereafter described as of Highgate, he evidently migrated there from Muswell Hill when he bought the Flask. When he died in 1747 his grandson, Charles, son of his son, John Lacey, took it under his grandfather's will.[115] In 1762 he appears as Charles Lacey of Turnstile, Holborn, cordwainer, when, with Elizabeth his wife, he sold it to William Carpenter, brewer, of Shoreditch.

There is a plate on the smaller existing building adjoining the inn which reads $\frac{\text{W.C.,}}{1767}$ for which William Carpenter was doubtless responsible. He may have made some alterations in the buildings at that date. From the fact disclosed in his will[116] that he had two brothers, Richard of Devizes and Thynn of Clack, near Frome, it may be supposed that he came from the West Country. His widow, Ann, succeeded him in 1783 and seems to have remained at Highgate until about 1803, in which year she was at South Lambeth, and in 1804 at Southampton Court, Queen's Square.[117] Their granddaughter, Maria, then Maria Fowle of Mitcham, widow, came into possession in 1807. In that year or the next she married the Rev. Thomas Aubrey Grantham and sold the Flask (and three cottages adjoining) to Thomas Marlborough Pryor and Robert Pryor, brewers, of Shoreditch, in 1812. They sold it in 1819 to John Tanner. He was succeeded by his son, George Tanner, in 1855, who died on 10th November, 1856. Thereafter it was in the hands of trustees under the will of John Tanner until 1917, when it was sold. The property then consisted of Nos. 24, 25, South Grove, No. 26, the Flask, and Nos. 27-32, South Grove.

The remaining portion of Carpenter's estate was sold in 1812 by the Rev. Thomas Aubrey Grantham, then of Rampisham otherwise Ransom, Dorset, to Thomas Brocksopp of Hornsey Lane, esquire. This land was the one-time Bowling Green. In 1840 the Brocksopp trustees sold it to Mark Beauchamp Peacock of the General Post Office, who lived at Southwood Lawn, Southwood Lane, and owned a great amount of property in Highgate. It consisted of a house on the site of the present Burlington Mansions, formerly in the occupation of Thomas Brocksopp, since of Ann Brocksopp, deceased, and late of Captain Ingram. Later occupants were Henry Charles Cowie, H. Longman and Miss Emma Hanbury (circa 1871). Between the garden of this house and the Flask was another garden extending from road to road, covering about a quarter of an acre, rented by William Bosher McPherson, nurseryman, who was also landlord of the Woodman Tavern.

When the sisters of Mary Hooper sold the Flask in 1716 they still possessed some land at

112

the north-west corner of the " island site " with which we are dealing, on which stand to-day Nos. 37 to 44, South Grove. The Hoopers were a well-to-do family living at Hurn Court, Christchurch, Hampshire, and these ladies were daughters of Mrs. Dorothy Hooper, sister of Anthony Ashley, 3rd Earl of Shaftesbury. Their mother's sister, Elizabeth, was grandmother of James, 1st Earl of Malmesbury, who became heir of their nephew, Edward Hooper, when he died unmarried. In 1733 Edward Hooper of Hurn Court succeeded after the death of his sisters, and there were then eight cottages on the land, three of them occupying approximately the site of Nos. 37, 38 and 39, while five others stood on the sites of Nos. 40-4. Edward Hooper was succeeded by his son, Edward Hooper, in 1751, and he died a bachelor in 1795, bequeathing this property to his " godson and friend," formerly his ward, Nathaniel Gundry, esquire, by whom it was sold in 1797 to John Hale, coachmaster, who gave the three cottages mentioned above to his son John, and pulled down the other five, erecting a house at the corner on the site of No. 44, and another house on the site of No. 40. Hale's stabling stood next to No. 40, beyond which was the entrance to his coachyard, in which stood other stabling, etc., backing on Mr. Brocksopp's house and garden. John Hale died in 1808 and was succeeded in the business by his younger son, Abraham Hale. Abraham Hale was one of the " homage " at the manor court held at the Angel on 18th April, 1843, and in the following September was dead, when trustees were admitted under his will. Mark Beauchamp Peacock bought the property in the same year, and, as he already owned the Brocksopp land (including the three houses sold in 1812 to Thomas Brocksopp by John Hale, junior), thus became possessed of the whole site, except the Flask.

The manor courts were often held at the Flask, but on 22nd April, 1740, the court was held at Kentish Town (doubtless at the Assembly House), when the jury imposed a fine of £5 on Nicholas Jefferies, esquire, " the lessee under the lord of the manor, for not allowing this jury sufficient wine according to the ancient and laudable custom." This was the court leet held once a year, and there was little business transacted beyond the election of officers and occasional presentments of nuisances and encroachments on the waste lands. The jury numbered twelve men, the main inducement to serve being the customary dinner given by the lord to his " tenants."

H

XXI—KEN WOOD

Murray, Earl of Mansfield

GROUND LANDLORD.

The mansion was bequeathed to the Nation by the 1st Earl of Iveagh and is administered by the Iveagh Trustees. It is used as a picture gallery, open to the public. All the other buildings on the estate are administered by the London County Council, and the grounds are utilised as a public open space.

GENERAL DESCRIPTION AND DATE OF STRUCTURE.

Ken Wood, though sometimes described as being at Hampstead, is equally claimed by Highgate, and as it lies almost entirely within the boundaries of the parish of St. Pancras is rightly included in this volume.

Robert Adam was employed by Lord Mansfield to add to a house which formerly belonged to Lord Bute. The extent of the original building can be judged from the hatched portions of the plan printed on Plate 98. In this undertaking* Adam found a work after his own heart, and in his *Works*† he dwells on the fine placing of the house on the summit of Hampstead, in a way which marks his appreciation of the locality.

" A great body of water covers the bottom, and serves to go round a large natural wood of tall trees rising one above another upon the sides of a hill. Over the vale, through which the water flows, there is a noble view let into the house and terrace, of the City of London, Greenwich Hospital, and the river Thames, the ships passing up and down, with an extensive prospect, but clear and distinct, on both sides of the river. To the north-east and west of the house and terrace, the mountainous villages of Highgate and Hampstead form delightful objects. The whole scene is amazingly gay, magnificent, beautiful and picturesque. The hill and dale are finely diversified; nor is it easy to imagine a situation more striking without, or more agreeably retired and peaceful within." While he ends his description with these words: " The decoration bestowed on this front of the house is suitable to such a scene. The idea is new and has been generally approved."

The scene at Ken Wood, however, has been completely changed by the growth of the trees all around, and the broad terrace along the south front no longer commands the extensive view which Robert Adam describes.

Approaching the house from the north, from the Spaniards Road, the present drive winds through fine trees on steep banks to end in a wide space in front of the great portico. Two wings have been added, but the body of the house, with the portico, remains unchanged and exactly corresponds with Adam's drawings in the *Works*.

The changes in the surroundings of the house are shown by a survey of 1793 (on which is a neat little sketch of the bridge), and a complete plan

* For the description of Adam's work we are largely indebted to Mr. Arthur T. Bolton, who has kindly granted permission for us to make use of his chapter on Ken Wood in *The Architecture of Robert and James Adam*.

† *The Works in Architecture of Robert and James Adam*, 1778-9, referred to briefly as the *Works*.

of 1797 (see Plates 96 and 97). It is not apparent whether any of the Adams were connected with this reconstruction of the grounds after the death of Robert Adam and of Lord Mansfield. Originally there was a long forecourt in front of the house, probably enclosed by walls, with a central entrance* from the road marked on the plan as " The old road." The present curved road of approach has been carried across the site of the old stables on the west, and the enclosure marked " Menagerie " (aviary) on the east and cuts away at least one-half of the original depth of the forecourt. The change is important, because the house is no longer visible from the main road, and the former forecourt must have given both importance to the portico and expression to the villa idea of the original Adam design.

In front of the house on the south was a lawn or pleasure garden, also apparently enclosed by walls extending down to an irregularly shaped lake,

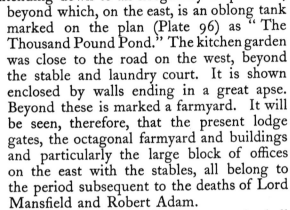

beyond which, on the east, is an oblong tank marked on the plan (Plate 96) as " The Thousand Pound Pond." The kitchen garden was close to the road on the west, beyond the stable and laundry court. It is shown enclosed by walls ending in a great apse. Beyond these is marked a farmyard. It will be seen, therefore, that the present lodge gates, the octagonal farmyard and buildings and particularly the large block of offices on the east with the stables, all belong to the period subsequent to the deaths of Lord Mansfield and Robert Adam.

From the portico we enter the hall (Plate 103). The ceiling, which was painted by Angelica Kauffmann, has ovals in chiaroscuro with reliefs of swags and medallions all bound together in a well-devised scheme. In the west wall is a fireplace of white marble having fluted pilasters and a frieze with a central medallion (carved with the head of Bacchus) between swags. The walls have a frieze enriched with ox-heads in medallions. The furniture delineated by Adam in his plates of Ken Wood published in the *Works* no longer remains.

East of the hall is the Adam staircase (Plate 112a). It is constructed of oak and has a good balustrade of open ironwork with scrolled uprights and honeysuckle ornaments of cast brass all painted black, and a plain mahogany handrail. The steps have enriched

---

* The entrance has been omitted in the view reproduced on Plate 94.

consoles at their ends and a running scroll ornament. The stair hall is open up to the roof and is lighted by an oval lantern decorated with festoons and covered by a glass dome.

The " Marble Hall " (Plate 115) adjoining is a small room with a domed ceiling which belongs to the later construction (*circa* 1795) and replaces the back court shown on the Adam plan of the house. A pair of doors communicates with the " Vestibule," in the south range, through a colonnade or screen. In this vestibule are two beautiful doorways (Plate 113), of which the more elaborate leads into the Adam Room, the other into the " Breakfast Room." The ceiling of the vestibule is coved and has a circular central panel enriched with festoons and a palm leaf ornament. In the south wall is the " Venetian " window described in the *Works*. To-day, instead of a niche a pair of great doors in keeping generally with the style of the period lead from under the colonnade into the so-called " Marble Hall " from which the paving of black and white marble squares has been removed. The vista is continued through into the dining-room in the east wing.

The magnificent Adam Room or Library (Plates 104 to 112a) ranks high among the great chambers to be found in England, and takes a leading place in the list of its architect's achievements. It is approached from the Ante-room through a pair of doors in the east wall.

Robert Adam's own account of it runs as follows: " The great room with its ante-room was begun by Lord Mansfield's orders in the year 1767 and was intended both for a Library and a ' room for receiving Company.' The circular recesses were therefore fitted up for the former purpose and the square part, or body of the room, was made suitable to the latter."

He continues by saying that the ceiling of the great room—" is in the form and style of those of the ancients. It is an imitation of a flat arch, which is extremely beautiful and much more perfect than that which is commonly called the coved ceiling when there is a height sufficient to admit of it, as in the present case. . . ."

Adam also tells us that " the stucco work of this ceiling and of the other decorations, is finely executed by Mr. Joseph Rose. The paintings (Plates 109 to 111) are elegantly performed by Mr. Antonio Zucchi, a Venetian painter of great eminence, and the grounds of the *pannels* and *freeses* are coloured with light tints of pink and green, so as to take off the glare of white, so common in every ceiling, till of late. This has always appeared to me so cold and unfinished, that I ventured to introduce this variety of ground at once to relieve the ornaments, remove the crudeness of the white, and create a harmony between the ceiling and the side walls, with their hangings pictures and other decorations." The grounds are now all pink.

A main feature of the room is the pair of great apses at the east and west ends, with their screens of Corinthian columns.* Continuity of design between them and the centre bay is promoted by a bold honeysuckle band at the base of the vault and of the apses. It recalls the narrower frieze of the

---

* The columns originally white are now painted a dark marbled brown : the capitals are gilded.

entablature. The apses are fitted with bookshelves* and are decorated above by three painted panels in enriched frames. The half-domes, very difficult to illustrate adequately, are masterly pieces of decorative stucco-work. The main frieze is decorated with running foliage, and lions, urns, and stags' heads alternately : the lions are the supporters and the stags' heads the crest of the family.

The fireplace (Plate 107) in the middle of the north wall in white statuary marble with pilasters, deer heads and sphinxes, remains exactly as illustrated in the *Works*. Above it was formerly a portrait of the 1st Lord Mansfield by David Martin set in an enriched frame. As shown in Adam's drawings there is a bottom border to balance the top cresting. A mirror which is now in the position formerly occupied by the painting is one of the two that originally occupied the recesses on either side of the fireplace. It is in three bays and has arched filigree ornament, all gilt. The large arched recesses are now book-lined. In the south wall are three sash windows. On the piers between them are two mirrors in carved wood and gilded frames with ornate crestings exactly as illustrated in Adam's *Works*.

The two oval mirrors which he also shows have disappeared.

The main vault, a large rectangular bay flanked east and west by narrower bays, contains in all fifteen painted panels. The central oval is the largest, filled with a classical or mythological subject. There are semi-oval panels at the edges of the large bay containing pairs of lovers, and between them other panels with similar subjects (Plates 109 to 111).† The narrower side bays have panels with conventional foliage and terminal figures of putti, flanked by painted subjects on polygonal panels. The paintings are very brightly coloured, executed in tones strong enough to stand the rich gilding which forms so large an element in the total effect. The carpet is red and the furniture was of gold and damask, so that it required judgment to ensure a general harmony of colour effect.

No record of the exact date of the earlier house has at present been found, but from the slender evidence left in the fabric itself it may be judged to have been reconstructed some forty or fifty years before it passed into the hands of Lord Mansfield. It seems to have been a long narrow building with an orangery (probably itself an addition) at its west end. Adam added his one-storey saloon at the east end to correspond with the orangery, built the portico, and increased the height of the old south range to agree with that of the northern range. He is said to have constructed the additional storey without removing the old roof—at least until the very end of the work so that occupation of the house was not interrupted during the progress of the alterations.

The rooms on the ground floor of the south range were fitted with

---

* Now carried down to the floor filling the formerly solid dado.

† The five photographs of panels painted by Zucchi from the ceiling of the Adam Room are reproduced by the courtesy of Trustees of the Iveagh Bequest, who gave permission for them to be photographed in 1933 by Dr. Nissen of Sweden for a work on Zucchi. The story of how the painter fell in love for the second time with Angelica Kauffmann while they were both working on the decoration of Ken Wood is well known.

new fireplaces, but were otherwise little altered. The " Breakfast Room " west of the ante-room has a typical fireplace of white marble decorated with urns and bulls' heads above the pilasters. The room is lighted by two south

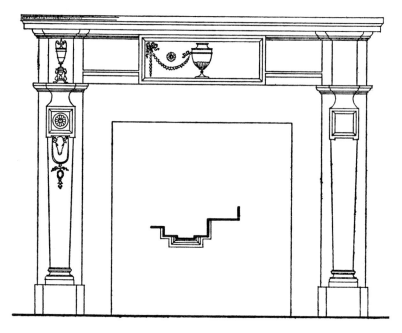

MANTEL IN BREAKFAST ROOM

windows. The " Library " next to it on the west has four south windows, but was originally divided into two apartments called on the Adam plan the drawing-room and parlour. The old " Tea Room " was also at one time divided into two with an angle fireplace in the principal apartment. Next comes the " Boudoir " (originally the housekeeper's room), corresponding to Adam's vestibule and with a similar Venetian window. Unfortunately the window has been robbed of most of its sash bars and its appearance has suffered thereby. In the north wall of this chamber are three round-headed recesses, the middle one containing a door to the western or back stair-hall. This range of rooms is connected by doors adjoining the north or inner wall. In the Adam plan these doors are on the opposite side of the fireplaces by the outer wall.

A doorway in the Boudoir now opens into the long orangery (once entered only from the garden by a door in its western wall) which has nothing very distinctive about it except that it is lighted by five round-headed windows in the south wall. The plaster ceiling is flat with a moulded cornice.

In the north range the large back stair-hall is a very plain structure rising to the second floor and of much later date. Above it is an oval lantern. Originally it was partly a store-room and partly a passage to the back-stairs which once butted against the eastern wall by the portico. North of the stair-hall is a narrow chamber known as the " Prayer Room " lighted by three north windows. In the two north angles are coved recesses. This room was formed out of the butler's pantry and the staircase referred to above.

On the first floor the large room over the entrance hall has doorways leading on to both staircases with doors of the Adam type. It is lighted by three windows below the north portico. In the west wall is a wooden fireplace (Plate 116a) in the Chinese style, differing from the Adam work and probably a later insertion or alteration.* It is treated with coloured panels in enamel: the pilasters are carved with terminal figures of men holding wyverns. The shelf or cornice is coved and enriched with a kind of palm-leaf ornament. The ceiling has a coved cornice with egg-and-tongue ornament.

Of the rooms in the south range, the eastern bedroom entered from the Adam staircase contains a large alcove with panelled doors on either side enclosing cupboards. In the west wall is a fireplace of wood treated with honeysuckle ornament. The walls have a plain frieze and a cornice enriched with egg-and-tongue ornament.

The adjoining chamber on the west was Lord Mansfield's bedroom. In the east wall is an Adam fireplace (see Plate 114b) of white marble, with twin Ionic fluted pilasters and a frieze decorated with paterae in beaded rings divided by double honeysuckle patterns. The next room has another typical fireplace of wood and pilasters with festoons and lintel with a honeysuckle and urn design. A small bathroom with a single south window leads out of this room and has a low ceiling with a coved and enriched cornice.

The eastern portion of the house which is entered off the west staircase contains a private office and an old staircase leading up to the second floor. This latter staircase (Plate 102) which may very well have been part of the original main staircase to the house dates probably from about 1720-30. It has a moulded handrail of that period filled in below with close panelling instead of balusters. As no early plan of the house above the main floor exists it is difficult to say what alterations may have taken place.

On the second floor there is a series of rooms in each of the two ranges. Those over the south range have their floor 17 inches higher than those of the north range, although the ceilings to the first floor are level with each other. This variation in the levels no doubt was caused by the necessity for leaving the old roof in position until Adam could complete the new roof. It is probable that this deeper floor space contains the earlier tiebeams left in place after the upper timbers of the original trusses were removed.

There are several Adam fireplaces with typical ornament in these rooms, one with bulls' heads, another with a lion's head and a third with rams' heads as decorations to the lintels : they are all of wood and retain the original hob-grates with urns and pine cones as ornaments.

Adam's roof construction is very simple: there is a great truss of king- and queen-post type between the two ranges in the middle.

* Mr. Arthur T. Bolton informs us that the 2nd Earl seems to have employed the painter I. C. Ibbetson (1759 to 1817) to make some alterations to the house and this fireplace may have been his work.

KEN WOOD

Subsequent additions to the house were made about 1795 by the 2nd Earl of Mansfield, who does not seem to have employed the successors of Robert Adam, possibly because of some disagreement. He threw out two wings on the north front, thus recessing the Adam front which had previously appeared as a projection on the older south range. The rooms are treated more or less after the Adam style but with a difference that only enhances the Adam craftsmanship. The western wing replaces the old kitchen and offices and the laundry court and leads into the orangery through an Ionic colonnade similar to that to the ante-room.

The north portico with its four fluted Ionic columns of wood sanded to represent stone carries an entablature which has its frieze decorated with swags. Above is a pediment in which is a circular panel containing a figure subject. The soffit is coffered. The main wall, which is also treated in cement, is of three storeys and has plain square windows, a fluted frieze and cornice. At the first-floor level is a plaster string course with guilloche ornament. The later north wings, to which reference has just been made, are built of a white brick above the ground level. Both end walls have Venetian windows to the ground floor and plain square upper windows.

The south front has its lowest storey treated with imitation rusticated masonry. Above it the wall has flat Ionic pilasters and a central pediment. The panels between the pilasters are plain, although shown in the Adam drawings as containing some form of decoration. The windows have plain square heads. The orangery and the Adam Room are treated alike in elevation: each having five round-headed bays divided by Ionic pilasters carrying a plain entablature.

In the lower level east of the house the basement of the north-east wing is built of a pleasant red-brown brick which has an earlier appearance than the white brick above, but is of the same period. The east wing is a two-storeyed building of the same red-brown brick containing the great kitchen, a fine large chamber, and other offices. It was once directly connected with the house, but is now entirely separated.

The two large rooms used as public refreshment rooms were originally the brewery and laundry. These offices took the place of an earlier range on the west side of the entrance forecourt. The kitchen in the days of the 1st Lord Mansfield butted against the north wall of the orangery.

The fruit and vegetable garden that lies alongside Hampstead Lane eastwards from the stables-block was probably formed between 1793 and 1797. The garden wall beside the lane which has been preserved by the London County Council is of interest as being one of the few examples extant near London of a wall designed for fruit-growing. It was not uncommon before the days of glasshouses to insert in such walls flues in which fires could be lighted to protect the trees from the effects of frosts in the spring. These flues and flue-doors can be seen at intervals along the length of the wall. Greenhouses, as indicated in the Ordnance Survey plans of 1875, were added later to a short length of the walling on the section nearest to Highgate.

A reference to the estate plan of 1797 shows three groups of outbuildings apart from the block of new offices adjoining the house itself. On the western boundary of the estate not far from The Spaniards was a farm planned as an octagon, of which only a fragment remains to-day (see Plate 119). To the south of this farm stood the dairy, consisting of three small buildings grouped round a forecourt, the one to the north being the dairy itself. These remain almost unchanged; Plate 118 gives the plan and elevation and Plate 117b a view of the centre building and the dairy block, picturesque brick structures with heavily overhanging eaves. Right away on the eastern boundary stand the stables, a view of which is given in Plate 117a. They were also built of brick round a square yard, the principal range being in two storeys; a large opening in the centre having a semicircular light above it crowned by a pediment. All the ground-floor windows show semicircular heads. These outbuildings are under the control of the London County Council and have been converted into tenements for the use of the staff employed upon the estate.

CONDITION OF REPAIR.
    Good.

HISTORICAL NOTES.
    For three centuries the Monastery of Christ Church, Aldgate, owned a large tract of wood and heath at the north-west corner of the parish of St. Pancras, including the present Ken Wood estate. In determining the acreage of it the ancient deeds of conveyance afford little help, the only boundaries which can be immediately identified being the boundaries of the parish where it abuts on Hampstead, Finchley and Hornsey. The greater part was occupied with the ancient " Cane Wood," which covered about 200 acres in the middle of the 16th century. The estate of Lord Mansfield as shown on the map of the parish in 1804 covered 230-odd acres, and may be taken as roughly co-extensive with the monastic property. It is probable that the southern boundary of the Christ Church property was where Mansfield Road now runs along the site of an ancient footpath from Kentish Town to Hampstead and that the wood itself extended southward to Parliament Hill. From the earliest times a farm lay to the south of the wood, but how near the eastern boundary of the estate approached the road (West Hill and Highgate Road) is uncertain. Millfield Lane and Sherricks Farm bounded it on the north-east. According to a terrier and survey [118a] of the manor of Tottenhall made in 1761 for the Hon. Charles Fitzroy (afterwards first Baron Southampton), Ken Wood as well as the adjoining estate of Sherricks lay within that manor. This is doubtless correct since it is impossible to believe that the manor (which certainly included Sherricks) did not originally include all the northern part of the parish outside the Manor of Cantlowes. If so, there must have been a grant from the Prebendary of Tottenhall to William de Blemont or his predecessor, but none has been found.

Holy Trinity Priory, Aldgate

    In the reign of Henry III the owners of this land were the great London family of Blémont or Cornhill[118b] (it will be observed that these two names are really the same, one being French and the other English). Hubert, who is said to have come from Caen, had at least three sons, namely :

    1. Alan, ancestor of the Fitz-Alan family ;
    2. Gervase of Cornhill, Justiciar of London in 1182, who died about 1184 ;
    3. William de Blemont or Blemund, *alias* le viel (elder).

Of these sons we are only concerned here with the last named. He had two sons, *viz.* :
    1. William de Blemont, afterwards a Canon of Holy Trinity or Christ Church ;
    2. Theodoric or Terry, who married Rose, daughter of Arnald le Rus, who was Sheriff in 1197 ;
    And possibly a daughter, Denyse, who married Arnald Fitz-Arnald her brother-in-law, son of Arnald le Rus.

121

KEN WOOD

It is possible that John Bucointe or Buccauncta (oily mouth), another important citizen, was predecessor of the Blemonts at Ken Wood; an inference drawn from the fact that in 1202 he conveyed to William de Blemont a carucate of land about three miles away, subsequently known as the manor of Blemundsbury, the present-day Bloomsbury.* Arnald Fitz-Arnald and Denyse his wife are of local interest since their descendants were lords of Bibsworth, a sub-manor of the adjacent Bishop of London's manor of Finchley.

"Cane Wood" does not appear under that name before the reign of Henry VIII, when it was in the possession of the Priory of Holy Trinity or Christ Church, Aldgate, which was founded by Matilda, wife of Henry I, in 1108, as a House of Augustinian Canons. Our only knowledge of Ken Wood in early days amounts to what we can glean from the documents by which it was conveyed to that monastery.

Although no record has been found showing that William de Blemund le viel owned Ken Wood, the dealings of his sons with it, as will appear, certainly imply that it came to them by inheritance. In an undated deed Theodoric, son of William de Blemont, quitclaimed to Sir William, his brother, his heath with the appurtenances, which his brother had granted to him for life, which heath lay between the wood of the canons of Holy Trinity, London, and the land which he (Theodoric) held outside the ditch likewise granted him by his brother on the south and between the wood of Hamstede and the land of William Dispensator on the east. For this grant he received 40s.[118c] In 1226 Theodoric de Blemont granted and confirmed to Sir William de Blemont his brother all his rights in lands, men, rents, services, hedges and ditches and appurtenances, next the wood of the Canons of Holy Trinity, London, in "Kentistun," in the parish of St. Pancras, in return for 17s. rent which Elwin Chese paid.[119] At that time such deeds were seldom dated exactly, and the time when they were executed can only be deduced from the names of the witnesses. The first-mentioned deed was witnessed by Robert de Halewic (Halliwic was in Friern Barnet), Eilwin Chese, William Dispensator, Peter Carect' (Carter), Robert de Haliwell, Terric Sokeling, Robert Remild, William de Stapelherst, Gilbert Safughel and others. Several of these can be recognised as local landowners, suggesting that the deed was witnessed in the manor court of Tottenhall or of Bloomsbury, but they do not enable us to fix the exact year. The second deed was witnessed by Richard Renger, mayor of London, Roger Duce, Martin Fitz-William, sheriffs of London, Andrew Bukerel, M. clerk (the sheriff of Middlesex), Henry Bokointe, Henry Fitz-William, Stephen de Strand, Master Robert de Tefont, Solomon his son, Eilwin Chese, William Dispensator, Ralph, servant of Terry, Edmund of Holy Trinity. From these names it would appear that the deed was executed in the Court of Hustings. After these preliminaries William, son of William de Blemont, in 1226, for the welfare of his soul and the souls of his ancestors and successors, granted and confirmed to Richard the Prior and the Convent of Holy Trinity (or Christ Church, Aldgate), London, all he possessed in the vil of "Kentiston" in the parish of St. Pancras, in wood and heath, men, homage, rents, services, liberties, common of pasture, ways, feeding-grounds, hedges and ditches and appurtenances, in free and perpetual alms, they to render him and his heirs half a mark yearly by instalments of 40d. at Michaelmas and 40d. at Easter.[120] In the same year Theodoric de Blemont confirmed his brother's grant in return for half a mark yearly payable at the church of Holy Trinity by payments of 40d. at Easter and 40d. at Michaelmas, and two marks paid down.[121] By another deed Theodoric de Blemont for the welfare of his soul and the souls of his ancestors and successors, confirmed to Richard the Prior and the Canons of Holy Trinity, London, the wood and heath, lands, rents and services which they had of the gift of Sir William de Blemont his brother in "Kentestun" in the parish of St. Pancras, rendering him and his heirs two marks yearly and also 37s. rent which they had of the gift of the same William in the city of London, in free and perpetual alms. Then Richard, Abbot of Westminster, granted and confirmed to Richard, the Prior, and the Convent of Holy Trinity, London, the wood, heath, lands, rents, service, homage, etc., which they had by reason of the gift of William de Blemont in the parish of St. Pancras of "Kentiston."[122] Finally, by charter dated 8th February, 1227, King Henry confirmed to the Priory all their wood and heath as enclosed on all sides with a ditch in the parish of St. Pancras of "Kentisseton," next the park of the Lord Bishop of London, towards the south, and William Uggel and his heirs and services.[123]

* The story of this estate and of the Blemund family can now be read in an article on the University site by Miss E. Jeffries Davis in the *London Topographical Record*, Volume XVII, 1936.

122

Theodoric de Blemont must have died soon after making over his interest to the Priory, since his widow, Rose, in 1229 entered an action against the Prior of Holy Trinity to secure her dower right (which she had with the assent of William de Blemont) in 26 acres of land, 60 acres of wood and 18s. rent in " Kentisseton."[124] Although William de Blemont conveyed all his rights to the Priory, some of the land was apparently not in his own possession. In 1226 he demised, granted and confirmed to Safugle, son of Dering, and his heirs, 12 acres lying next to the grove of Sirewic for a rent of 2s. 6d. yearly by quarterly payments of 7½d., as well as 4s. down " in gersumma."[125] According to an endorsement on this deed Safugle was the father of Gilbert, evidently the Gilbert mentioned in the next deed and a witness to the first deed mentioned above. Until recent times there was a " Sherricks Wood " and farm lying between Ken Wood and Highgate Village ; the grove of Sirewic mentioned here is therefore very interesting since it must refer to Sherricks. By a deed of uncertain date, but obviously following the last mentioned, Robert de Tephont with the assent and free will of his wife, Lucy, confirmed to Richard de Stanes and Margery, his wife, all his land in " St. Pancras of Kentisseton " of the fee of William de Blemont, as well as the land which Gilbert Safugle demised and granted to him and his wife, Lucy, called la Dune, and a croft which he held of William, son of Robert Spencer (Dispensator), next the same land.[126] The croft of William Spencer mentioned must be related to the " land of William Spencer " mentioned in the release by Theodoric to his brother. Spencer's land would appear to have been south of Sherricks, fronting West Hill. In 1325 Richard de Stanes and Margery, his wife, conveyed to Richard, the Prior, and the Convent of Holy Trinity, all her right in 24 acres in " Cantisseton."[127] This grant was confirmed by Margery after the death of her husband to John the Prior (successor of Prior Richard) and to the Convent.[128]

There was still another portion of Blemont's land, dealt with in the following undated deed. Agnes, formerly the wife of John Wallis of " Kentissetun," sold to Richard the Prior and the Canons of Holy Trinity, London, all her dower of the tenements which her late husband held in the said town of the fee of William de Blemont. For this she received 8s. The names of the witnesses show that this must have been soon after Blemont's donation. Master Robert de Teffunt, John and Solomon, sons of Master John de Lyesnes, Roger de Beuchedrey, Robert Hunte, William Stephen, Ralph his son, William Huggel, Richard his son, Richard Bruy, Gilbert, Nicholas, Ralph, brothers. William Huggel is possibly the William Uggel of the royal charter of 1227, and the names also suggest that the deed was witnessed at the Priory.[129]

William de Blemont's son, Terry, had a daughter, Egidia, who married firstly Richard Viel and secondly William de Kent. She had a son, Thomas Viel, and a daughter, Margery de Kent.[130] The Manor of Bloomsbury descended to Thomas Viel when his father died, whilst he was still under age, but was forfeited because it was alleged that he was one of the King's enemies and associated with the barons who rebelled under Simon de Montfort against Henry III. He afterwards pleaded that during the time of these disturbances he was in the custody of Stephen Buckerel,[131] and ought not to have incurred a forfeiture of his lands. Egidia Blemund is noted as holding a fee in the soke of Blemund in 1242-3,[132] some 21 years before the Battle of Lewes, which means that she was then a widow ; her son, Thomas Viel, seems to have come of age about 1254. William Belet, one of the serjeants of the King's table and a knight who held much property in Norfolk and elsewhere, had been given the forfeited Manor of Bloomsbury by Henry III in 1265. As a result of Thomas Viel's plea in 1277, William Belet in 1278 conveyed to him for life rents amounting to £3 13s. 4d., including the half-mark from Ken Wood, but kept the manor of Bloomsbury. In 1288 Margery de Kent, sister and heir of Thomas Viel, citizen of London, remised to the Priory of Holy Trinity the wood, etc., formerly of William de Blemont her ancestor, in Kentish Town in St. Pancras, and this half a mark rent.[133] In an assessment of ecclesiastical property made in 1291 the goods of the Priory in " Kentisseton " were valued at £3 19s. 3d.[134]

At this distance of time and in the absence of other records one cannot pretend to place on the map exactly the separate properties dealt with in these ancient deeds. What William de Blemont gave to the Priory was his rights as landlord, but the interests of those who held under him and of his relatives had to be gathered in separately. In 1328 Henry de Seccheford, citizen of London, conveyed to John de Oxford, vintner and citizen of London, a messuage and six acres of land and meadow in the vil of " Kentisshetonn."[135] Henry de Seccheford, mercer, was Alderman of Aldersgate Ward 1319 to 1336 and of Cripplegate Ward in 1336, and M.P. for London in 1324, 1325, 1327 and 1336. John of Oxford was sheriff in 1323 and Mayor in 1341, when he died. He was evidently a very wealthy man, judging from the bequests in his will. In 1335 he had licence to alienate to the Priory of Holy Trinity two tofts of land, one mill, 50 acres of land and two acres of wood in Kentish Town, of the yearly value of 20s. 3d.[136] This, presumably including the six acres purchased from Henry Seccheford, was said to be holden of the Monastery in chief by John of Oxford by service of 8s. 7d. a year.[137]

The whole estate dealt with in the records cited above remained in the possession of the monastery of Christchurch, Aldgate, and there is nothing to record until the Dissolution two hundred years later, except a grant by Nicholas, the Prior, and the Convent, to Nicholas Gray, yeoman, of Highgate, on 15th August, 1525, of the office of woodwardship, bailyship and keeping of their two woods of " Cane Wood " and " Gyll Holt."[138] Omitting the legal phrases, the effect of this long and interesting document is as follows. Nicholas Gray was to oversee the woods, and if any cattle or beasts came into them he was to drive, bring or carry (if not prevented) all such cattle and beasts to the Lord's pound, there to remain until the masters or owners agreed with him for the damage done. He was to receive for his diligence all the profit of distraining beasts or cattle so pounded. If any person was to hew, cut, fell or carry away any woods, underwoods, boughs or poles, Nicholas was to take them if he could, or to report their names to the Prior. He was to receive for his diligence any wood so cut and the tools used. The ditches, hedges and fences belonging to the two woods and also the great ditch between the upper end of the two fields called Mylfeld and Huntfeld and Hamsted Heth, he was to make, scour, cleanse and amend as he should think necessary at the cost of the Priory. For ditching a new ditch he was to receive 12d. a pole, for mending or scouring a ditch 8d. He was to take in the woods any stuff required for mending the hedges, ditches and fences. From 1st November to 30th April every year he might fell, cut down, make and square longwood, polewood, lashbaven, talwood and timber to the number of 290 loads or more, 200 being for the use of the monastery according to the old custom. For every load of polewood and longwood he was to receive 3d. felling money ; for every load of talwood and baven 4d. felling money, and for every timber tree felled and made in loads 4d. His annual fee was 25s. 8d. paid quarterly, with one load of talwood, two loads of longwood or polewood and all faggots called bush baven made of holy thorns, brambles, briers, bushes and tops of trees, all manner of bark, windfalls and chips. He had all the profit of the grass, herbage, feeding and pannage. The Priory was to give him three broad yards and a half yard good measure of woollen cloth for a coat 21 days before the following Easter, and four broad yards and a half good measure of woollen cloth for a gown 21 days before Easter, 1526, or they were to pay him 14s. in lieu of the coat cloth and 20s. in lieu of the gown cloth. Once a year for six days (six days warning being given by the Prior) he was to ride with the Prior when he kept courts, finding himself horse, saddle and bridle. The Priory would find him honest meat, drink and lodging with good and sufficient bate, provin and litter for his horse during these six days. Four times in the year he was to wait on the Prior in the monastery, from Christmas Day to Twelfth Day, three holy days in Easter week, three holy days in Whitsun week and on Trinity Sunday. At these four times he was to have within the monastery honest, good and sufficient meat and drink and to sit at mess, meat and table with the cellerer or rentgatherer and to have assigned to him a chamber and " wooddraught," with honest bedding and all other stuff necessary. The grant of this office was for life, and for a year after the Michaelmas following his death. Talwood mentioned in this grant meant wood in billets for firewood, and bavin was a bundle of brushwood or other light combustible matter for kindling, fencing, draining, etc. For centuries the predecessors of Nicholas Gray had been working in these woods according to the regulations set out, felling timber in the winter months from November to April, preparing timber for building and the smaller wood for fuel, keeping the watercourses clear and the hedges mended. The office was one of considerable importance and it will be noticed that his precedence in the retinue of the Prior is laid down with reference to his place at table with the cellarer and rentgatherer, and that he had a uniform or livery to wear.

Nicholas Gray was the last woodward appointed by the Priory. In 1532 it was dissolved and its possessions vested in the Crown. Soon afterwards King Henry VIII granted " a serteyne ferme called Cane Feildes and the woode called Cane woodes " to the monastery of Waltham Holy Cross in exchange for Copped Hall Park, which he wished to own for " the great consolacon and comforde of his moste royall person."[139] In his accounts for the two years ended Michaelmas, 1535, the Receiver of Rents, William Cavendish, claimed to be allowed £5 off the amount due from

Waltham Abbey

him on account of the "manor of Canefeldes," because it had been taken out of his hands and granted to the Abbot of Waltham.[140] Our next record concerns the farm that lay southward of Ken Wood, which must have covered what is now Parliament Hill Fields. On 10th March, 1535, the Abbot of Waltham leased to John Palmer of "Kentychtown" lands in St. Pancras on the south side of "Cane Wood and Gyllys Hawte, now called Millefeldes or Canewode Feyldes otherwise Myllefeyldes, Huntsfeld, Fernefeld, Gutterfeyld and Knyzhtes Grove," and certain small crofts adjoining, lately in the tenure of Nicholas Gray by lease from the Prior of Christ Church, London, all of which abutted on Hatch Lane and "Canewode Lane" and the lands of John Palmer on the east, and the said "Canewode" and "Gyllys Hawte" on the north and "Hampstead Heyth" on the west, and on land late of "Whetnalles" on the south, for 41 years at £5 a year. The monastery of Waltham Holy Cross was dissolved in its turn in 1540 and Ken Wood again came into the king's hands, John Hyghame, Receiver-General, accounting for £13 for the year ended Michaelmas, 1540, on account of "Canelandes."

The first portion of the estate disposed of by the Crown was the farm land on the south leased to John Palmer. John Taw, esquire, and Edward Taylor, esquire, on 12th July, 1543, signed what would be called now a "contract note" to purchase "Canefeldes" with the woods growing there, "parcell of ye possessions of the late monasterye of Walthame" of the yearly value of £5. Allowing for tithe 10s. the net income was £4 10s., which, rated at 20 years' purchase, amounted to £90 to be paid by them. In the surveyor's note it is stated that the lands were "no parcel of any manor, lordship or farm" and lay within four miles of London or thereabouts.[141] The purchase was concluded by the issue to them of letters patent dated 14th September, 1543. The tithe of 10s. reserved on the land was granted by patent dated 23rd September, 1546, to Thomas Wriothesley, lord Wriothesley. On 8th January, 1546, Messrs. Taw and Taylor took out a licence to alienate this property to the said Thomas Wriothesley, K.G., Lord Wriothesley, Lord Chancellor. Taw and Taylor had many similar grants of monastic lands and appear to have been speculators.

Wriothesley

Turning now to the northern portion, Ken Wood itself, we find that the Monastery of Waltham Holy Cross had leased it to John Slannyng of Hampstead on 20th May, 1536, for 40 years, at £8 a year. Slannyng came from Devonshire, where he owned considerable property near Plymouth. There is no doubt that Slanning acquired the woods as an investment pure and simple, and he found that it was more profitable to sell the timber on the land and employ the cleared site for grazing than to preserve the woods. The diminution of woods was a frequent complaint by writers of that time, and Parliament in 1543 passed an Act intended to compel owners to maintain woods in the public interest. Mr. Slannyng's activities are recorded in a presentment made presumably to Quarter Sessions on 28th March, 1556, by "William Gennings and his fellows of all such offences as do come to their knowledge." They presented "John Slannyng for keeping 140 acres in Hampsteed and also for keeping to pasture another farm called Chawcotts [Chalk Farm] containing 120 acres in the same parish, which land he lets to butchers and innholders of London. For selling and felling woods without leaving 'storyars' according to the statute, John Slannyng of Hampsteed, gentleman, for cutting down 20 acres of wood in a wood called Cayne Wood two years since and for now suffering horses and mares and other cattell as doth appear to destroy the springes of the same wood" and also "for cutting down 14 acres of wood in Wyldes Wood for two years past and putting on his cattle. . . ."[142] Similar presentments of destruction of woods were made about this time at the manor courts of Hornsey and Tottenham. The Act had provided that in woods felled at 24 years' growing or under there should be left standing for every acre of wood felled 12 standils or storers of oak likely to be timber trees or an equal number of elm, ash, asp or beech if no oak trees were growing there. Such trees were not to be felled before they had attained the size of ten inches square within three foot of the ground. Also all trees under the age of 14 years were to be protected from destruction by cattle or beasts. By neglecting to leave standing twelve storers in each of the 20 acres felled in "Cayne Wood" Slannyng had incurred a penalty of 3s. 4d. for each one felled, and a like penalty for every rood left unprotected from cattle.

Whether the statutory penalties were exacted from Slannyng we do not know, but there is an undated plan in the Public Record Office[143] which may have been made at this time. On it is written : "This woode is knowen by the name of Cane woode and conteyneth one hundred fowerer score and tenne acres, all wast and pathes deducted, and is devided into Tenne falls of diuerse groathes with the valew of evearie fall at Tenne yeares groath." The ten falls with

125

their respective acreage, value per acre and total value are set out in a table, which may be summarised as follows : (1) 18 acres, 50s.-£45 ; (2) 18 acres, 50s.-£45 ; (3) 18 acres, 53s. 4d.-£48 ; (4) 18 acres, 53s. 4d.-£48 ; (5) 18 acres, 53s. 4d.-£48 ; (6) 18 acres, 53s. 4d.-£48 ; (7) 18 acres, 53s. 4d.-£48 ; (8) 23 acres, 33s. 4d.-£35 6s. 8d. ; (9) 23 acres, 33s. 4d.-£35 6s. 8d. ; (10) 18 acres, 50s.-£45 ; Total £445 13s. 4d. Then follows : " Note that there was 500 principalls felled at the last fall which by the Statute ought to have been preserved and were worth 16d. a pece . . . £33 6s. 8d." The plan, which measures about 17 inches by 13 inches, consists entirely of straight lines, each of the ten " falls " being marked with its number and the acreage. Outside the northern boundary is written " Hornesey Park," the western boundary " White Burche," the north-eastern " Sherewick," the eastern " Sherewick Lane " and south-eastern " Millfield." These meagre topographical details can be identified on the modern map. " White Burche " is in Hampstead against the parish boundary and it is notable that in a valuation of that manor made in 1312[144] are mentioned " woods called Wytebirche, Brockehole and Tymberhurst in sevralty in which is neither pasture nor pannage." In the survey of Tottenhall, mentioned above (p. 121), Brockhill is marked in the field that contained Parliament Hill, to the south of the land which was opposite " White Burch." We can therefore locate the wood called Brockhole in 1312 as in the neighbourhood of South Hill Gardens, Hampstead, and Wytebirche as north of that between Spaniards Road and Ken Wood. There were thus three woods adjoining, Sherricks Wood to the east (named after an early owner), White Birch Wood to the west (obviously so called from the trees growing in it) and Ken Wood or Cane Wood between them. In Anglo-Norman-French " keynes en le boys " meant " oaks in the wood," in modern French " bois de chênes " is an oak wood, and it does not seem far-fetched to suppose that Cane Wood, the earliest form of the name so far found, simply means " oakwood." * Sherewick Lane was the present Millfield Lane, and Sherewick approximately lay within a triangle formed by lines adjoining Caenwood Towers, Beechwood and Southampton Lodge. Hornesey Park abutted on Ken Wood along the parish boundary from Sherricks to The Spaniards.

John Slannyng died on 28th September, 1558,[145] and left to Dorothy Mallett, a daughter of Michael Mallett, property at Umberleigh in Devon and his lease of " Cane Wood."[146] Dorothy Mallet married John Wood on 22nd August, 1564.[147] The freehold of the property belonged to the Crown until the year 1565 when it was bought by one Robert Hall at 30 years' purchase, namely £240.[148] Hall was a nominee of Sir Nicholas Throckmorton of Congleton, Warwick, whose son Robert Throckmorton, gentleman, of London, sold it in 1588 for £300 to Roger Puleston, gentleman, of Highgate.[149] He was elected a governor of the Grammar School in 1586 and died intestate on 11th May, 1592, leaving a widow, Dionisia. Her first husband had been William Hodges, who was elected a governor of the Grammar School on 16th June, 1581, and died on 9th January, 1582. His daughter, Anne, married William Birchinshaw, gentleman, and apparently she was married a second time, to the Rev. Thomas Westfield, afterwards Bishop of Bristol. William Birchinshaw and Anne had four daughters, Sarah, Margaret, Anne and Susanna, of whom Sarah married Robert Story, citizen and clothworker of London, and dying in the lifetime of her mother, left a daughter, Anne, aged five in 1622. The estate was sold in 1616 to John Bill, the King's Printer. It was conveyed to him by Thomas Westfield, S.T.P., and Anne his wife, Robert Story and Sarah his wife, Margaret, Anne and Susannah Birchinshaw. The property was then described as containing 30 acres of land, 20 acres of meadow, 40 acres of pasture, 350 acres of wood and 20 acres of furze and heath, in St. Pancras, Kentish Town, Hampstead and Hornsey. This was far more than the Ken Wood

---

* Various attempts have been made to explain the origin and meaning of the name—Cane till the 18th century, then Caen or Ken—attached to this estate, but none has met with general acceptance. Dr. Mawer, Hon. Secretary of the Place-Name Society, writes : " We have not got sufficient evidence to come to any positive conclusion as to the right etymology." Mr. E. Williams, the venerable author of *Early Holborn* (1927), whose extensive studies in St. Pancras topography inspire respect, firmly maintains that the stream flowing from the ponds through Kentish Town must have been called the Ken, hence Kentish Town and Ken Wood. Mr. J. G. Muddiman has energetically urged " Caen " Wood, which was also the view of Mr. J. H. Lloyd. Mr. Fred Hitchin Kemp, going farther back, suggests a still more far-fetched derivation, from the British " Iceni." Miss Jeffries Davis has tentatively put forward " Canons' " Wood as the origin, but is now inclined to agree with Mr. John Neville Keynes, who proposed the derivation mentioned in the text.

estate and it undoubtedly included a leasehold interest in part of the Great Park in Hornsey from the Bishop of London.[150]

It will be observed that in the conveyances up to this date no mention is made of a house. We may therefore conclude that the first house there was built by Mr. Bill. The following information concerning him is taken from an excellent account communicated by Colonel Prideaux to *Notes and Queries* in 1897. John Bill was a man of some mark in his day. From a comparatively humble position he was enabled, by his industry and ability, to attain the highest rank in his calling, and to take a place amongst the gentry of Middlesex, while his son and successor not only made his mark in the political world, but became allied with one of the most distinguished families among the aristocracy of England. He was born in 1576 the son of Walter Bill of Spittle Street, Much Wenlock, Salop, husbandman, and came to London at 15 years of age being then apprenticed to John Norton, citizen and stationer of London, for the term of eight years. At the expiration of his apprenticeship, in 1601, he was admitted a freeman of the Company of Stationers. The date of his first registered publication was in 1604 and some years afterwards, in conjunction with Bonham Norton, he purchased the office of King's Printer from the Barker family. His printing office seems originally to have been situated in St. Paul's Churchyard and was afterwards removed to Blackfriars, on the site of the present Printing House Square. His first wife was Anne, daughter of Thomas Mountford, D.D., vicar of St. Martin's-in-the-Fields, who was famous for her skill in music. She died on 3rd May, 1621, aged 33. His second wife was Jane, daughter of Henry Franklin, who survived him. He died on 13th May, 1630, leaving an annuity of £300 to his wife.[151] To Robert Graves and Grace his wife, he left 40s. for their care at "Canewood." His eldest son, John Bill, who was born on 30th May, 1614, succeeded him in the business and in the ownership of Ken Wood. In the October following his death, Mrs. Jane Bill had become the wife of Sir Thomas Bludder.

When John Bill the second was 28 years of age the Civil War began and he joined the royal army. Four years later he addressed a petition dated 18th April, 1646, to the Committee for Compounding with Delinquents as follows: "That your petitioner was master of a regiment of horse under the command of the Lord Hopton, in which service he acted until about the month of March last upon the Treaty of Truro with his Excellency Sir Thomas Fairfax he deserted his employment promising never to bear arms against the Parliament. That he is heartily sorrowful for his errors and humbly submits to the mercy of Parliament and prayeth he may be admitted to a favourable composition for the discharge of the sequestration of his estate."

The annual value of his St. Pancras property before the Civil War was stated to be £79 9s. 6d., consisting of certain lands and woodlands called "Cainewood." In Hornsey he had a lease or rather sub-lease of part of the Great Park, worth £30 a year, out of which he paid John Oldbury a ground rent of £19 6s. 6d. He held jointly with Mr. Roger Norton the King's Printing House at Blackfriars, part being occupied as a dwelling house by Sir Samuel Luke and part by the printing works. His half share of the office of King's Printer was said to be worth £600 per annum "before these troubles." There were two printing presses with type formerly sent to York by the King's command and afterwards to Exeter, where they fell into the hands of the Parliamentarians and were sold to Mr. Egelesfeild of London, bookseller. His debt amounted to £2,000.[152] Despite the heavy fine he had to pay for his "delinquency" he took part in another effort on behalf of the royal cause, and his estate was again sequestered, on 16th October, 1648. After having been for some time imprisoned in Peter House, Aldersgate Street, he was removed in November, 1648, to the Counter, in Southwark.[153] On 17th April, 1649, John Bill again petitioned the Parliamentary Commissioners, stating that "since his former composition with the Honourable Committee he hath been unhappily engaged in the late Insurrection in Surrey with the late Earl of Holland against the Parliament." "Cainewood" was now worth only £49 a year to him because he had been obliged to lease it for 40 years towards raising the money to pay his fine. This time he was ordered to pay £1,500. From another petition received from him on 27th September, 1651, when he is described as of Reigate, Surrey, he appears to have claimed £1,500 as owing to him by Sir Walter Roberts, baronet, and suggested that the Commissioners for Kent should levy the money out of the rents of Sir Walter and hand over the surplus to him for subsistence. Roberts denied all knowledge of the debt. A reminder that in John Bill's time his land abutted north on the road following the boundary between St. Pancras and Hornsey Park appears in a presentment made by the jury of the Hornsey Court Leet in 1653 : " Mr. Bill and Mr. Siddon for setting up gates for passage into the way that leadeth from Hamsteed Heath to Highgate through Holliocke Hill Wood are amerced for each gate ten shillings apiece." Mr. Siddon was the tenant of Sherricks Farm at that time.[22]

On the authority of some modern transcripts (now in St. Pancras Public Library) of papers said to have belonged to the Vane family, it has been stated that Sir James Harington sold Ken Wood to John Bill at the Restoration. In 1658, it is said, Sir Harry Vane (who lived at Hampstead) wrote to John Bill : " The estate at Ken Wood appeared to him to require handling well, the home domain being peculiarly good, and capable of much improvement but he felt that the price asked too great by £100 . . . as that little castle of ruinous brick and stone could only be used for material to build another house, near thirty acres in waste, as ponds and the moate, a deal of great trees to be cut down and many serious expenses he had not yet considered." In June 1660 Mr. Bill purchased the estate of Sir James Harington. It then consisted of 280 acres of land well covered with large timber, and is set out as a capital messuage of brick, wood and plaster, eight cottages, a farm-house and windmill, fishponds, etc. Mr. Bill states he had formed a place that he could live in with comfort and surrounded 25 acres with a brick wall. All this is entirely lacking in any evidence to show how far it is authentic and there must be something wrong with the story in face of the known facts. Ken Wood belonged to John Bill by bequest from his father, and there is no evidence that he ever sold it to Sir James or anybody else. He owned it as we have seen in 1645 and still owned the reversion in 1649. The statement, therefore, that Sir James sold it to him requires corroboration. Turning to Sir James Harington we find that he had children baptised at Highgate in 1640 and 1642, implying residence there then. In 1643 Sir Edmund Wright, of Swakeleys, his father-in-law, died, leaving that house to his daughter, Harington's wife. In 1647, 1653 and 1654, children of Sir James were buried at Swakeleys ; his father also was buried there in 1652. It is evident, then, that Sir James Harington went to live at Swakeleys in 1643 or soon after.[87] In 1653 it was Mr. Bill who was fined ten shillings for making a gate from Ken Wood and not Harington.

Sir John Finch, writing to Lord Conway on 11th January, 1661, stated that on Sunday, 50 Fifth Monarchy men went to Mr. Johnson, a bookseller, near St. Paul's, and demanded the church keys. Being refused they broke open the door and setting sentries demanded of passengers whom they were for ; one answered for King Charles, on which they replied they were for King Jesus, and shot him through the heart ; they put to flight some musketeers sent to reduce them and the Lord Mayor came in person with his troop, whereupon they retreated to Highgate ; on Wednesday morning they returned to the city with mad courage, fell on the guard, and beat the Life Guard and a whole regiment in half an hour, refusing all quarter. Venner their Captain was taken with nine more, and 20 slain ; six got into a house, and refusing all quarter, were slain.[154] Other accounts show that it was at " Cane Wood " these fanatics bivouacked.

In the Hearth Tax assessments John Bill's house was rated at 24 hearths in 1665 and 20 in 1674, showing that his house was nearly as large as Dorchester House. He married Diana, daughter of Mildmay Fane, 2nd Earl of Westmorland, and widow of Edward Pelham of Brocklesby, Lincs, esquire. In 1661, Diana, their daughter, was baptised at " Caen Wood." John Bill was buried at Hampstead on 4th October, 1680. It is evident from his will[155] that he was in a good financial position at his death, 32 years after his second " delinquency " in fighting for King Charles. A hint of family disagreement is seen in the half-crown he left to his " unkind brother," Henry Bill, but he left Henry's two sons, John and Henry, £50 and £20 respectively. His daughter, Diana (mentioned above), who had become the wife of Captain Darcy Savage, got £2,000. His son, Charles, was to have his printing business and everything at " Caine Wood " after his mother's death. On 25th April, 1681, Charles, then about 19 years old, had licence to marry Elizabeth, daughter of Robert Hampson, serjeant at law.[156]

In 1685 Lady Diana Bill for £6,000 surrendered to her son, Charles Bill " of St. Giles-in-the-Fields," esquire, her rights in " Canewood," viz. a " capital messuage at Canewood, and a farm house called Little Canewood and the woods called Canewood and Gills Haute, late in the occupation of John Bill and William Nicholls, containing 155 acres."[157] In 1658 William Nicolls of " Cane Wood " was presented at the Hornsey Court Leet for pasturing sheep upon the common in that manor and amerced ten shillings.[22] In 1685 again Brook Bridges, esquire, and Samuel Bridges, suffered a " recovery " of two messuages, 108 acres of land, 100 acres of meadow, 100 acres of pasture and 60 acres of wood, in St. Pancras, Hornsey and Hampstead, Diana Bill, widow, Charles Bill and Elizabeth his wife, warranting the title."[158] This included Ken Wood, and indicates, possibly, a mortgage by Charles Bill to Bridges. In 1690, after his mother's death, Charles Bill of St. Giles-in-the-Fields, esq., son and heir of John Bill, late of "Canewood," esquire, deceased, by the Right Hon. the Lady Diana his wife, deceased, and Elizabeth Bill now the wife of Charles Bill, conveyed to Brook Bridges of St. Andrew's, Holborn, esquire, for £3,400, the capital messuage at Ken Wood with the gardens, containing 4 acres 3 roods, the farm-house called "Little Canewood" with Barnefeild containing 2 acres 2 roods, Barnefeild South, 3 acres, Long Cherry Ground 1 acre 1 rood, an arable close of 5 acres, Eight Acre close 8 acres 2 roods, Eighteen Acre close, 20 acres, Gills Hart 5 acres 1 rood, Gills Hart 6 acres, Cane Wood Pasture 10 acres 1 rood, Small Gains 3 acres, Fourteen Acre Field 12 acres, Great Broomfeild 7 acres 3 roods, Broomfeild 5 acres, Five Acre Mead 8 acres 1 rood, Little Cherry Ground 1 acre, Great Cherry Ground 3 acres 3 roods, Cane Wood 61 acres, part of which was lately grubbed up. In all 169 acres 3 roods.[159] The equity of redemption was mentioned.

Lord Berkeley of Stratton

Apparently Brook Bridges was a relative of "William Bridges of Canewood," the next owner, son of Robert Bridges and Mary (Woodcock) his wife. William Bridges was elected a governor of the Grammar School on 21st May, 1694. He was Surveyor-General of the Ordnance at the Tower of London, and M.P. for Liskeard. He died on 23rd October, 1714. In 1705[160] William Bridges sold Ken Wood to John Walter of London, merchant, and in 1711 John Walter for £3,600 sold to William, 4th Lord Berkeley of Stratton in Cornwall, "Cane Wood House" with four ponds containing two acres, land adjoining the kitchen garden containing two acres, and woodland containing 22 acres, and £5 rent, part of £15 rent receivable from the owners of the Waterworks on the Ponds under their lease.[161]

Writing on 29th July, 1712, to Thomas Wentworth, Earl of Strafford, Lord Berkeley said : " You cannot imagine how I enjoy myself at Cane Wood, after this hurry, and how quiet and pleasant it is." A few days later he wrote to the same correspondent (12th August) : " Your Lordship will wonder to hear I have sold Cane Wood. A Lord Blantyre of Scotland offer'd me 4000 pounds for it, which I thought worth hearkening to, considering the little time I stay out of town, and that a place of half that sum might serve me. I wish I may get a house in your neighbourhood of Twitnam, for I was always fond of that part of the country. I am still at Cane Wood, but would be glad to remove since it is none of my own. It seems 'tis the D. of Argyle hath bought it under another name, and I am desir'd to stay till the goods are valued, part of which he desires to buy. . . ."[162] Anne, daughter of the said Duke of Argyll, married William, the son of Lord Strafford. Berkeley conveyed the estate to Walter, Lord Blantyre, on 2nd August.[163] Three days later Lord Blantyre conveyed it to John Campbell, 2nd Duke of Argyll.[164] Three years later the Duke conveyed it to his brother, Archibald Campbell, Earl of Ilay, P.C., and his brother-in-law, James Stuart, 2nd Earl of Bute, who had married their sister, Anne.[165] Five years later, on 13th May, 1720, they sold it to William Dale of St. Paul's, Covent Garden, esquire, for £3,150. Writing about this time, Daniel Defoe, under the name of Macky, says, " Adjoining to this village [Hampstead] the Duke of Argyle has a fine seat called Caen Wood. . . . It now belongs to one Dale, an upholsterer, who bought it out of the Bubbles."[166] On 7th April, 1720, the famous South Sea Act was passed for redeeming the National Debt, and the Directors of the South Sea Company by various means raised the original £100 shares to the price of £1,050. By 29th September it had sunk to £150 and thousands of families were reduced to beggary. William Dale was one of the victims. On 15th October, 1720, he mortgaged Ken Wood House for £1,575 to Archibald, Earl of Ilay. His daughter, Dorothy, who is said to have lost £20,000 in the South Sea Bubble, married William Forbes, 13th Baron Forbes, during this year, and he lent his father-in-law another £1,000 on the property. Neither principal nor interest was paid by Dale. In February, 1721, the Earl of Ilay filed a bill in Chancery stating that Dale, who owed him £1,575, gave him a bond dated 27th May, 1720, and afterwards mortgaged the estate as better security.[167] He said that Dale had suffered the house to run to ruin, had felled a great quantity of timber, committed great waste and threatened to commit more. Dale said that he was ready to pay off the mortgage as soon as he was able to raise the money and that the premises were worth double the amount owing to the plaintiff. He denied committing waste and prayed for a reasonable time to redeem the mortgage. On 29th October, 1724, judgment to foreclose was given against Dale, and on 4th February, 1725, against Lord Forbes on his second mortgage. Lord Ilay

Stuart, Lord Bute

I

got back the estate, but it was certainly worth much more than the £2,575 advanced by him and Lord Forbes, with interest added.

After the disappearance of the unfortunate Dale the house appears to have been occupied by a George Middleton. In 1746 Archibald, 3rd Duke of Argyll, conveyed his interest to his nephew, John Stuart, 3rd Earl of Bute, son of Anne, the Duke's sister.[168] This Earl of Bute is known to fame as the most unpopular Prime Minister England has ever known and, more creditably, as the son-in-law of the celebrated Lady Mary Wortley Montagu. He was born in 1713 and married Mary, only daughter of Edward Wortley Montagu, esquire, of Wortley, Yorks, and Mary his wife, daughter of Evelyn Pierrepont, esquire, afterwards Duke of Kingston. Lord Bute was a minister of the Crown from 1737 until he resigned in 1763. Lady Bute's mother, who was living in Italy, writing on 20th August, 1749, to the Countess of Oxford said : " My daughter writes me word she has fitted up that house near Hampstead, which I once had the honour to see with your ladyship ; I hope it is a proof she is in no want of money." Writing two days later to her daughter she said : " I very well remember Caenwood House, and cannot wish you a more agreeable place. It would be a great pleasure to me to see my grandchildren run about in the gardens. I do not question Lord Bute's good taste in the improvements round it, or yours in the choice of the furniture." In the following November she remarks : " I believe you have some leisure hours at Caenwood, where anything new is welcome," and writing on 16th February, 1752 : " I hope it will find you at Caenwood ; your solitude there will permit you to peruse, and even to forgive all the impertinence of your most affectionate mother."[169]

On 8th August, 1754, Lord Bute conveyed the estate to William Murray, esquire, H.M. Attorney-General, for £4,000. The rest of the 170 acres formerly owned successively by Bill, and Bridges, was sold by Walter in 1715 to William Cox of Bouldham, Kent, gentleman, and now forms a considerable part of Parliament Hill Fields as well as of Ken Wood. In the tenure of Mrs. Carter, formerly of John Walter and afterwards of John Carter, was a messuage and two acres and a pond containing one rood. In the tenure of Richard Watts and the Company for the Waterworks and John Cox of Stanstead, Kent, gentleman, a messuage, barn, two stables, yards, gardens, etc., and Barnfield, 4 acres 2 roods, Brickfield 2 acres 2 roods, Arable closes 2 acres, Eight Acre close 8 acres, Eighteen Acre close 18 acres, Great Gills Heart and Little Gills Heart 11 acres, and two ponds in Eighteen Acre close containing two acres. In the tenure of John Cox, formerly in the tenure of William Bilson, late of Edward Fletcher, was " Cane Wood Pasture " containing 18 acres. Finally, in the tenure of John Cox, formerly in the tenure of Jeffery Gibbons, late of Edward Fletcher and —— Ambridge, Wallfield 6 acres, Little Broomfield 7 acres, Great Broomfield 14 acres, Small Gains 4 acres, Little Woodfield 5 acres, Peafield 10 acres, and Great Woodfield 14½ acres. All this was subsequently acquired by William Murray, who became Baron Mansfield and Lord Chief Justice of England on 8th November, 1756. He became Earl of Mansfield in 1776. His first purchase from the Cox estates was in September, 1757, when he acquired from John Cox of Fairseat, Stanstead, Kent, esquire, only son and heir of John Cox late of Fairseat, 1 acre 1 rood 15 perches of land adjoining " Cane Wood " House on the west and on the east a road from Hampstead Lane to " Cane Wood " Farm House.[170]

Lord Mansfield was a younger son of David Murray, 5th Viscount Stormont and 3rd Lord Balvaird by Margery his wife, only daughter of David Scott of Scottarvet, Fifeshire, and was born at Scone on 2nd March, 1705. He was educated at Westminster School and became a barrister in 1730. As the youngest son of an impecunious Scottish nobleman his advancement in life must have depended on his own exertions and abilities, but a Westminster schoolboy who spent his holiday in the house of the married daughter of Robert Harley, Earl of Oxford, and was befriended by Bishop Atterbury, can hardly have lacked influential friends. He possessed a pleasant voice, and practised elocution under Alexander Pope, and was called " the silver-tongued Murray." In 1745 it became his duty as Solicitor-General to act as counsel for the government against his cousin, Lord Lovat, who was implicated in the rising in favour of the Young Pretender. Lord Lovat himself at the trial characterised Mr. Murray as an honour to his country and said he had heard him with pleasure, though he was against him. There is no doubt that he was a brilliant and accomplished advocate, and after he became Lord Chief Justice exhibited on the Bench great independence and strong common sense, delivering many judgments advantageous to the cause of freedom and religious toleration. A decision in favour of the right of a Catholic priest to say mass led the mob in the 1780

THE EARLS OF MANSFIELD

Gordon Riots to burn his house in Bloomsbury Square, destroying his valuable law library. Some critics have accused him of being grasping in money matters, yet he refused any pecuniary compensation from public funds for this loss. When the mob went to Ken Wood with the intention of burning down that house also, they were headed off by the expedient of supplying them with all the intoxicants they liked to take at The Spaniards. By the time a party of soldiers arrived they were in no condition to resist. Lord Mansfield married in 1738, Elizabeth, daughter of Daniel, Earl of Winchelsea and Nottingham, but died without issue on 20th March, 1793, in his 89th year.

The first Lord Mansfield was succeeded by his nephew, David, 7th Viscount Stormont, son of David, 6th Viscount Stormont, brother of the 1st Earl. David, 2nd Earl of Mansfield, was born 9th October, 1727. He married as his second wife in 1776, Louisa, 3rd daughter of Charles, 9th Lord Cathcart, by whom he had three sons and a daughter. He died on 1st September, 1796, and was succeeded by his son, William, as 3rd Earl of Mansfield.

Tracing the ownership of Ken Wood we are in contact with the main current of English history from the days of Henry III to Victoria. In William de Blemond we have a characteristic member of the military aristocracy ruling the city of London in early days. Retiring from the world and becoming a canon of the monastery of Holy Trinity, Aldgate, he reminds us of those religious institutions that occupied such a great place in the nation's life until they were swept away by the outburst we call the Renaissance and Reformation. For centuries the essentials of life appeared to change but little, and Ken Wood in monastic ownership reflected that static life. Then it suddenly came into lay hands. The old order of things implied in the woodwardship of Nicholas Gray disappeared, the estate was split up and its new owners proceeded to commercialise it according to the new spirit of the age. In the indictment of Slannyng for felling and grubbing up the wood we see an incident in the initial stages of the struggle then commencing between the interests of enterprising financiers and the welfare of the community. During its ownership by three successive King's Printers, its story is interwoven with that of the Civil War, first in the downfall of John Bill, the second, with the royalty he fought for, and secondly in his triumphant reinstatement with the restored king. The Bridges family following represented the quasi-aristocratic class of place-men then growing rich and providing one of the strongest bulwarks of the Hanoverian régime with which their welfare was identified. The Duke of Argyll was a foremost general under the triumphant Marlborough, and in the interlude of Dale we are brought into touch with the famous South Sea Bubble. Lord Bute, again, filled a prominent place in the struggle of royalty to rule and the efforts of the middle classes to acquire political power. Even with the replacement of Bute by Lord Mansfield we see the emergence of one who is said to have laid the foundation of that commercial law and civil freedom required by developing wealth and commerce. Finally the supersession of Lord Mansfield as a representative of the land-holding class by the London County Council on behalf of the people of London, may be regarded as significant of the times. The people now own this beautiful corner of England and may study its history as a mirror of the nation's life through the ages.

Its acquisition may be regarded as the consummation of the efforts which have been made over a long series of years to preserve the northern heights of London as open spaces. It is just over a century since the first agitation for the preservation of Hampstead Heath commenced, culminating in the Hampstead Heath Act of 1871, some 40 years after public feeling had been first aroused by the threatened conversion of this famous pleasure resort into a building estate. By this Act about 240 acres of land were secured at a cost of £45,000. In 1889 a further 267 acres of Parliament Hill Fields were purchased, at a cost of £302,000, of which more than half was contributed by the Metropolitan Board of Works. In 1897 came the purchase of Golders Hill Park of 37 acres for £38,500, the whole of the money being raised by private subscription, and a few years later Wylde's Farm of 80 acres was added to the Heath at a cost of £36,000.

In 1914 it became known that Lord Mansfield was negotiating for the sale of Ken Wood to a building syndicate. Steps were taken to form a purchasing committee, but the war put a stop to further proceedings at that time.

From 1916 onwards, however, the efforts were continued at intervals which eventually resulted in the purchase of 121 acres and in the protection by stringent restrictive covenants of a further nine acres. The 121 acres included the whole of the tract of woodland known as Ken Wood and the adjacent lakes, and on the 27th May, 1924, the London County Council agreed to take over as a public open space the portions of the estate offered to it by the purchasing committee, which was

KEN WOOD

Guinness, Earl of Iveagh

known as the Kenwood Preservation Council, while on the 18th July, 1925, the newly acquired area was opened to the public by His late Majesty King George V, accompanied by Her Majesty Queen Mary.

But a further act of generosity was to follow when the house itself and 89 acres of the surrounding woodlands were purchased by Edward Cecil Guinness, 1st Earl of Iveagh, at a cost of £189,000, who bequeathed the whole estate to the nation at his death or at the expiration of ten years. He died (within a short while of making the purchase) in October, 1927, and on 16th July, 1928, the house, slightly altered to its new purpose, was opened to the public. It contains a magnificent collection of pictures, principally of the Flemish, Dutch and English Schools, with furniture and other objects of art. The 89 acres of meadow and woodland were added to the area already administered by the London County Council.

NOTES AND REFERENCES TO RECORDS

All the land in Highgate dealt with in this volume (with the exception of Ken Wood and Fitzroy Farm) was formerly held of the prebendal Manor of Cantlowes or Kentish Town by copy of court roll, consequently the court rolls of the manor are the source from which our knowledge of owners and occupiers is derived. There are a good many rolls in the Public Record Office dating from 1480 to 1595, but the series is incomplete. The remainder of the rolls are in the hands of the Ecclesiastical Commissioners, beginning in 1609. From 1656 to date they are almost complete. Detailed references to entries are, from the nature of the record, unnecessary, and would, indeed, be hardly practicable. After land had become freehold by "enfranchisement" changes of ownership can usually be found in the Land Registry.

Another source of information is a transcript, in the possession of W. McB. Marcham, of a MS. formerly belonging to the late Col. Robert Edmund Chester Waters. This contains extracts from the Registers of Highgate Chapel and Hampstead Chapel (many by "Adams," who was the well-known G. E. Cokayne) and also a complete list of the governors of Sir Roger Cholmeley's Free School at Highgate—referred to as the Grammar School—with many biographical details, dates of death and monumental inscriptions. There are also two important collections of materials relating to local history, namely that of the late George Potter which is now in the British Museum and the Heal Collection in the St. Pancras Public Library, Chester Road.

Biographical material as to the aldermen of the city of London is derived from the authoritative record published by the Corporation in 1908 (vol. 1) and 1913 (vol. 2), edited by the Rev. A. B. Beaven, and general information as to well-known historical persons is taken from the *Dictionary of National Biography*, the *Complete English Peerage*, Burke's *Peerage*, etc. Where no specific authority is quoted the facts will usually be found in these standard works of reference.

§ 1.

1. Note Book of the steward of the Manor of Cantlowes. Rawlinson MSS. B 368, fo. 13. Edward Stafford, esquire, owning 15 acres of land, appears to have been the Edward Stafford, ambassador to France, who wrote a letter from Highgate, dated 2nd November, 1582, to Lord Burleigh (printed in the *Hist. MSS. Com. Cal. of the Cecil papers at Hatfield*). His father was Sir Edward Stafford of Grafton, Staffs. He was born in 1552. In October, 1583, he was knighted. He married Roberta, daughter of one Chapman, and the record cited suggests that she brought this land to him.

2. Monumental inscription in Christ Church, Newgate Street, recorded in Strype's *Stow* (1720).

3. Will of John Povey. P.C.C. 92 Kidd.

4. P.R.O., S.P.Dom., James I, vol. 62, no. 27.

5. Public Record Office, S.P.Dom., James I, vol. 62, nos. 30 and 39.

6. P.R.O., E. 351/2800.

7. Will of Sir Henry Hobart. P.C.C. 56 Hele.

8. *Registers of All Hallows Honey Lane*. Harl. Soc., vols. 44 and 45 (1914-5).

9. P.R.O., S.P.Dom., Interr. vols. A 46, pp. 38, 67 ; A 21, p. 276 ; A 123, pp. 51-3, 55-6, 59-63.   10.   *Ibid.*, vols. A 17, pp. 10, 44, 47, 61, 88 ; A 11, p. 169.

11. *Journals of the House of Lords* (printed). The Judgment of the Court, 20th November, 1660, was that the Plaintiffs be reinstated (Ireton's lease having expired) and Ireton was left to seek in the ordinary courts any remedy he might claim.

12. *A Historical Catalogue of the Pictures, Herse-cloths, and Tapestry at Merchant Taylors Hall*, by Frederick J. Fry, Master of the Company for 1895-6 (1907).

13. Will of Sir William Prichard. P.C.C. 155 Gee. His three houses were situate at Little Minories, Highgate, and Great Linford, Bucks.

14. Will of Edward Pauncefort. P.C.C. 151 Plymouth.

15. *Charity Commission Reports*, vol. 18, p. 393.   16.   *Ibid.*, vol. 32, Pt. vi, p. 823.

17. Brit. Mus. Cole's MSS., vol. xxxv, p. 159.

18. Land Registry, Middlesex Memorials, 1756/2/531.

19. *The History and Antiquities of the County of Buckingham*, George Lipscomb, M.D. (1847). A side-light on the occupation of the house is thrown by the evangelist John Wesley, who notes in his Journal, under date Friday, November 29th, 1782, " I preached at Highgate in the palace built in the last century by that wretched Duke of Lauderdale, now one of the most elegant boarding houses in England."

20. *Episodes of my Second Life*, A. Gallenga (1884).

21. Wills of George Pryor and Dorothy Prior, P.C.C. 69 and 102 Dycer.

22. *Court Rolls of the Bishop of London's Manor of Hornsey*, W. McB. and F. Marcham (1929).

23. *The Register of Admissions to Grays Inn*, Joseph Foster (1889) and Cansick's *Epitaphs*.

24. Will of Mary Charnells. P.C.C. 177 Wake.

25. *A Collection of Curious and Interesting Epitaphs*, 3 vols. Frederick Teague Cansick (1869, 1872, 1875).

26. See also Burke's *Landed Gentry*. Will of Sir Nathaniel Herne. P.C.C. 107 King.

27. Will of Paul Sinderye. P.C.C. 27 Penn.

§ 2.

28. P.R.O., C7/427/137.

29. *Visitation of London*, 1633-4. Harl. Soc., vol. 15 (1880).

30. Deed of Ann Gower, 12th April, 1687 on Court Roll for 1687.

31. Abstract of the Court Rolls of Stoke Newington and Digest of the same in Stoke Newington Public Library (W. McB. Marcham).

32. Land Registry, Midd. Mem., 1733/2/68.

33. Will of Robert Harrison. P.C.C. 256 Anstis.

34. Land Reg. Midd. Mem., 1764/3/153 ; also 1756/2/377 and 1757/2/589.

35. *Ibid.*, 1774/1/131.   36. *Ibid.*, 1861/11/900.

§ 3.

37. P.R.O., C 142/216/65.   38. P.R.O., C 6/149/58.

39. P.R.O., C 33/210, p. 947.

40. Pedigree of Gould. *Notes and Queries* 6th Series, Vol. ix, p. 293.

41. Will of Peter Heywood. P.C.C. 378 Tebbs.

§ 4.

42. Rate Books of St. Pancras in St. Pancras Public Library, Chester Road, and the Land Tax Assessments.

43. *Nonconformity in Highgate*, Josiah Viney (1858).

44. Land Reg. Midd. Mem., 1811/5/684.

§ 5.

45. Will of Mary Welbe. P.C.C. 51 Pett.

46. Will of William Brown. P.C.C. 65/66 Fox.

47. *Novum Repertorium Ecclesiasticum Parochialis Londinense*, Rev. George Hennessy (1897).

48. *Calamy Revised*, Oxford University Press (1934).

49. *Alumni Cantabrigienses*, vol. 3. Venn. (1927).

50. Will of John Wynne. P.C.C. 228 Auber.

51. Will of Mark Wynne. P.C.C. 106 Pett.

52. Will of Peter Storer. P.C.C. 25 Busby.

53. Will of Peter Storer. P.C.C. 282 Arran.

54. Will of Sir John Hawkins. P.C.C. 259 Macham. The tenancy of David Duveluz ended in 1779. Robert Johnson was occupier in the following year.

REFERENCES

55. *Dictionary of National Biography.*

56. *The History, Topography and Antiquities of Highgate in the county of Middlesex,* by John H. Lloyd, Honorary Secretary of the Highgate Literary and Scientific Institution (1888). Printed by subscription on behalf of the Library Fund in celebration of the Jubilee of the Institution. This well-written work, though free from the cramping pedantry that sometimes tends to make such publications a bald *précis* of records, is not always reliable as to facts, and contains statements which research has shown to be unfounded. Two outstanding errors are the statement adopted from Prickett that Arundel House stood on the east side of the High Street in Hornsey, and the assumption that Sir William Bond's house was Arundel House—which lead to some confusion as to the place and time of certain events. His errors regarding Cromwell House were rectified in the London Survey Committee's monograph on the house. Lloyd's work contains much of interest concerning local inhabitants at the end of the last century.

§ 6.

57. The will of John Gilpin was proved 10th May, 1591. P.C.C. 31 Sainberbe.

58. Will of John Wetherley. P.C.C. 132 St. John.

59. Will of Roger Coise. P.C.C. 12 Bacon. He died 30th January, 1579 (P.R.O., C 142/186/31).

60. Will of Thomasine Coyce. P.C.C. 7 Dixy.

61. Will of Dr. Elisha Coish. P.C.C. 2 Lloyd. *Merchant Taylors' School Register.* E. P. Hart, 1936.

62. Will of Hester Harrison. P.C.C. 117 Mico.

§ 7.

63. *Hist. MSS. Com. Cal. of the Cecil papers at Hatfield.*

64. P.R.O., Req. 2/144/77 and Req. 2/26/76.

65. P.R.O., C 11/2163/62.

66. P.R.O., C 11/2236/69.

67. P.R.O., C 33/358 fo. 23.

68. P.R.O., C 11/378/147 ; C 11/2290/116.

§ 8.

69. P.R.O., C 2 Eliz. /S26/46.

70. *Hist. MSS. Com. Cal. of the MSS. of the Marquis of Salisbury* (1905).

71. *Progresses of Queen Elizabeth,* Nichols (1823).

72. *The Annals of St. Helen's Bishopsgate,* Rev. J. E. Cox (1876).

73. P.R.O., S.P.Dom., Jas. I., vol. 92, no. 70.

74. Brit. Mus. Harl. MSS. 1551. Harl. Soc., vol. 65 (1914).

75. P.R.O., C 7/555/65.

76. Register of Highgate Chapel.

77. *History of Hertfordshire,* John Edwin Cussans (1881).

78. *Merlinus Anonymus.* Brit. Mus. E 1488.

79. Will of John Bill. P.C.C. 124 Bath.

§ 9.

80. P.R.O., C 66/3375/9.

81. *Marriages in Grays Inn Chapel,* Joseph Foster (1883).

§ 10.

82. Will of Andrew Campion. P.C.C. 22 Reeve.

83. This is supported by the description given when Henry Isherwood was " admitted " of a strip of land heretofore part of a road leading to Sandpit Field, adjoining to the garden of Thomas Bromwich and lately laid thereto and enclosed within a brick wall.

§ 11.

84. Will of John Shorte. P.C.C. 150 Mico.
85. Manuscript plan of the estate of Thomas Bromwich, esquire, finished in 1776, *penes* F. Marcham.
86. Land Reg. Midd. Mem., 1733/2/49.

§ 12.

87. *Swakeleys, Ickenham*, Walter Godfrey, F.S.A. (1933). London Survey Committee.
88. *A General History of the Kemp and Kempe Families*, Fred. Hitchin Kempe (1902).
89. Will of Robert Osbaldeston. P.C.C. 54 Fox.
90. *London Marriage Licences*, Joseph Foster. Will of Dame Child, P.C.C. 6 Spurway.
91. Land Reg. Midd. Mem., 1821/6/706.   92. *Ibid.*, 1727/3/134.
93. Admon. of William Bridges, 19th March, 1741-2. P.C.C.
94. Land Reg. Midd. Mem., 1810/6/651.
95. *Memoirs of Miss Mellon*, Mrs. Cornwell Barron-Wilson (1887).
96. Will of John Hillman. P.C.C. 653 Bearde.

§ 13.

97. P.R.O., C 54/4962 (6).
98. *Middlesex County Records* I, p. 50.
99. Land Reg. Midd. Mem., 1733/2/326.   100. *Ibid.*, 1890/2/326.
101. Will of Henry Woodfall. P.C.C. 109 Bogg.

§ 14.

102. The Warner family belonged to the parish of All Hallows, Lombard Street. Their wills were proved in the P.C.C. as follows. John Warner, alderman of London, 1511 (38 Bennett). He left 100 marks towards making part of the aisle and steeple. Robert Warner, his son, 1555 (29 More). Mark Warner, son of Robert, 1583 (28 Butts).
103. *Baronetage*, G.E.C.
104. *Middlesex County Records*, vol. III, p. 291.
105. Vestry Minutes of St. Clement's Danes, and St. Giles-in-the-Fields, quoted by Lloyd.
106. Land Reg. Midd. Mem., 1866/9/624.
107. *Middle Temple Records*, Charles Henry Hopwood, K.C. (1905).
108. *The Roll of the Royal College of Physicians*, William Munk, M.D. (1878).
109. Will of Catherine Nicoll. P.C.C. 261 Eedes.

§ 16.

110. P.R.O., S.C. 6/1140/m19, and S.C. 6/1139/m11.
111. P.R.O., Star Chamber Proceedings, Henry VII, no. 51.
112. *Middlesex County Records*, vol. III, p. 281. Will of Elizabeth Symonds, proved 14th March, 1700-1 (P.C.C. 43 Dyer).

§ 17.

113. Land Reg. Midd. Mem., 1728/1/396.

§ 20.

114. *Ibid.*, 1750/1/496.
115. Will of Charles Lacey. P.C.C. 233 Potter.
116. Will of William Carpenter. P.C.C. 125 Rockingham.
117. Land Reg. Midd. Mem., 1803/5/505; 1804/6/32.

§ 21.

118a. Muniments of Lord Southampton.
118b. Brit. Mus. Add. MS. 14252, fo. 127d.
118c. P.R.O., E 40/A 8778.   119. *Ibid.*, A 2233.   120. *Ibid.*, A 2231.
121. *Ibid.*, A 2243.   122. *Ibid.*, A 2238, A 2244.

REFERENCES

123. P.R.O., C53/18 m34.   124. P.R.O., K.B. 26/101. m8d.
125. P.R.O., E 40/A 2230.   126. *Ibid.*, A 2234.   128. *Ibid.*, A 2237.
127. P.R.O., C.P., 25, H.III./121.   129 P.R.O., E 40/A2092.
130. *Lond. Topog. Record* XVII.
131. P.R.O., K.B. 27/29.m.3.
132. *Book of Fees (Testa de Nevill)*, 1923 ed. pp. 897, 899.
133. P.R.O., C.P. 40/70/m. 19.   134. *Taxatio Ecclesiastica.* (1802).
135. P.R.O., E 40/A 2235.   136. P.R.O., C 66/185. m 27.
137. P.R.O.., C 143/235/13.   138. P.R.O., E 303/London 3.
139. Brit. Mus. Harl. MSS. 3739, ff. 427-9, *Statutes of the Realm* 3.529.
140. P.R.O., E 315/, vol. 279 fo. 5 and E 303/Essex, 214.
141. P.R.O., E 318/1104.
142. *Hist. MSS. Com.* 15th Report, pp. 258-261.
143. P.R.O., S.P. Dom. James I, vol. 190, no. 5.
144. *The Manor and Parish Church of Hampstead*, J. Kennedy (1906), p. 118.
145. P.R.O., C 142/ vol. 130, no. 39.
146. Will of John Slannyng. P.C.C. 63 Noodes.
147. P.R.O., C 3/197/49.   148. P.R.O., E 318/2365 and C 66/1027 (6).
149. P.R.O., C 54/1324 and C.P. 25/31/2 Eliz. Mich.
150. P.R.O., C.P. 43/135. m. 60.
151. Will of John Bill. P.C.C. 124 Bath, and P.R.O., C 142/768/20.
152. P.R.O., S.P. Dom. Interr., vols. G 188 (35), G 188 (44), G 188 (51):
153. P.R.O., S.P. Dom. Interr. G 68. p. 267, 271, 273.
154. *Cal. of S.P. Dom.*, Chas. II, 1660-1 (1860), p. 270-1.
155. Will of John Bill. P.C.C. 124 Bath. His widow appears to have got into financial difficulties, even to the extent of being imprisoned for debt (P.R.O., C 8/415/28).
156. *Vicar Gen. Marr. Lic.* Harl. Soc. vol. 60 (1890).
157. P.R.O., C.P. 43/409.m.9d.   158. *Ibid.*, 411.m.24.
159. P.R.O., C 54/4713(35).   160. *Ibid.*, 4930(4).
161. *Ibid.*, 5015(1).
162. *Wentworth Papers*, 1705-1739. James J. Cartwright (1883).
163. P.R.O., C 54/5032(18).   164. P.R.O., C.54/5032(17).
165. Deed in St. Pancras Library.   166. P.R.O., C 54/5160(27).
167. Land Reg. Midd. Mem., 1720/1/253 ; P.R.O., C 11/2380/36 ; P.R.O., C 33/343, pp. 4, 107.
168. Land Reg. Midd. Mem., 1746/2/730.
169. *Letters from the Right Hon. Lady Mary Wortley Montagu*, 1709-1762. Everyman Edition (1914), pp. 379, 380, 382, 409.
170. Land Reg. Midd. Mem., 1754/3/75 ; 1754/4/427 ; 1757/4/351 ; 1715/5/26.

Except in the case of State Papers, Domestic series, the references to documents in the Public Record Office give the pressmarks only. In these C. denotes a Chancery record : C.53 are Charter Rolls, C.54 Close Rolls, C.66 Patent Rolls, C.142, 143, volumes or files of Inquisitions. C.P. denotes a record of the Court of Common Pleas : C.P. 25 are Feet of Fines, C.P.40 De Banco plea Rolls, C.P.43 Recovery Rolls. E. denotes an Exchequer record : E.40 Ancient Deeds preserved in that department, E.301-330 records of the Augmentation Office, E.351 Declared Accounts. K.B. denotes a record of the Court of King's Bench : K.B.26 Curia Regis Rolls, K.B.27 Coram Rege Rolls. Req. denotes a record of the Court of Requests, S.C. a record in some special collection, S.C.6 being Ministers Accounts, S.C.11 Rentals and Surveys.

APPENDIX I

THE WILL OF GILES EUSTACE. 1495

(*Commissary Court of London.* 91 *Harvy.*)

IN THE NAME OF GOD AMEN the secunde Day of the monyth of Aprill' the yere of our lord god Mlcccc lxxxxv^{to}.

I, GYLES EUSTAS in hoole mynde and parfite memory being Laude and preysing be vnto almighti god. Make ordeyne and dispose this my present testament conteynyng my last will in manere and forme as folowith.

First I bequeth and recommend my soull vnto almighti god my maker and redemor to the gloryouse virgyn and Lady Saint Mary his moder and to all the blessed company in Hevyn.

And my Body to be buried in the chirch of Sainte Pancrace in the ffelde before the ymage of our blissed Lady ther

And I bequeth vnto the High Auter of the same chirch for my tithes and oblacionns w^t holden or neglegently forgotten in discharging of my soull and consciens vjs viij^d.

Item I bequeth to the High Auter of the parishe chirch of Haringey to haue my soull in Remembrannce vjs viij^d.

Item I bequeth to the High Auter of the parishe chirch of Islington' in like wise vjs viij^d

Item I bequeth to William Eustas my brother to pray for my soull xx^s in money

Item I bequeth to Henry Checheley in like condicion' xx^s in money

Item I bequeth to Thomas Hoo the younger xx^s in money and a Gowne of must de Velys to haue my soull in his prayer and remembrannce

Item I bequeth to Thomas Hoo the elder in like forme to pray for my soull vjs viij^d in money and a gowne of Tawny

Item I bequeth to Richard Baker Heremyte of the Chapell of Hygate to pray for my soull vjs viij^d in money

And as towching the disposicion' of my Landis I will that Johan my Wiff haue all my said Landis and Tenements lying w^{t}in the shire of midd' in eny place w^t there Appurtenannces to theme belonging to haue and to holde to her terme of her lyff Excepte the bequestes vndre rehersed And aftir her decesse I woll that Myles my sonne haue my Tenement which I dwell in lying in Hygate w^t the Appurtenannces and xv acres of Lande adionyng vnto the same called the morys And a Closse callid Kingges Crofte lying in Hygate And a Orchard callid the Kingges gardyn And a Closse callid Brodfelde cont' xij Acres to haue and to holde to the saide myles my Sonne his heires and assignes for euermore

Item I woll that Thomas my Sonne have ij tenementes lying at Hygate in the parishe of Haringey in one of the which dwellith one Collyer and in the other one Robert Leke w^t the Appurtenannces therto belonging And a Closse lying besyde Hygate Lane in the parishe of Islyngton conteynyng vj Acres of Lande and a Closse lying in the parishe of Haringey callid the Parke Hill and a Closse callid Pedaker in the same parish to my saide Sonne Thomas his Heires and assignes for euermore

Item I will that John' my Sonne haue a Tenement in Haringey called May Howsse and the Closse nexte adionyng behinde it And a Closse callid Campisborne w^t all my Landis and Tenementes vnder Southwode and in the vale of Haringey and Mawswell Hill to my saide Sonne John' his Heires and assignes for euermore

Item I will that Alice my Doughter shall haue whanne she shall come to her lawfull age or be maryed a Tenement which John' Wekyng Dwellith in w^t a nother Tenement nexte adioynyng vnto it which Henry Kyrkby dwellith in with their Appurtenannces to theme belonging to her assignes and heires foreuermore w^t x marke of money to her mariage

Item I will that Amy my Doughter haue a Tenement lying at Hygate grene which John' Dryver dwellith in w^t the Appurtenannces and x marks in money as afore is rehersed And which of theme ouerlyth other to be the heire as well to the Landis as to the money

The Residew of all my goodis meuable above not bequest I gyff and bequeith Vnto Johan my wiff therwith to doo her owne fre will as w^t her owne propre goodis foreuermore Which saide Johan I make and ordeyne my soole executrice of this my present testament and last will and William Eustas my brother to be her ouerseer

Witnesses Sir Edward Dukfelde parishe prest of Haringey William Eustas Squyer Thomas Hoo yonger William Sheperd Henry Checheley Richard Hoo Richard Baker w^t other moo

138

APPENDIX II

HEARTH TAX ROLLS FOR HIGHGATE (ST. PANCRAS)

The figures after the names indicate the number of hearths on which the occupier had to pay.

1665		1673		1674	
				Empty, Mr Pryor owr	02
Earl of Lodderdale	26			Empty, Duke of Lotherdale	26
George Pryer	07			Mr Pryor	07
Maior Grinstone	15			Empty, Thom: Gunstone owr	15
Robt. Lea	04			Rob. Leay	04
Paul Ginderley	07			Mr Ffilkins	07
Ric. Gower	11			Mr Goare	11
Geo. Whitten	04			Geo. Whitton	04
Wm Read	02	— Duckett	02	Cha. Hatton	02
Martin Stappilles	02	Empty	02	Wm Smyth	02
John Shuley	01	Empty	02	Wdd. Hutton	01
— Miller	04	John Miller	04	John Miller	04
				John Foster	02
Wm Branson	02	W. Bramson	03	Wm Branson	03
				Wdd. Coggesell	02
		Empty	07	Jona. Cook	07
Edw. Greene	02			— Stanell	02
Rich. Weekes	04	Ricd Weekes	05	Empty	04
				Ralph Sharwood	02
		Thomas Greene	02	Thom. Greene	02
John Storrey	03	Mr. Storye	09	Mr Stoney	09
Owen Lewis	09	Empty	03	Empty	07
		W. Brogden	06	Wm. Bragden	06
Mrs White	09			Empty, Mr White owr	09
Robt. Clarke	12	Robert Clarke	12	Mr Clarke	06
				Mr Willam	06
Wdd : Smith	02	Widow Smith	02	Wd. Smyth	02
Mrs Bateman	04	Edwd Thompson	04	Edw. Thompson	04
Nich : Baker	02	Ricd Baker	02	Richd Baker	02
Wm Homes	02	Thos : Stones	02	Thom. Smith	02
Beni Arthur	10	Kaye Esq	10	Esqr : Kage	10
				John Branson	02
Wm Riles	02	Wm Ryles	02	Wm Rayles	02
				Mr Plowman	07
Owen Cope	02	Owen Cope	02	Owen Cooper	02
Baron Turner	23	Mr Johnson	10	Mr Johnson	10
		Mr Hinde	11	Empty, Mr Blocke ownr	11
John Ives	07	John Ives	07	John Ives	07
Francis Blake	13	Francis Blake	13	Fran. Blacke	13
Sam. Boxter (*sic.*)	07	Simon Baxter	07	Simo. Baxter	07
Wm Bitterfeild	02	W. Butterfield	02	Wm Butterfeild	02
Mrs Skillett	02	John Foster	02	John Tayler	02
		Empty, Poulson ownr	04	Empty	04
Wdd. White	06	Wid : White	02	Wd. White	02
				Wdd. Burden	02
		W. Crosse	02	Rich. Finder	02
Anth. Odam	02	Anth Odam	03	Ano Odum	03
				Wm. Lewis	05

THE VILLAGE OF HIGHGATE

Marquisse of Dorchester	31	Marq. of Dorchester	31	Marques of Dorchester	31
Tho. Collett, esq.	11	Empty	11	Thom : Collett Esqr	10
— Coppenger	05	M. Beaumont	05	Mr Beomont	05
W. Prue	04				
Chr. Keemer	02	Mr Keymer	04	Mr Keymor	04
Edw. Thompson	02	Robt. Poulsen	02	Robt. Poulson	02
Tho. Weden	02	John Taylour	02	Thom. Kirke	02
Tho. Barnes	02	Thos : Barnes	03	Thom : Barnes	02
Nic : Andrews	04	Nich : Andrewes	04	Mich. Andrews	04
Wm Nicholls	06	Empty	06	Wm. Nicholls	06
John Bill	24	John Bill	23	John Bill Esqr	20
— Flood	02	— Flood	02	— Flood	02
Thos Conce	04	Thos. Sconce	04	Tho. Sconne	05

The order of the names in the lists of 1665 and 1673 has been modified to tally with that for 1674.

APPENDIX III

HIGHGATE SCHOOL ROLL

GOVERNORS

Sir WILLIAM HEWETT, Lord Mayor, 1559	Died	1567
Sir ROGER MARTEN, Lord Mayor, 1567	„	1573
ROGER CAREW	„	1586
RICHARD HEYWOOD	„	1570
RICHARD HODGES	„	1572
JASPER CHOLMELEY	„	1587

The above mentioned were named in the Letters Patent of Queen Elizabeth, dated 6th April, 1565.

Elected

1567.	Sir JOHN LANGLEY, Lord Mayor, 1576	Died	1578
1570.	John KITCHEN	„	1586
1572.	JOHN DRAPER	„	1576
1574.	WILLIAM LAMB, Founder of Sutton Valence School	„	1580
1574.	JOHN DUDLEY	„	1580
1576.	Sir WILLIAM CORDELL, M.P., Speaker of the House of Commons, Master of the Rolls	„	1581
1578.	JOHN MARTYN	„	15—
1580.	JOHN GUILPINE	„	1591
1581.	WILLIAM HODGES	„	1582
1582.	WILLIAM CLARK	„	1587
1586.	ROGER PULESTON	„	1592
1587.	OWEN LLOYD	„	1589
1587.	JOHN CHOLMELEY	„	1589
1587.	Rt. Rev. WILLIAM COTTON, Lord Bishop of Exeter	„	1621
1589.	WILLIAM LINFORD	„	1599
1589.	JOHN POVIE	„	1599
1591.	Sir WILLIAM CORNWALLIS	„	1611
1592.	Sir HUGH PLATT	„	1609
159–.	RICHARD SKEVINGTON	„	1597
1598.	Sir NICHOLAS KEMPE	„	1624
1599.	Sir WILLIAM WAAD, Lieut. of the Tower	„	1623
1599.	WILLIAM CHOLMELEY	„	1642
1609.	THOMAS EDWARDS, D.C.L., Chancellor of Diocese of London	„	1619
1611	EDWARD FORSETT	„	1630
16—	Sir THOMAS FOWLER	„	1625
1620.	Rt. Rev. THOMAS WESTFIELD, Lord Bishop of Bristol	„	1644
1621.	Sir BAPTIST HICKS, Bart., afterwards Viscount Campden	„	1629
1624.	EDWARD ALLEN, Alderman of London	„	1626
1625.	SAMUEL ARMITAGE	„	1636
1626.	Rev. THOMAS WORRALL, D.D.	„	1639
1629.	JOHN SMITH	„	1656
1630.	Sir JOHN WOLLASTON, Lord Mayor, 1644	„	1658
1636.	Sir THOMAS GARDINER, Solicitor-General, Recorder of London	„	1652
1639.	Sir RICHARD SPRIGNELL, Bart.	„	1659
1642.	BASILL NICOLL	„	1648
1644.	RICHARD CHAMBERS, Alderman of London	„	1658
1648.	EDWARD TAYLOR	„	1660
1652.	Sir THOMAS ALLEN, Lord Mayor, 1660	„	1681

141

1656.	JOHN IRETON, Lord Mayor, 1659	Died	1690
1658.	GEORGE PRIOR	„	1675
1658.	Colonel THOMAS GOWER	„	1676
1659.	THOMAS COLLETT	„	1675
1660.	Sir THOMAS ROWE	„	1685
1675.	Sir JOHN MUSTERS	„	1689
1675.	Sir NATHANIEL HERNE, Sheriff of London, 1674-5	„	1679
1676.	Sir PAUL PAYNTER	„	1686
1679.	Sir FRANCIS PEMBERTON, Lord Chief Justice of England	„	1697
1681.	EDWARD ALLEN	„	1692
1685.	WILLIAM SHENTON	„	1692
1686.	RICHARD CRADOCK	„	1712
1689.	Sir WILLIAM PRITCHARD	„	1705
1690.	Sir JAMES SMYTH	„	1708
1692.	THOMAS DICKINS	„	1719
1692.	Lieut.-Col. EDWARD BEAKER	„	1694
1694.	WILLIAM BRIDGES	„	1714
1697.	Sir WILLIAM ASHURST, Lord Mayor, 1694	„	1720
1705.	JAMES BUCK	„	1712
1709.	WILLIAM THATCHER	„	1728
1712.	EDWARD PAUNCEFORT	„	1726
1712.	WILLIAM, 4th Lord BERKLEY of STRATTON (afterwards Visct. Fitzharding)	„	1741
1714.	Sir EDWARD GOULD, a Justice of H.M. Court of Common Pleas	„	1728
1719.	JOHN TOWNSEND	„	1720
1720.	HUMPHREY HENCHMAN, LL.D., Chancellor of Diocese of London	„	1739
1725.	WILLIAM BRIDGES (of the Stamp Office)	„	1741
1726.	JOHN SCHOPPENS	„	1728
1728.	THOMAS BAYLY	„	1749
1728.	FRANCIS ANNESLEY	„	1750
1728.	CHARLES SHALES	„	1734
1734.	JOHN EDWARDS	„	1769
1739.	ROBERT THOMAS	„	1776
1741.	WILLIAM TOWNSEND	Resigned	1747
1741.	WILLIAM THATCHER	Died	1743
1743.	SAMUEL FORSTER	„	1752
1747.	MATTHEW LANGLEY	„	1758
1749.	ROBERT BOOTLE	„	1758
1750.	WILLIAM PHILLIPS	„	1755
1752.	THOMAS NASH	„	1752
1752.	Sir THOMAS BURNET, a Justice of H.M. Court of Common Pleas	„	1753
1753.	HAMMOND CROSS	Resigned	1756
1755.	PETER STORER	Died	1759
1756.	EDMUND BYRON	„	1778
1758.	RICHARD WILBRAHAM BOOTLE	„	1796
1758.	BENDALL MARTYN	„	1761
1759.	ROBERT PAUL	„	1762
1762.	Hon. CHARLES YORKE, Lord High Chancellor, 1770	„	1770
1762.	WILLIAM (first) Earl of MANSFIELD, Lord Chief Justice	„	1793
1770.	Sir THOMAS CAVE, Bart.	„	1780
1770.	THOMAS BROMWICH	„	1787
1776.	Gen. the Hon. CHARLES FITZROY (first) Lord SOUTHAMPTON	„	1797
1778.	CHARLES CAUSTON	„	1811
1780.	WILLIAM BAYNES	Resigned	1781
1781.	THOMAS SAUNDERS	„	1794

THE SCHOOL GOVERNORS

1787.	ALEXANDER ANDERSON	Died	1796
1793.	DAVID (second) Earl of MANSFIELD	„	1796
1796.	ROBERT MENDHAM	„	1810
1796.	Colonel JOHN BRETTELL	„	1801
1796.	THOMAS WALKER, Accountant-General in Chancery	„	1802
1796.	WILLIAM (third) Earl of MANSFIELD	Resigned	1828
1779.	DAVID DUVELUZ	Died	1808
1801.	BENJAMIN PRICE	„	1820
1802.	WILLIAM BELCHER	Resigned	1842
18—.	ABRAHAM LANGFORD	Died	1817
18—.	HENRY ISHERWOOD	„	18—
18—.	WILLIAM BLOXAM	„	1814
1812.	ROBERT ISHERWOOD	„	1837
1816.	RICHARD NIXON	„	1835
1817.	THOMAS HURST	Resigned	1832
1820.	GEORGE KINDERLEY	Died	1847
1828.	Rev. THOMAS HENRY CAUSTON	„	1854
1832.	WILLIAM DODGE COOPER COOPER	Resigned	1857
1836.	CHARLES (third) Lord SOUTHAMPTON	„	1859
1837.	Rev. CHARLES MAYO	„	1847
1842.	HARRY CHESTER	„	1860
1847.	CHARLES JOHN BLOXAM	„	1881
1847.	GEORGE ABRAHAM CRAWLEY	Died	1862
1854.	NATHANIEL BASEVI	Resigned	1859
1857.	JOHN LAWRENCE TATHAM	Died	1886
1859.	WILLIAM FORD	„	1889
1859.	HENRY LAKE	„	1863
1860.	WILLIAM WALTER LEGGE, (fifth) Earl of DARTMOUTH	Resigned	1876
1862.	Sir ROUNDELL PALMER, Q.C. afterwards (first) Earl of SELBOURNE, Lord High Chancellor	Died	1895
1863.	WILLIAM GLADSTONE	„	1873
1873.	Lieut.-Col. Sir GEORGE ARCHIBALD LEACH, R.E., K.C.B.	Resigned	1908
		Died 18th June, 1913	

Under the scheme for the administration of the School which came into operation in 1876, the number of Governors was increased from six to twelve. Of these, six were Co-optative and six Nominated; one each by the Lord-Lieutenant of Middlesex, the Lord Bishop of London, the Lord Chief Justice of England, and the Universities of Oxford, Cambridge and London.

1876.	GEORGE BADEN CRAWLEY (Lord-Lieutenant)	Died	1879
1876.	The Venerable JAMES AUGUSTUS HESSEY, D.C.L., Archdeacon of Middlesex (Bp. of L.)	Resigned	1891
1876.	JAMES STEPHEN (L.C.J.)	„	1880
1876.	CHARLES MARSHALL GRIFFITH, Q.C. (Oxf.)	„	1888
1876.	Rev. JOHN LLEWELYN DAVIES (Camb.)	„	1889
1876.	TIMOTHY SMITH OSLER (Lond.)	Died	1905
1876.	WILLIAM HENEAGE, Viscount LEWISHAM, M.P., afterwards (sixth) Earl of DARTMOUTH (Co-op.)	Resigned	1900
1880.	Rev. ROBERT TOWNSEND CRAWLEY (Lord-Lieut.)	„	1903
1880.	BENJAMIN GREENE LAKE (L.C.J.)	„	1891
1882.	JOHN BRADLEY DYNE (Co-op.)	Died	1909
1886.	THOMAS CLARKE TATHAM (Co-op.)	„	1914
1889.	Major-Gen. Sir JOHN FRETCHEVILLE DYKES DONNELLY, R.E., K.C.B. (Co-op.)	„	1902
1889.	CHARLES GEORGE, Lord LYTTELTON, afterwards Viscount COBHAM (Camb.)	Resigned	1902

1889.	BENJAMIN BICKLEY ROGERS (Oxf.)	Resigned	1898
1891.	The Ven. ROBINSON THORNTON, D.D., Archdeacon of Middlesex (Bp. of L.)	Resigned	1903
1891.	WALTER SCRIMGEOUR (L.C.J.)	,,	1898
1896.	HENRY SAMUEL BENBOW PRICE (Co-op.)	Died	1898
1898.	EDWARD BOND (Oxf.)	,,	1920
1898.	CHARLES PONSONBY WILMER (L.C.J.)	,,	1903
1898.	ARTHUR RANKEN FORD (Co-op.)	Resigned	1919
1900.	WILLIAM DAVID (fifth) Earl of MANSFIELD (Co-op.)	Died	1906
1902.	ROGER GASKELL (Camb.)	,,	1912
1902.	Rt. Rev. CHARLES HENRY, Lord Bishop of Islington, D.D. (Co-op.)	,,	1923
1903.	CHARLES GEORGE, Viscount COBHAM (Lord-Lieut.)	Resigned	1908
1903.	LEONARD CHARLES WAKEFIELD (L.C.J.)	,,	1918
1903.	The Ven. H. E. J. BEVAN, Archdeacon of Middlesex (Bp. of L.)	,,	1930
1905.	DAVID SING CAPPER (Lond.)	,,	1920
1906.	CHARLES GRANT CHURCH (Co-op.)	,,	1929
1908.	Colonel THOMAS MYLES SANDYS, M.P. (Lord-Lieut.)	Died	1911
1908.	Hon. LAWRENCE JOHN LUMLEY, Earl of RONALDSHAY, M.P. (Co-op.)	Resigned	1916
1909.	Rev. HENRY RICHARD COOPER SMITH, D.D. (Co-op.)	,,	1930
1912.	Major-Gen. EUSTON HENRY SARTORIUS, V.C., C.B. (Lord-Lieut.)	,,	1915
1912.	RUDOLPH CHAMBERS LEHMANN (Camb.)	,,	1919
1914.	Brig.-Gen. HAROLD PEMBERTON LEACH, C.B., D.S.O. (Co-op.)	,,	1928
1916.	ROLAND LYONS NOSWORTHY MICHELL, C.M.G. (Lord-Lieut.)	,,	1929
1917.	ROGER GASKELL HETHERINGTON, C.B., O.B.E. (Co-op.)		
1918.	CHRISTOPHER KEMPLAY TATHAM (L.C.J.)		
1919.	GEORGE NEWTON PITT, O.B.E., M.D., F.R.C.P. (Camb.)	Died 23rd Feb.,	1929
1919.	Admiral Sir HERBERT EDWARD PUREY CUST, K.B.E., C.B. (Co-op.)		
1920.	FREDERICK AUGUSTUS DIXEY, M.D., F.R.S. (Oxf.)		
1920.	JOHN LEIGH SMEATHMAN HATTON (Lond.)		

Under the provisions of the School Teachers (Superannuation) Act, 1918, the Board of Education nominated three additional Governors, thus increasing the number from twelve to fifteen, but their appointments lapsed in September 1923.

		Appointment lapsed	
1921.	WILLIAM WALTER KELLAND (B. of E.)	Sept. 1923	
1921.	Right Hon. Sir WILLOUGHBY DICKINSON, K.B.E. (B. of E.)	,, ,,	
1921.	Sir FREDERICK WILLIAM ANDREWES, O.B.E., M.D., F.R.S. (B. of E.)	,, ,,	
1923.	Sir FRANCIS NUGENT GREER, K.C.B. (Co-op.)	Died 1925	
1925.	The Hon. Mr. Justice FRANK DOUGLAS MACKINNON (Co-op.)		
1928.	GEORGE KEMP (first) Lord ROCHDALE (Co-op.)		
1929.	Sir ARTHUR HENRY CROSFIELD, Bart. (Co.-op.)	Resigned 1930	
1929.	ARCHIBALD VIVIAN HILL, O.B.E., G.B.E., D.Sc., F.R.S. (Camb.)		
1929.	Sir CHARLES GRANT ROBERTSON, C.V.O. (Lord-Lieut.)		
1930.	EDWARD JOHN WILLIAM JEUDWINE (Co-op.)		
1930.	CHARLES TATE REGAN, D.Sc., F.R.S. (Co-op.)		
1930.	The Ven. F. N. THICKNESSE, Archdeacon of Middlesex (Bp. of L.)		
1930.	BERNARD EUSTACE CUTHBERT DAVIS (London University)		
1933.	Right Rev. GUY VERNON, Lord Bishop of Willesden (Bp. of L.)		
1934.	WILLIAM SEAFORD SHARPE (Co-op.)		

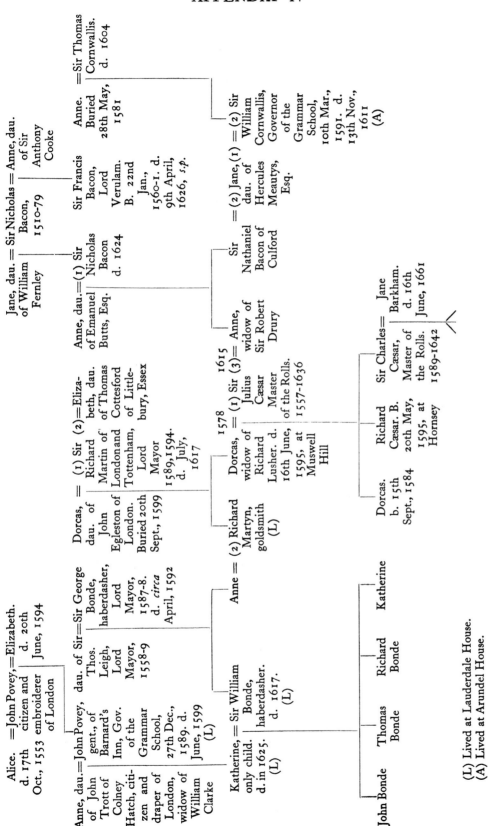

APPENDIX V

PEDIGREE OF EUSTACE AND HART

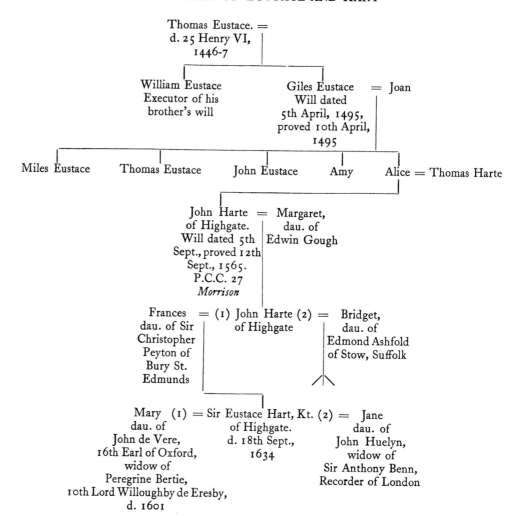

Thomas Eustace. =
d. 25 Henry VI,
1446-7

William Eustace
Executor of his
brother's will

Giles Eustace = Joan
Will dated
5th April, 1495,
proved 10th April,
1495

Miles Eustace   Thomas Eustace   John Eustace   Amy   Alice = Thomas Harte

John Harte = Margaret,
of Highgate.   dau. of
Will dated 5th   Edwin Gough
Sept., proved 12th
Sept., 1565.
P.C.C. 27
Morrison

Frances = (1) John Harte (2) = Bridget,
dau. of Sir   of Highgate   dau. of
Christopher   Edmond Ashfold
Peyton of   of Stow, Suffolk
Bury St.
Edmunds

Mary (1) = Sir Eustace Hart, Kt. (2) = Jane
dau. of   of Highgate.   dau. of
John de Vere,   d. 18th Sept.,   John Huelyn,
16th Earl of Oxford,   1634   widow of
widow of   Sir Anthony Benn,
Peregrine Bertie,   Recorder of London
10th Lord Willoughby de Eresby,
d. 1601

APPENDIX VI

PEDIGREE OF CHOLMELEY

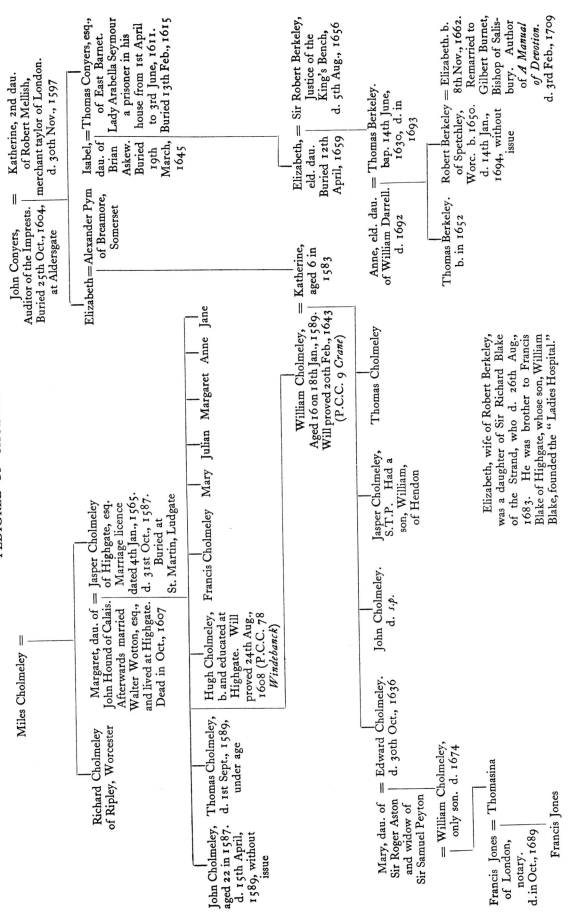

Miles Cholmeley =

John Conyers, Auditor of the Imprests. Buried 25th Oct., 1604, at Aldersgate. = Katherine, 2nd dau. of Robert Mellish, merchant taylor of London. d. 30th Nov., 1597

Isabel, = Thomas Conyers, esq., of East Barnet. Lady Arabella Seymour a prisoner in his house from 1st April to 3rd June, 1611. Buried 13th Feb., 1615. dau. of Brian Askew. Buried 19th March, 1645

Elizabeth = Alexander Pym of Breamore, Somerset

Richard Cholmeley of Ripley, Worcester

Margaret, dau. of John Hound of Calais. Afterwards married Walter Wotton, esq., and lived at Highgate. Dead in Oct., 1607 = Jasper Cholmeley of Highgate, esq. Marriage licence dated 4th Jan., 1565. d. 31st Oct., 1587. Buried at St. Martin, Ludgate

Hugh Cholmeley, b. and educated at Highgate. Will proved 24th Aug., 1608 (P.C.C. 78 *Windebanck*)

Francis Cholmeley   Mary   Julian   Margaret   Anne   Jane

Elizabeth, eld. dau. Buried 12th April, 1659 = Sir Robert Berkeley, Justice of the King's Bench, d. 5th Aug., 1656

Katherine, aged 6 in 1583 = William Cholmeley, Aged 16 on 18th Jan., 1589. Will proved 20th Feb., 1643 (P.C.C. 9 *Crane*)

Anne, eld. dau. of William Darrell. d. 1692 = Thomas Berkeley. bap. 14th June, 1630, d. in 1693

Robert Berkeley of Spetchley, Worc. b. 1650. d. 14th Jan., 1694, without issue = Elizabeth. b. 8th Nov., 1662. Remarried to Gilbert Burnet, Bishop of Salisbury. Author of *A Manual of Devotion*. d. 3rd Feb., 1709

Thomas Berkeley. b. in 1652

John Cholmeley, aged 22 in 1587, d. 15th April, 1589, without issue

Thomas Cholmeley, d. 1st Sept., 1589, under age

Thomas Cholmeley

Jasper Cholmeley, S.T.P. Had a son, William, of Hendon

John Cholmeley. d. s.p.

Mary, dau. of Sir Roger Aston and widow of Sir Samuel Peyton = Edward Cholmeley. d. 30th Oct., 1636

= William Cholmeley, only son. d. 1674

Francis Jones = Thomasina of London, notary. d. in Oct., 1689

Francis Jones

Elizabeth, wife of Robert Berkeley, was a daughter of Sir Richard Blake of the Strand, who d. 26th Aug., 1683. He was brother to Francis Blake of Highgate, whose son, William Blake, founded the "Ladies Hospital."

PEDIGREE OF BLAKE

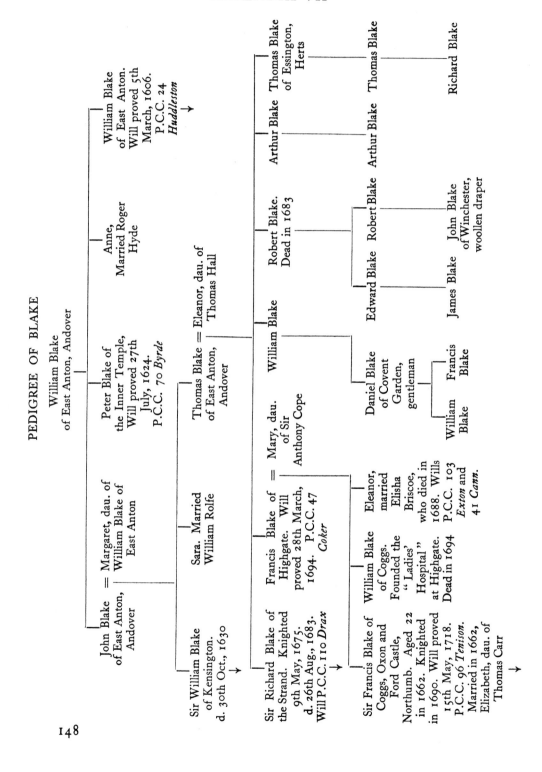

148

INDEX TO NAMES

NOTE.—The pedigrees referred to are only of a "skeleton" nature, intended to illustrate the relationships between the principal Highgate families.

149

154

L

166

Plates, Nos. 1 to 119

PLATE I

HIGHGATE *circa* 1804

PLATE 2

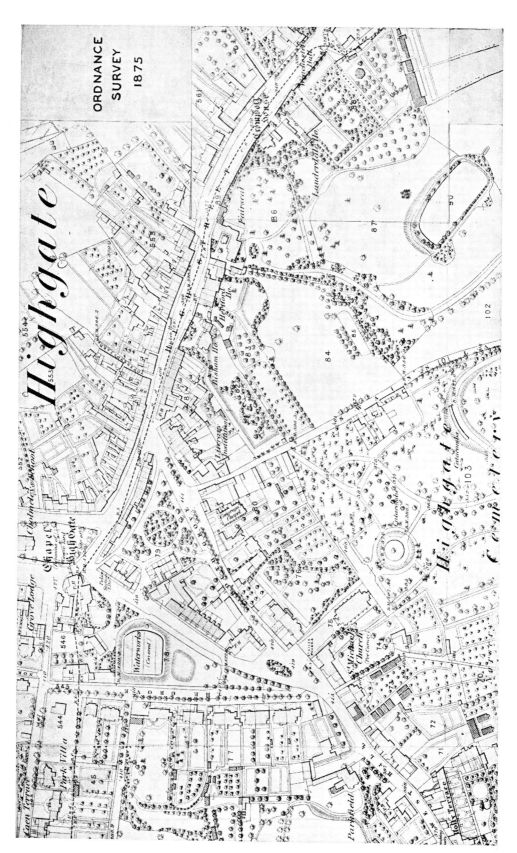

ORDNANCE
SURVEY
1875

HIGHGATE, 1875

PLATE 3

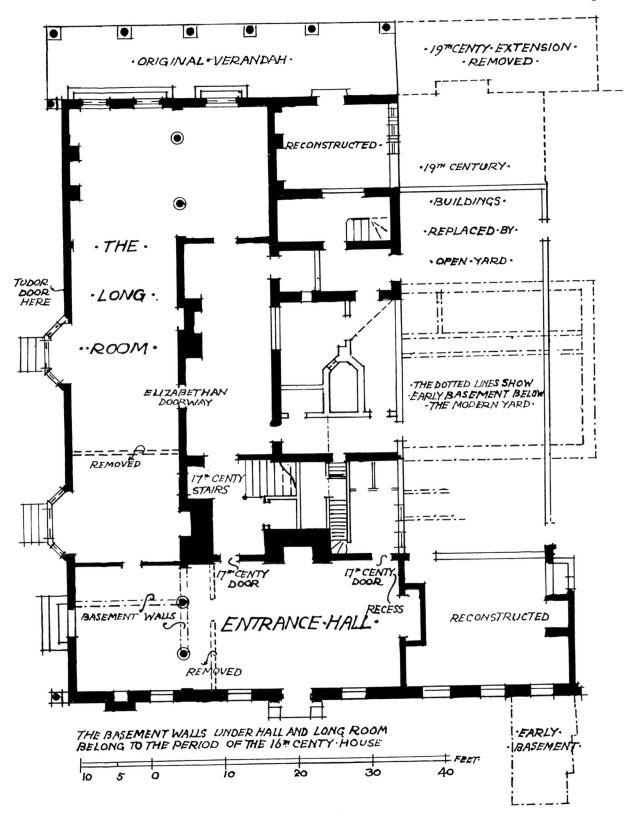

·ORIGINAL·VERANDAH·

·19ᵀᴴ·CENTY·EXTENSION· ·REMOVED·

·RECONSTRUCTED·

·19ᵀᴴ CENTURY·

·BUILDINGS·

·REPLACED·BY·

·OPEN·YARD·

·THE· ·LONG· ·ROOM·

TUDOR DOOR HERE

ELIZABETHAN DOORWAY

·THE DOTTED LINES SHOW ·EARLY BASEMENT BELOW ·THE MODERN YARD·

REMOVED

17ᵀᴴ CENTY STAIRS

17ᵀᴴ CENTY DOOR

17ᵀᴴ CENTY DOOR

RECESS

RECONSTRUCTED

BASEMENT WALLS

·ENTRANCE·HALL·

REMOVED

·EARLY· ·BASEMENT·

THE BASEMENT WALLS UNDER HALL AND LONG ROOM BELONG TO THE PERIOD OF THE 16ᵀᴴ CENTY·HOUSE

10 5 0 10 20 30 40 FEET

PLAN OF LAUDERDALE HOUSE (*p. 7*)
BASED ON LONDON COUNTY COUNCIL SURVEYS OF 1893

BLACK═ORIGINAL OR RECONSTRUCTED WALLS OF THE RESTORATION HOUSE
PLAIN═MODERN ADDITIONS
DOTTED LINES═BASEMENT WALLS OR WALLS THAT HAVE BEEN REMOVED

PLATE 4

LAUDERDALE HOUSE (*pp.* 7-8)

PLATE 5

LAUDERDALE HOUSE
FIREPLACE IN ENTRANCE HALL (*p.* 8)

PLATE 6

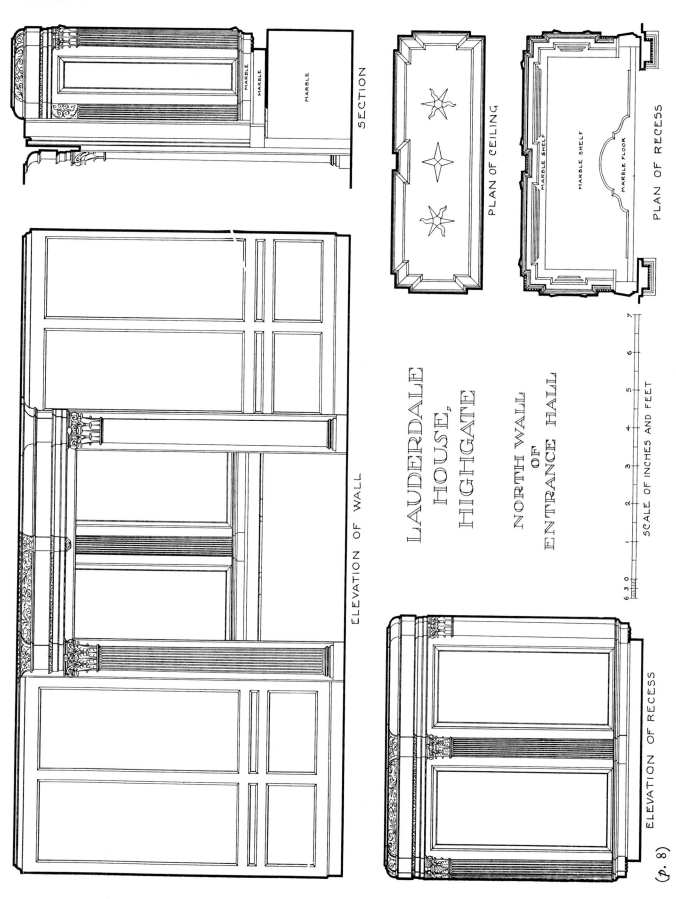

SECTION

MARBLE

MARBLE

PLAN OF CEILING

MARBLE SHELF

MARBLE SHELF

MARBLE FLOOR

PLAN OF RECESS

ELEVATION OF WALL

LAUDERDALE HOUSE, HIGHGATE

NORTH WALL OF ENTRANCE HALL

6 3 0   1   2   3   4   5   6   7

SCALE OF INCHES AND FEET

ELEVATION OF RECESS

(p. 8)

PLATE 7

LAUDERDALE HOUSE
RECESS IN ENTRANCE HALL (*p.* 8)

PLATE 8

LAUDERDALE HOUSE
SOUTH-WEST CORNER OF LONG ROOM ON
GROUND FLOOR (*p.* 7)

PLATE 9

LAUDERDALE HOUSE, HIGHGATE,
DOOR & PANELLING ON GROUND FLOOR

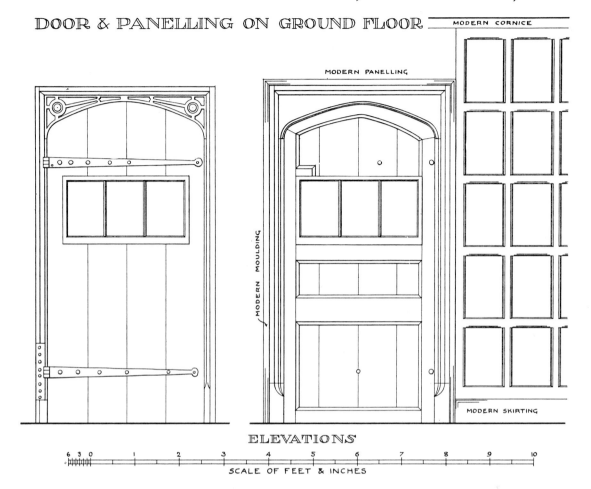

MODERN CORNICE

MODERN PANELLING

MODERN MOULDING

MODERN SKIRTING

ELEVATIONS

6 3 0   1   2   3   4   5   6   7   8   9   10

SCALE OF FEET & INCHES

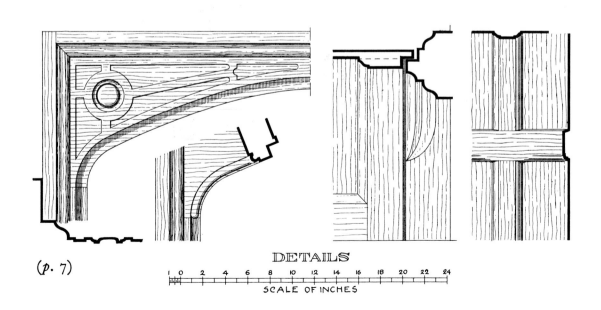

(p. 7)

DETAILS

1 0 2 4 6 8 10 12 14 16 18 20 22 24

SCALE OF INCHES

PLATE 10

LAUDERDALE HOUSE
MAIN STAIRCASE (*p.* 7)

PLATE II

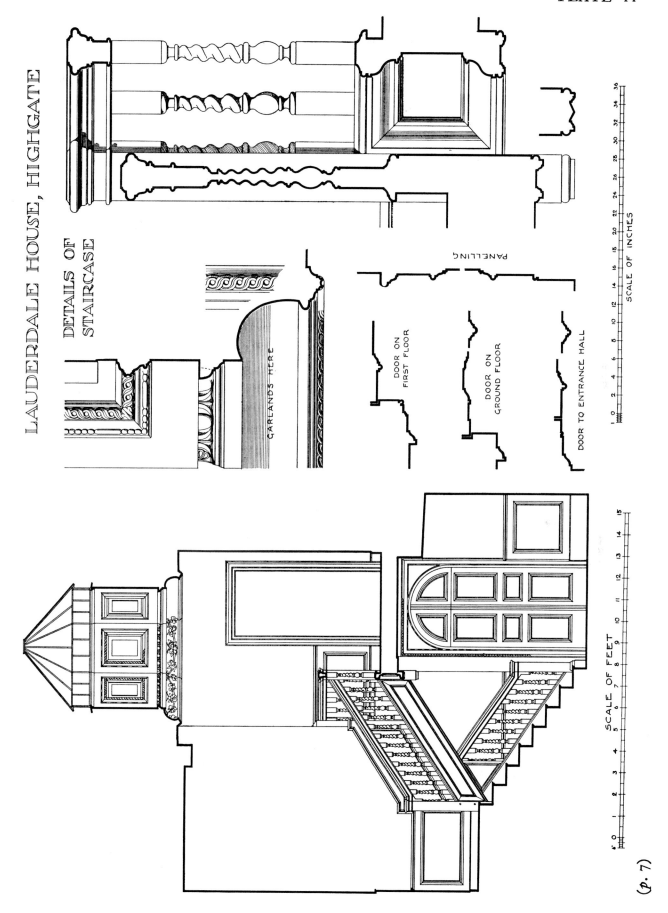

LAUDERDALE HOUSE, HIGHGATE

DETAILS OF STAIRCASE

GARLANDS HERE

PANELLING

DOOR ON FIRST FLOOR

DOOR ON GROUND FLOOR

DOOR TO ENTRANCE HALL

SCALE OF INCHES

SCALE OF FEET

PLATE 12

LAUDERDALE HOUSE
(*a*) LANTERN OVER STAIRS (*p.* 8)
(*b*) GARDEN VASE (*p.* 8)

PLATE 13

(*a*) "ANDREW MARVELL'S COTTAGE"
(*b*) THE SAME FROM THE GARDEN (*p.* 16)

PLATE 14

Nos. 17, 19 AND 21, HIGH STREET (*p.* 19)

PLATE 15

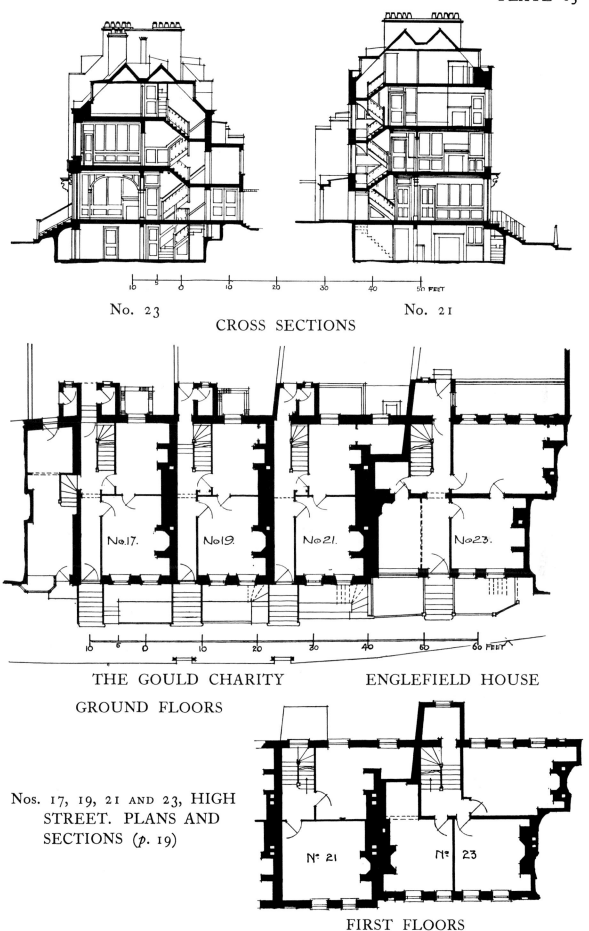

No. 23   CROSS SECTIONS   No. 21

THE GOULD CHARITY   ENGLEFIELD HOUSE

GROUND FLOORS

Nos. 17, 19, 21 and 23, HIGH STREET. PLANS AND SECTIONS (*p.* 19)

FIRST FLOORS

PLATE 16

No. 23   No. 21   No. 19   No. 17

No. 17   No. 19   No. 21   No. 23 STREET

HIGH

GOULD CHARITY ESTATE   ENGLEFIELD HOUSE

(*p.* 19)

PLATE 17

21 HIGH STREET HIGHGATE VILLAGE

DETAILS OF STAIRCASE AND ENTRANCE HALL

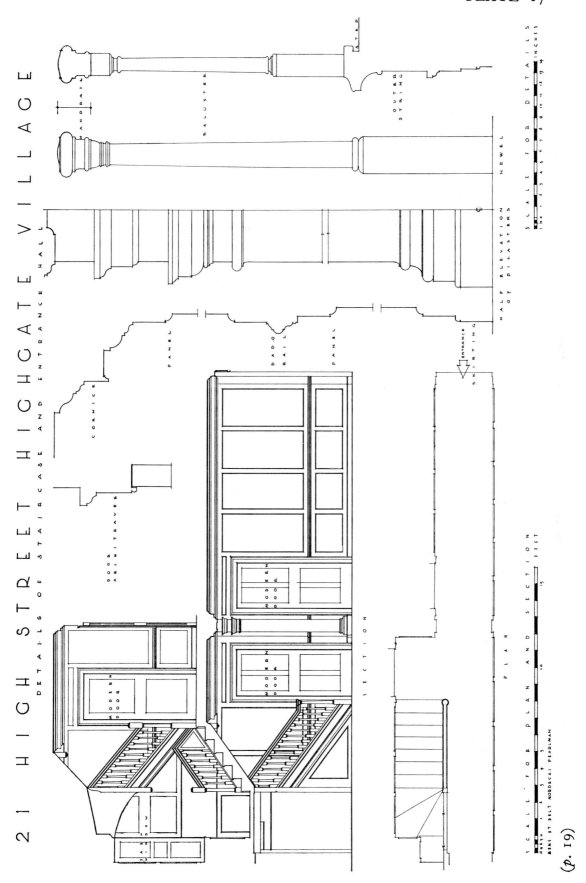

HANDRAIL

BALUSTER

STEP

OUTER STRING

NEWEL

HALF ELEVATION OF PILASTERS

SCALE FOR DETAILS INCHES

CORNICE

DOOR ARCHITRAVES

PANEL

DADO RAIL

PANEL

ENTRANCE SKIRTING

SECTION

PLAN

SCALE FOR PLAN AND SECTION FEET

MENS ET BELT MORDECAI PEARLMAN

(p. 19)

PLATE 18

No. 23, HIGH STREET
ENGLEFIELD HOUSE (*pp.* 22-3)

PLATE 19

No. 23, HIGH STREET, ENGLEFIELD HOUSE (*p. 23*)

(*b*) HOB GRATE ON FIRST FLOOR

(*a*) STAIRCASE

C

PLATE 20

Chimney Piece in the Drawing Room, Englefield House at Highgate.

Measured & Drawn by Wm W. Comfrey, March 1913.

Scale 1½" = 1'·0"

PLATE 21

No. 23, HIGH STREET
ENGLEFIELD HOUSE—CHIMNEY PIECE ON GROUND FLOOR (*p.* 23)

PLATE 22

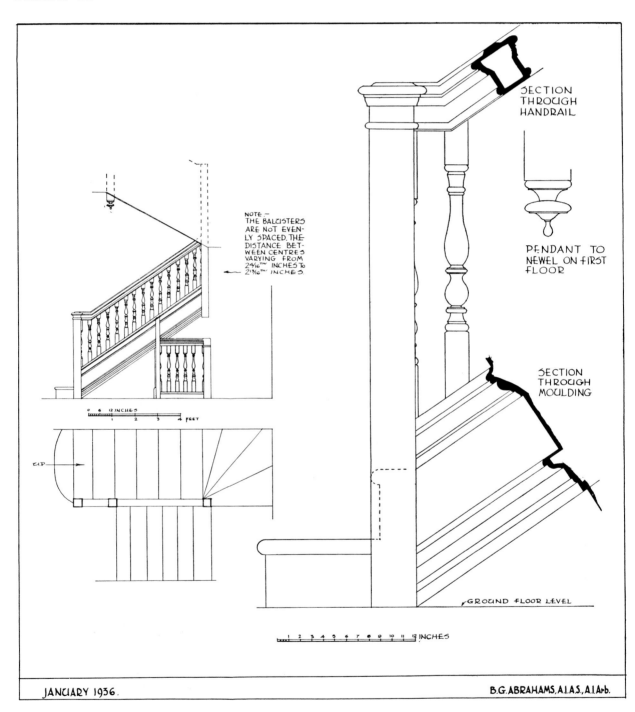

SECTION
THROUGH
HANDRAIL

NOTE —
THE BALUSTERS
ARE NOT EVEN-
LY SPACED. THE
DISTANCE BET-
WEEN CENTRES
VARYING FROM
2⁴/₁₆ᵀ INCHES TO
2¹³/₁₆ᵀ INCHES.

PENDANT TO
NEWEL ON FIRST
FLOOR

SECTION
THROUGH
MOULDING

0 6 12 INCHES
1   2   3   4 FEET

UP

GROUND FLOOR LEVEL

1 2 3 4 5 6 7 8 9 10 11 12 INCHES

JANUARY 1936.

B.G. ABRAHAMS, A.I.A.S., A.I.Arb.

No. 23, HIGH STREET
ENGLEFIELD HOUSE—STAIRCASE (*p.* 23)

PLATE 23

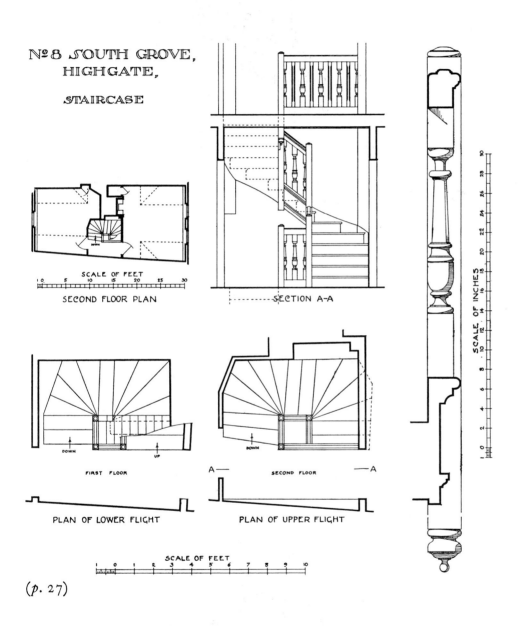

Nº 8 SOUTH GROVE,
HIGHGATE,
STAIRCASE

SCALE OF FEET

SECOND FLOOR PLAN

SECTION A-A

DOWN   UP

FIRST FLOOR

DOWN

SECOND FLOOR

A —   — A

PLAN OF LOWER FLIGHT

PLAN OF UPPER FLIGHT

SCALE OF FEET

SCALE OF INCHES

PLATE 24

No. 9, SOUTH GROVE, RUSSELL HOUSE (*pp.* 27-8)

(*a*) GENERAL VIEW OF FRONT

(*b*) GARDEN VIEW

PLATE 25

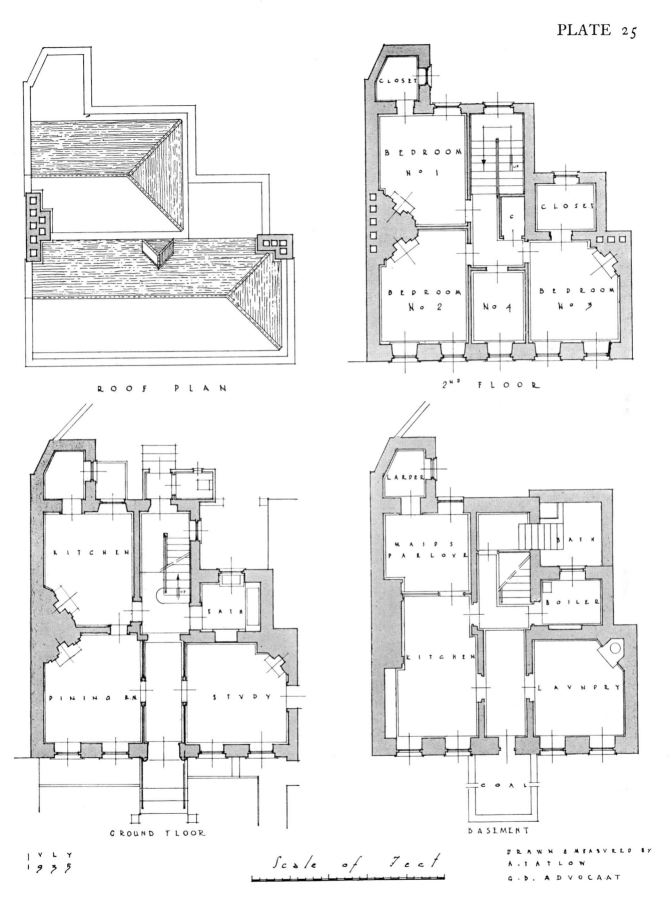

ROOF PLAN

2ᴺᴰ FLOOR

CLOSET

BEDROOM Nº 1

CLOSET

C

BEDROOM Nº 2   Nº 4   BEDROOM Nº 3

GROUND FLOOR

KITCHEN

UP

BATH

DINING RM.   STUDY

BASEMENT

LARDER

MAIDS PARLOUR   BATH

BOILER

KITCHEN   LAVNDRY

COAL

JVLY 1935

Scale of Feet

DRAWN & MEASVRED BY
A. TATLOW
G. D. ADVOCAAT

No. 10, SOUTH GROVE, CHURCH HOUSE (p. 33)

PLATE 26

FRONT ELEVATION   BACK ELEVATION

SECTION   SECTION

JULY
1935

Scale of Feet

DRAWN & MEASURED BY
A. TATLOW.
C. D. KOVOKRAT

No. 10, SOUTH GROVE, CHURCH HOUSE (*pp.* 32-3)

PLATE 27

No. 10, SOUTH GROVE, CHURCH HOUSE (*pp.* 33-4)

(*a*) GENERAL VIEW OF FRONT

(*b*) VIEW FROM GARDEN

PLATE 28

No. 10, SOUTH GROVE, CHURCH HOUSE
ENTRANCE GATE AND RAILINGS (*p.* 34)

PLATE 29

No. 10, SOUTH GROVE, CHURCH HOUSE
ENTRANCE DOORWAY (*pp.* 32-3)

PLATE 30

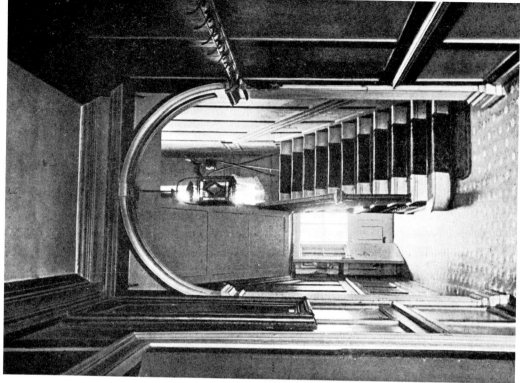

No. 10, SOUTH GROVE, CHURCH HOUSE (*p.* 33)

(*b*) ENTRANCE HALL

(*a*) STAIRCASE

PLATE 31

POND SQUARE WITH
MORETON HOUSE AND
No. 15 BEFORE
ITS DEMOLITION (*p.* 41)

PLATE 32

No. 14, SOUTH GROVE, MORETON HOUSE (*p.* 41)

PLATE 33

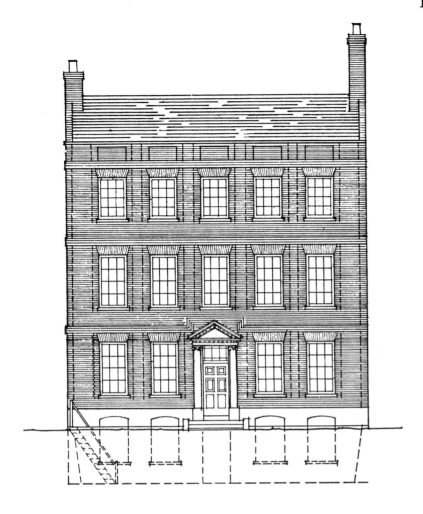

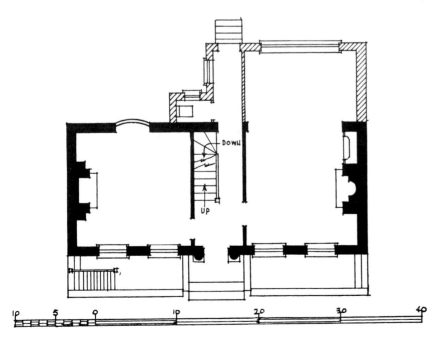

No. 14, SOUTH GROVE, MORETON HOUSE (*p.* 41)

PLATE 34

No. 14, SOUTH GROVE, MORETON HOUSE (*p.* 41)

PLATE 35

SCALE OF SECTION IN FEET

SCALE OF DETAILS IN INCHES

CYNTHIA WOOD. 1935

No. 14, SOUTH GROVE, MORETON HOUSE (*p.* 41)

PLATE 36

Earl of Arundel's House Highgate

Lord Ch:. Bacon died at the Earl of Arundel's house at Highgate 1626

A Back View of South Grove Establishment, Highgate. Middlesex

(Brignon & Halls School)

adjoining Old Hall

(*a*) ARUNDEL HOUSE (*pp.* 50, 54)
(*b*) No. 16, SOUTH GROVE (NOW DEMOLISHED) (*pp.* 46, 48-9)

PLATE 37

No. 17, SOUTH GROVE, OLD HALL (*pp.* 46-7)

PLATE 38

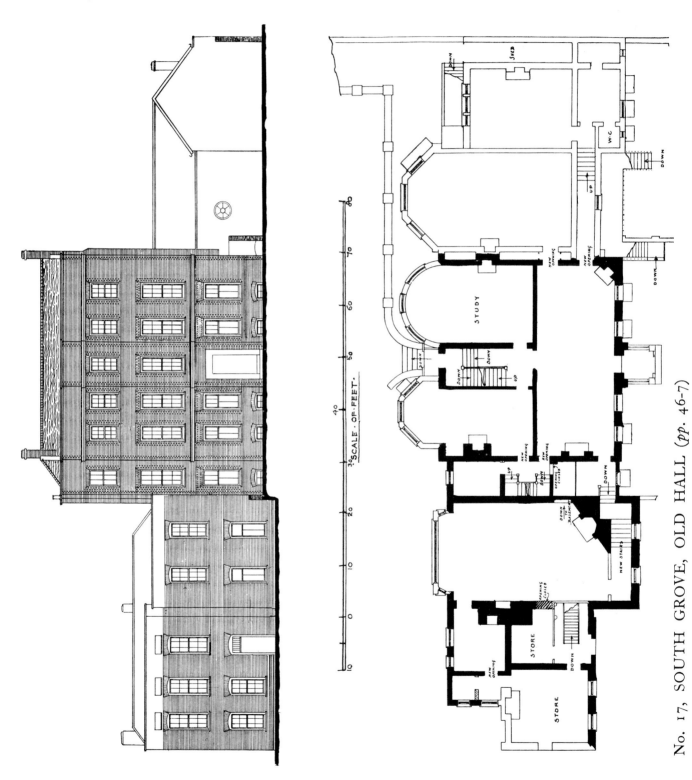

SCALE · OF · FEET ·

No. 17, SOUTH GROVE, OLD HALL (pp. 46-7)

PLATE 39

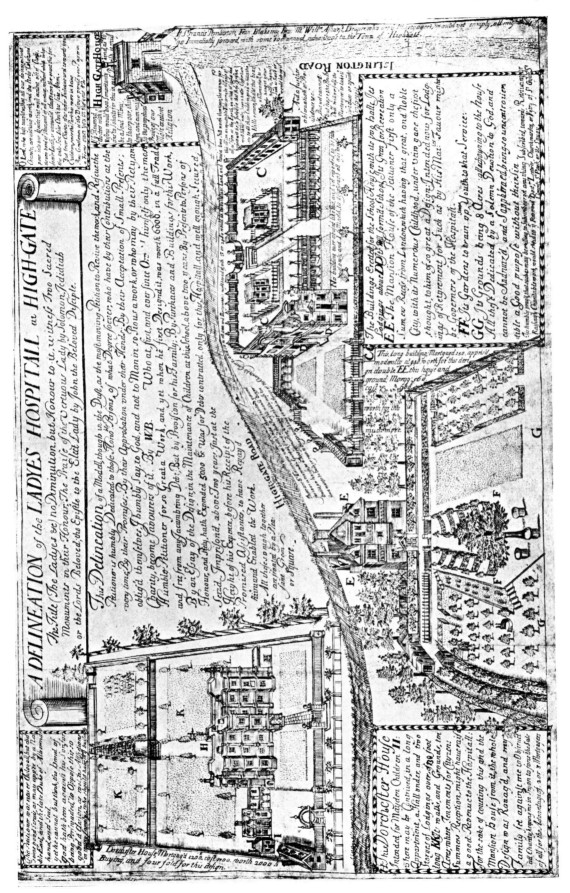

WILLIAM BLAKE'S PLAN OF HIGHGATE SHOWING
DORCHESTER HOUSE AND GARDENS AND HIS OWN HOUSE (LATER ASHURST) (pp. 52, 54, 77, 89)

PLATE 40

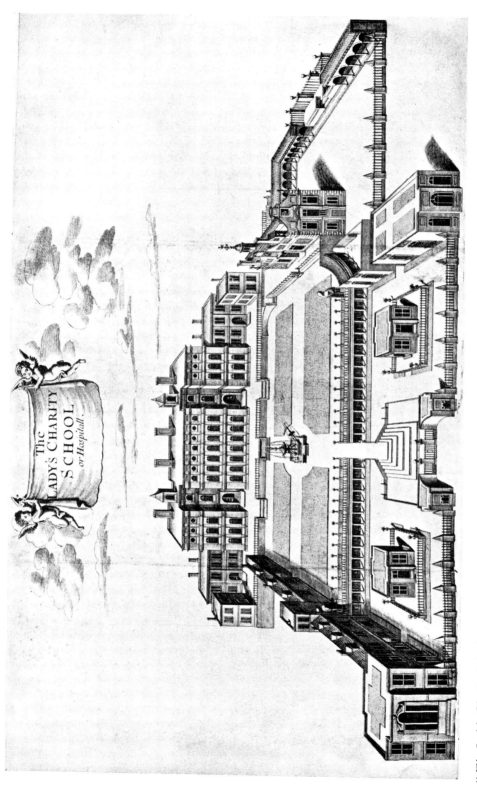

"The Lady's Charity School, so pleasantly situated on Highgate Hill near London, being built and more especially dedicated to them for their most Christian Charity and Praise, and to the honour of our Protestant Religion, for Poor and Fatherless Children, Boys or Girls (which either they or their Honble. Husbands, Lords, Knights, Gentlemen, Governors or other good Benefactors shall recommend) being about 9, 10 or 11 years of age, who shall be all decently clothed in blue lin'd with yellow, and everything answerable. The Boys taught the art of Painting, Gardening, Casting Accompt and Navigation or put forth to some good handicraft trade. The Girls taught to Read, Write, Sew, Starch, Raise, Paint and Dress yt they may be fitt for any good service. And any Person above said may send in from any place, Boy or Girl, French or English, who either hath or will procure to be given 50 Pounds to the said School. And if everything succeed not to their comfort and satisfaction they shall command 3 parts of their money back at ye year's end, their being many Honble. and Worthy Governors and if at this time a few Children of the persecuted French Protestants should be admitted, it would be great Charity to them and advantageous to both in matter of Language. If 2 or 3 Persons joyne together and send one in, it is the same thing. Likewise they who give 5, 10 or 20 guineas towards the Building or Endowing the said School shall also have their Names fairly registered to be read of all in future ages, for Promoters of so Honourable, and so Pyous a Designe."

(p. 54)

PLATE 41

ASHURST HOUSE *circa* 1710 (*p.* 54)

PLATE 42

(*a*) ASHURST HOUSE *circa* 1820
(*b*) ASHURST HOUSE *circa* 1830 (*p.* 54)

PLATE 43

ST. MICHAEL'S CHURCH
JOHN SCHOPPENS MEMORIAL (*pp.* 58-9)

PLATE 44

EXTENDED ELEVATION

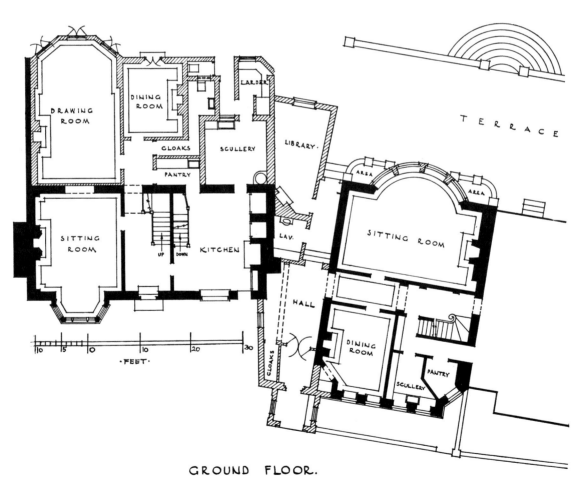

GROUND FLOOR.

Nos. 18 AND 19, SOUTH GROVE
VOEL AND SOUTH GROVE HOUSE (*p.* 63 *ff.*)

PLATE 45

No. 18, SOUTH GROVE, VOEL (*p*. 63)

PLATE 46

No. 18, SOUTH GROVE, VOEL HOUSE (*p.* 63)

PLATE 47

VOEL HOUSE
STAIRCASE

SECTION THROUGH
STAIRCASE

DETAILS OF
BALUSTER ETC

SCALE FOR SMALL SECTION
FEET

MENS ET DELT

SCALE FOR LARGE DETAILS
INCHES

B. H. PEAKE

No. 18, SOUTH GROVE (*p.* 63)

PLATE 48

No. 19, SOUTH GROVE
SOUTH GROVE HOUSE (DEMOLISHED) (*pp.* 64-5)

PLATE 49

(a) THE FOX AND CROWN *circa* 1840
(b) THE FOX AND CROWN *circa* 1880 (*pp.* 74-5)

PLATE 50

(a) PARKFIELD (pp. 72-3)
(b) GROVE BANK (DEMOLISHED)
SITE OF "DORCHESTER HOUSE" (p. 74)

PLATE 51

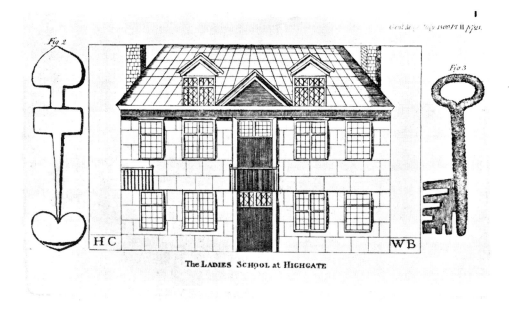

The LADIES SCHOOL at HIGHGATE

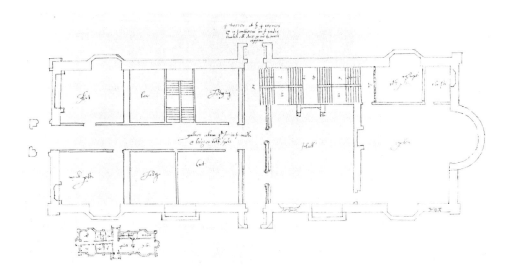

(a) THE LADIES SCHOOL AT HIGHGATE (p. 78)
(b) "DORCHESTER HOUSE" PLAN
(JOHN THORPE ARCHT.) (p. 89)

E

PLATE 52

THE GROVE BEFORE 1930
SITE OF GARDENS OF "DORCHESTER HOUSE" (*pp.* 77 *ff.*)

PLATE 53

Nos. 1 and 2, THE GROVE (*p.* 79)

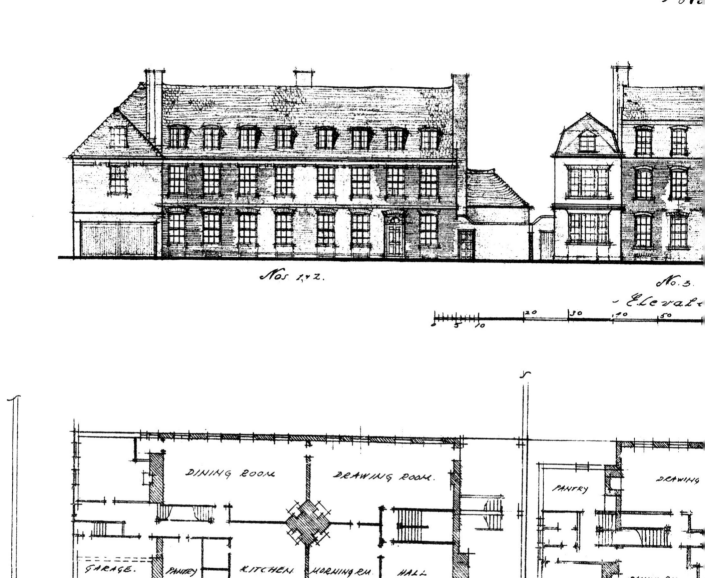

Nos 1, + 2.   *No. 3.*

— Elevat

20   30   40   50
0   5   10

DINING ROOM   DRAWING ROOM.   PANTRY   DRAWING

GARAGE.   PANTRY   KITCHEN   MORNING RM.   HALL   DINING RM.

CHILDREN'S
ROOM.

Nos 1. + 2.   *No. 3.*

The

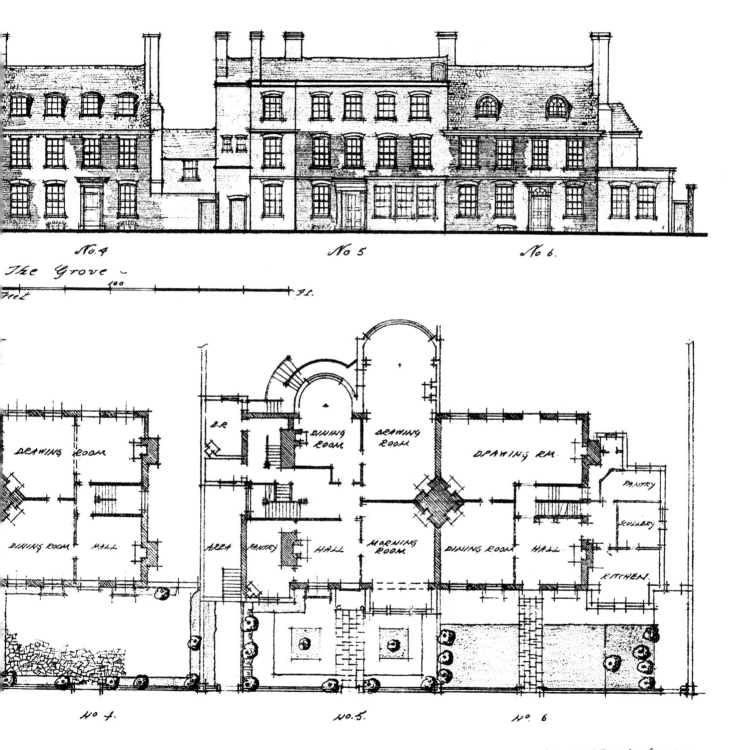

No.4   No 5   No 6.

The Grove ~

Feet   100   31.

DRAWING ROOM

DINING ROOM   HALL

D.R.

DINING ROOM

DRAWING ROOM

DRAWING RM.

PANTRY

SCULLERY

AREA   PANTRY   HALL   MORNING ROOM   DINING ROOM   HALL

KITCHEN.

No 4.   No.5.   No. 6

Original Work hatched

Grove

L.A.P.

PLATE 55

Nos. 1 AND 2, THE GROVE
ENTRANCE GATE (*p.* 79)

PLATE 56

Nos. 3 and 4, THE GROVE (*pp.* 79 *ff.*)

PLATE 57

GROUND FLOOR

DRAWING ROOM

DINING ROOM

HALL

PANTRY

SECOND FLOOR

NURSERY

BED ROOM

BED ROOM

BED ROOM

BED ROOM

W C

BASEMENT PLAN

LARDER

STORE

MAIDS ROOM

WINES

KITCHEN

FIRST FLOOR

BOUDOIR

BED ROOM

CUPBOARD

BED ROOM

BATH ROOM

BED ROOM

POWDER CLOSET

J D F PICKEN
W G MADDISON

FEET 0   3   6   9   12

No. 4, THE GROVE (*pp.* 79 *ff.*)

PLATE 58

FRONT ELEVATION

FEET 0 6 12

W G MADDISON
I D F PICKEN

BACK ELEVATION

FEET 0 6 12

No. 4, THE GROVE (*pp.* 79 *ff.*)

PLATE 59

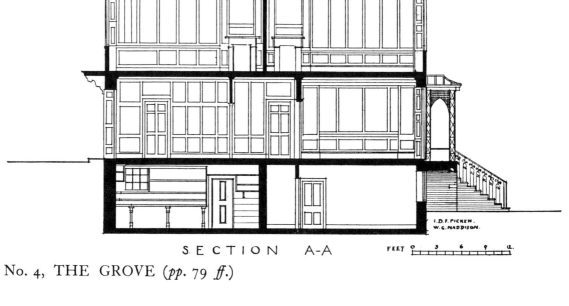

SIDE ELEVATION

SECTION A-A   FEET 0   3   6   9   12

I.D.F.PICKEN.
W.G.MADDISON.

No. 4, THE GROVE (*pp.* 79 *ff.*)

PLATE 60

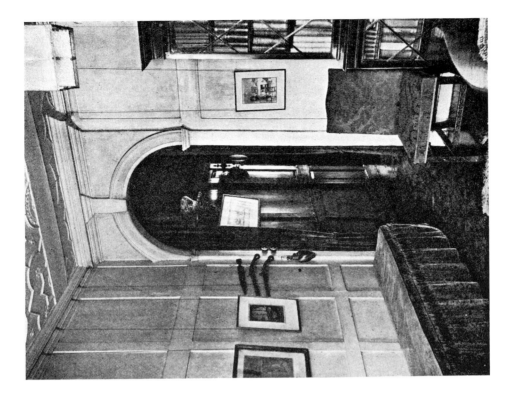

No. 4, THE GROVE (*pp.* 77 *ff.*)
(*b*) HALL

(*a*) EXTERIOR

PLATE 61

STAIRCASE AT Nº4 THE GROVE

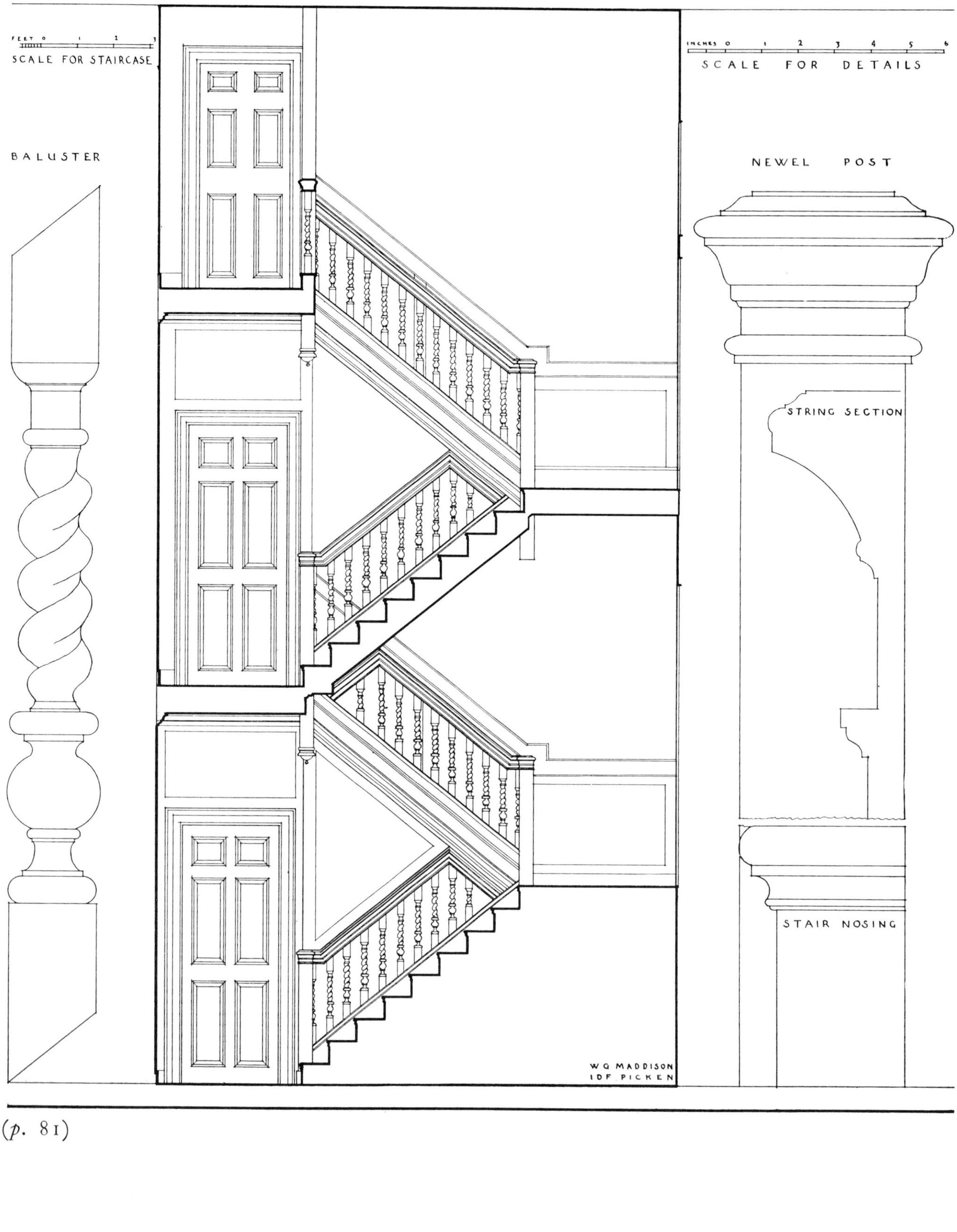
FEET 0 1 2 3
SCALE FOR STAIRCASE
INCHES 0 1 2 3 4 5 6
SCALE FOR DETAILS
BALUSTER
NEWEL POST
STRING SECTION
STAIR NOSING
W G MADDISON
I D F PICKEN

(p. 81)

PLATE 62

Nos. 5 AND 6, THE GROVE
BEFORE RECONSTRUCTION OF No. 5 (*pp.* 83 *ff.*)

PLATE 63

No. 5, THE GROVE
BEFORE RECONSTRUCTION (*p.* 83)

PLATE 64

No. 5, THE GROVE—STAIRCASE
BEFORE RECONSTRUCTION (*p.* 83)

PLATE 65

No. 5, THE GROVE—STAIRCASE
BEFORE RECONSTRUCTION (*p.* 83)

PLATE 66

No. 5, THE GROVE
WALLPAPER. EXAMPLE "A" (*p.* 84)

PLATE 67

No. 5, THE GROVE
WALLPAPER. EXAMPLE "B" (*p.* 85)

PLATE 68

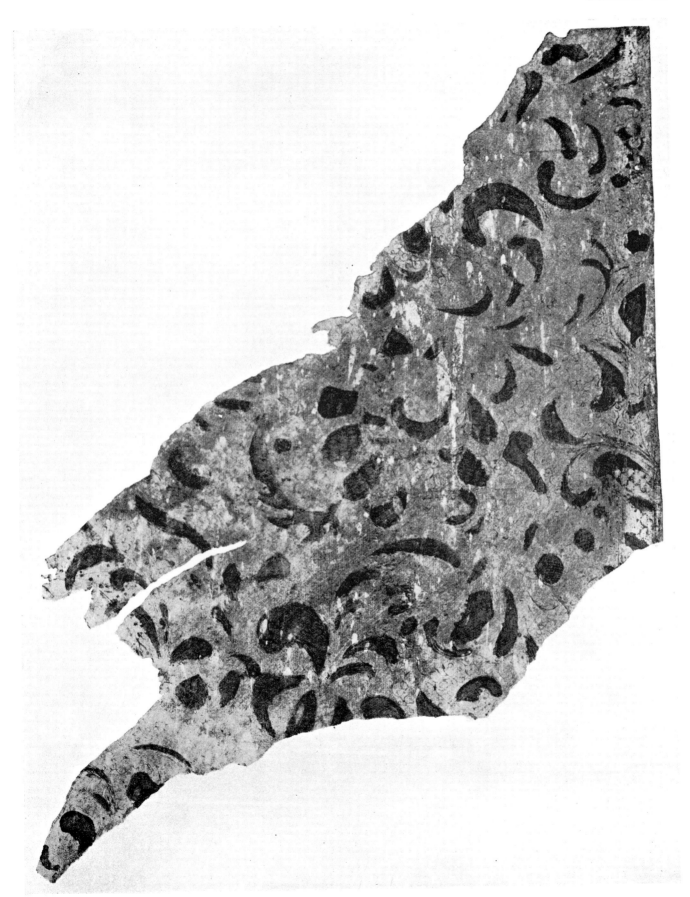

No. 5, THE GROVE. WALLPAPER. EXAMPLE "C" (p. 85)

PLATE 69

No. 5, THE GROVE
WALLPAPER. EXAMPLE "D" (*p.* 85)

PLATE 70

DETAILS OF
NEWEL

DETAILS OF
BALUSTER

6, THE GROVE
STAIRCASE

SCALE FOR SMALL SECTION

SCALE FOR LARGE DETAILS

FEET

INCHES

MODERN

DETAILS OF STRING

SECTION THROUGH STAIRCASE

MENS ET DELT BH PEAKE

(p. 87)

F

PLATE 71

No. 52, SOUTH GROVE (*pp. 95 ff.*)

PLATE 72

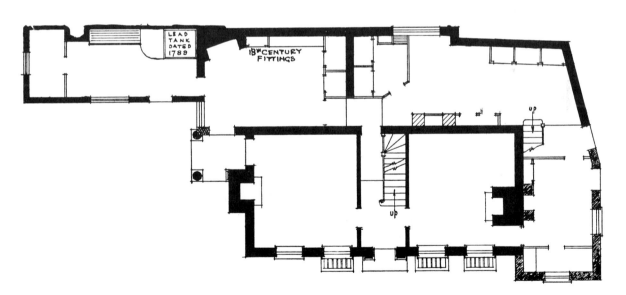

LEAD
TANK
DATED
1789

18ᵀᴴ CENTURY
FITTINGS

UP

UP

No. 52, SOUTH GROVE (*p.* 95)

PLATE 73

No. 52, SOUTH GROVE
PORCH TO GARDEN (*p. 96*)

PLATE 74

No. 52, SOUTH GROVE
PORCH TO GARDEN (*p.* 96)

PLATE 75

No. 52, SOUTH GROVE (*p. 96*)

PLATE 76

Nº 52 SOUTH GROVE, HIGHGATE

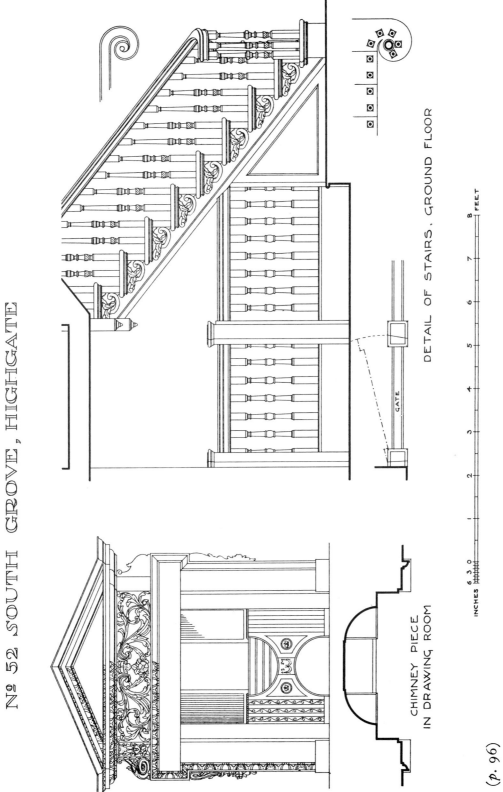

DETAIL OF STAIRS, GROUND FLOOR

GATE

CHIMNEY PIECE
IN DRAWING ROOM

INCHES 6 3 0   1   2   3   4   5   6   7   8 FEET

(p. 96)

PLATE 77

N⁰ 52 SOUTH GROVE, HIGHGATE,

DETAILS OF MANTEL & STAIRS

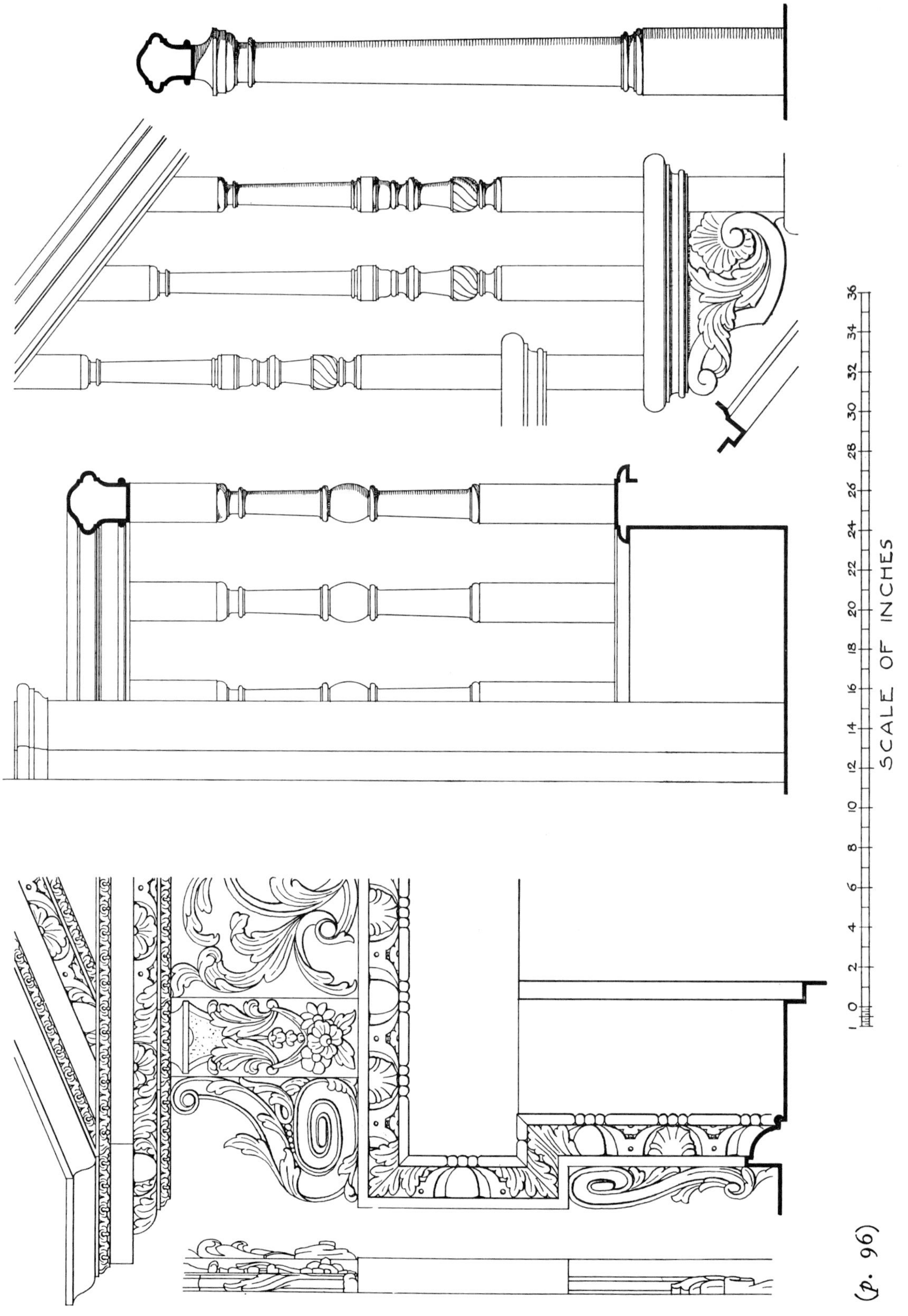

SCALE OF INCHES

0 2 4 6 8 10 12 14 16 18 20 22 24 26 28 30 32 34 36

(p. 96)

PLATE 78

Nos. 53 AND 54, SOUTH GROVE (*pp.* 97 *ff.*)

PLATE 79

Nos. 53 and 54, SOUTH GROVE
(*a*) BACK ELEVATION (*p*. 98)
(*b*) LEAD RAINWATER HEAD (*p*. 97)

PLATE 80

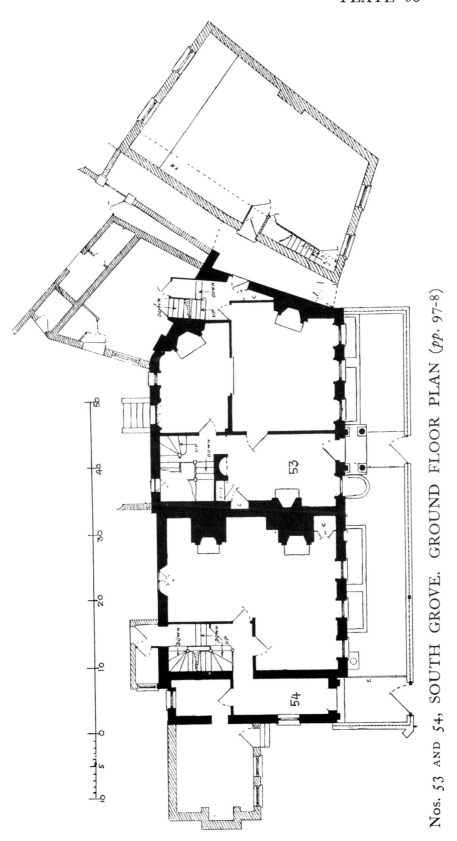

Nos. 53 AND 54, SOUTH GROVE. GROUND FLOOR PLAN (*pp.* 97-8)

PLATE 81

ELEVATION

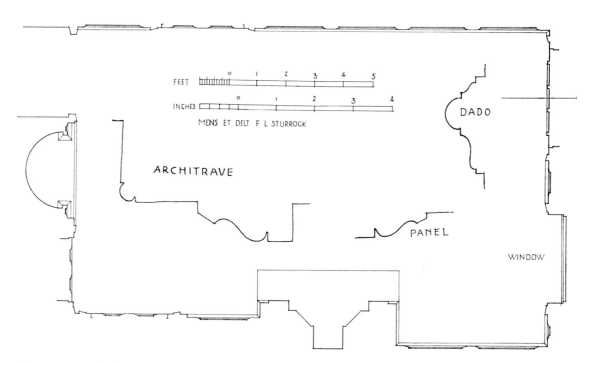

FEET

INCHES

MENS ET DELT F L STURROCK

ARCHITRAVE

DADO

PANEL

WINDOW

No. 53, SOUTH GROVE
ENTRANCE HALL (*p.* 98)

PLATE 82

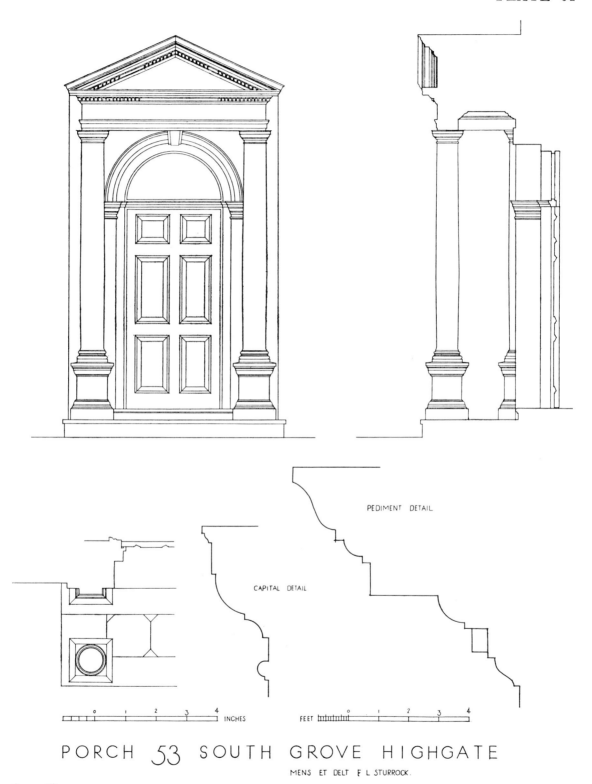

PEDIMENT DETAIL

CAPITAL DETAIL

INCHES

FEET

PORCH 53 SOUTH GROVE HIGHGATE

MENS ET DELT F L STURROCK.

(p. 98)

PLATE 83

No. 54, SOUTH GROVE (*p*. 99)

PLATE 84

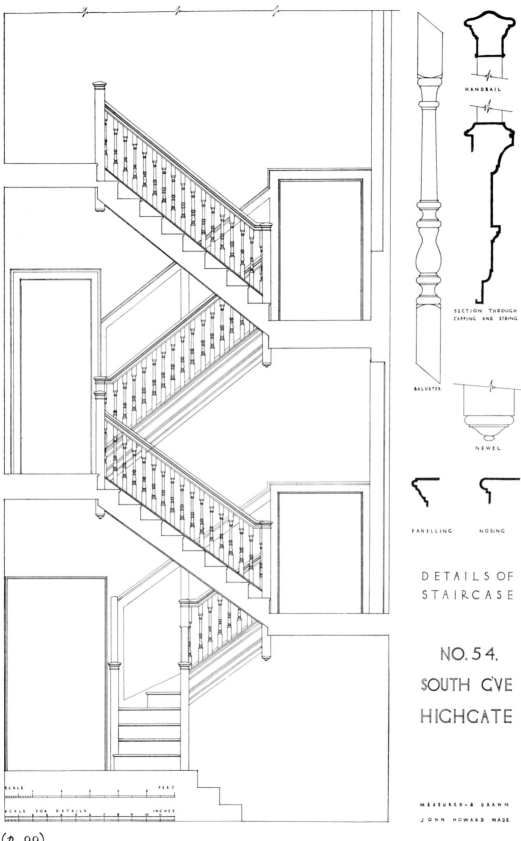

HANDRAIL

SECTION THROUGH
CAPPING AND STRING

BALUSTER

NEWEL

PANELLING   NOSING

DETAILS OF
STAIRCASE

NO. 54,

SOUTH G'VE

HIGHGATE

MEASURED & DRAWN

JOHN HOWARD WADE

SCALE   FEET

SCALE FOR DETAILS   INCHES

PLATE 85

THE OLD GATE HOUSE (*p.* 103)

(*a*) *circa* 1840

(*b*) *circa* 1900

PLATE 86

THE OLD GATEHOUSE
STAIRS TO PASSAGE OVER GATE (*p.* 103)

PLATE 87

(a) THE OLD FORGE
DESTROYED 1896 (p. 105)
(b) POND SQUARE, 1845 (p. 110)

PLATE 88

(*a*) Nos. 1 to 6, POND SQUARE, 1909
(*b*) Nos. 4 and 5, POND SQUARE, 1909
(*pp.* 109-10)

PLATE 89

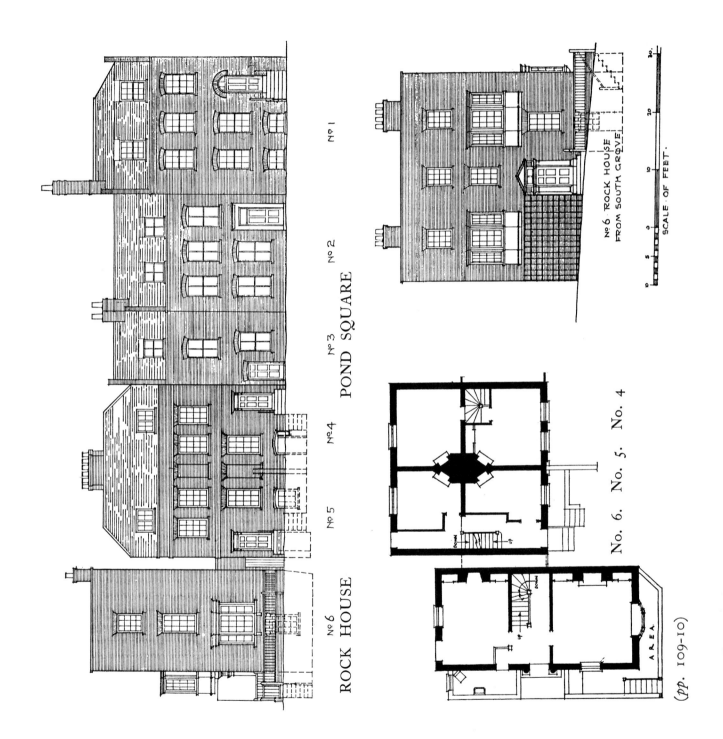

No 1

No 2

No 3

POND SQUARE

No 4

No 5

No 6
ROCK HOUSE

No 6. ROCK HOUSE
FROM SOUTH GROVE

SCALE · OF · FEET.

No. 6. No. 5. No. 4

AREA

(pp. 109-10)

PLATE 90

No. 6, POND SQUARE
ROCK HOUSE (*p.* 110)

PLATE 91

THE FLASK TAVERN (*pp.* 111 *ff.*)

PLATE 92

EXAMPLES OF IRONWORK

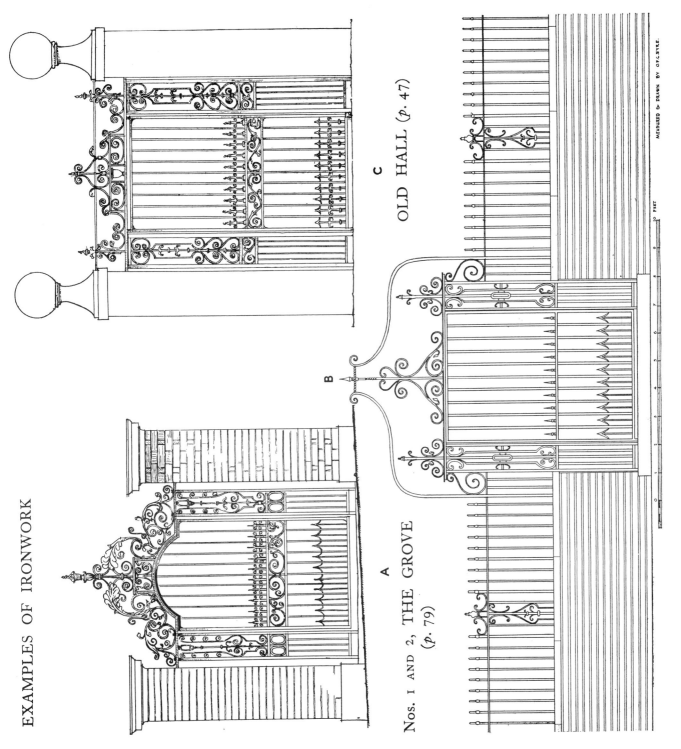

C

OLD HALL (*p.* 47)

A

Nos. 1 AND 2, THE GROVE
(*p.* 79)

B

No. 10, SOUTH GROVE. CHURCH HOUSE (*p.* 34)

MEASURED & DRAWN BY OT. G. EYLE.

PLATE 93

Lord Southampton's Lodge, at Highgate, Middlesex.
Published according to Act of Parliament by Rob.t Sayer & C.o Fleet Street London.

FITZROY HOUSE, THE SEAT OF LORD
SOUTHAMPTON (*p.* 2)

PLATE 94

The Earl of Mansfields, at Caen Wood, near Hampstead, Middlesex.

Published as Sept 1792, by Rob Sayer, & Co Fleet Street London.

PLATE 95

KEN WOOD. THE SOUTH FRONT AND TERRACE *circa* 1770 (*p.* 120)

PLATE 96

PLAN OF KEN WOOD, 1793 (*p.* 114)

PLATE 97

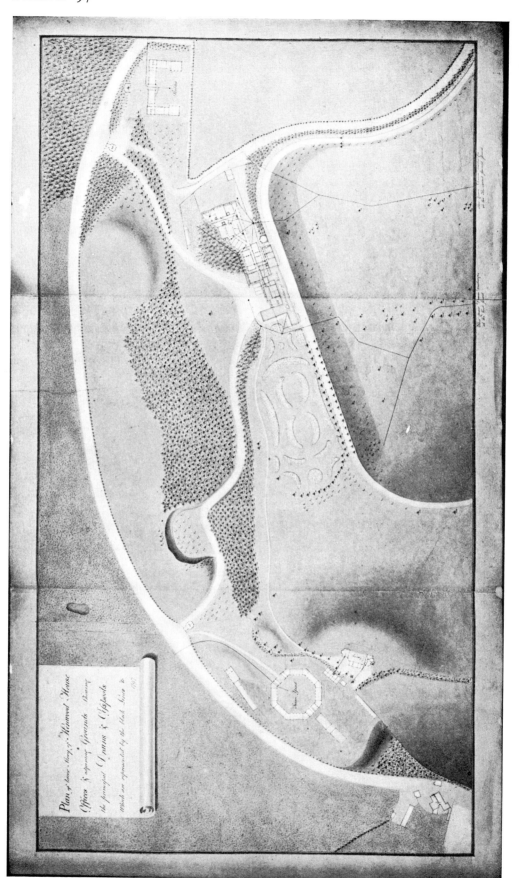

PLAN OF KEN WOOD, 1797 (*p.* 115)

PLATE 98

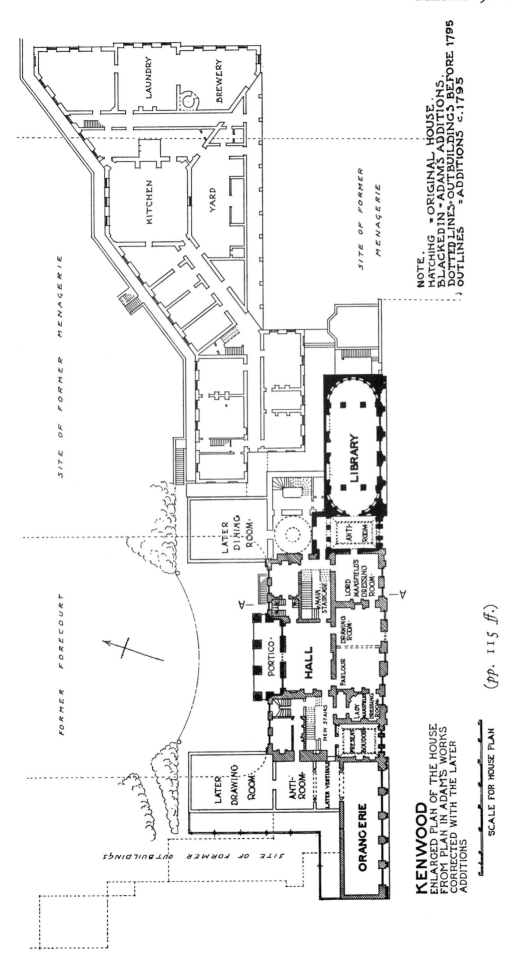

LAUNDRY

BREWERY

KITCHEN

YARD

SITE OF FORMER MENAGERIE

SITE OF FORMER MENAGERIE

SITE OF FORMER MENAGERIE

FORMER FORECOURT

LATER DINING ROOM.

LIBRARY

ANTE ROOM

NEW STAIRCASE

MAIN STAIRCASE

LORD MANSFIELD'S DRESSING ROOM.

A— —A

DRAWING ROOM.

PARLOUR

LADY MANSFIELD'S DRESSING ROOM.

PORTICO.

HALL

PRESENT BOUDOIR

LATER VESTIBULE

NEW STAIRS

LATER DRAWING ROOM.

ANTE-ROOM.

ORANGERIE

SITE OF FORMER OUTBUILDINGS

NOTE.
HATCHING = ORIGINAL HOUSE.
BLACKED IN = ADAM'S ADDITIONS.
DOTTED LINES = OUTBUILDINGS BEFORE 1795
OUTLINES = ADDITIONS c.1795

KENWOOD
ENLARGED PLAN OF THE HOUSE
FROM PLAN IN ADAM'S WORKS
CORRECTED WITH THE LATER
ADDITIONS

(pp. 115 ff.)

SCALE FOR HOUSE PLAN

PLATE 99

KEN WOOD. THE ENTRANCE FRONT (*p.* 120)

PLATE 100

KEN WOOD. SOUTH FRONT (*p.* 120)

PLATE 101

KEN WOOD. THE KITCHENS AND OFFICES
ADDED *circa* 1795 (*p.* 120)

PLATE 102

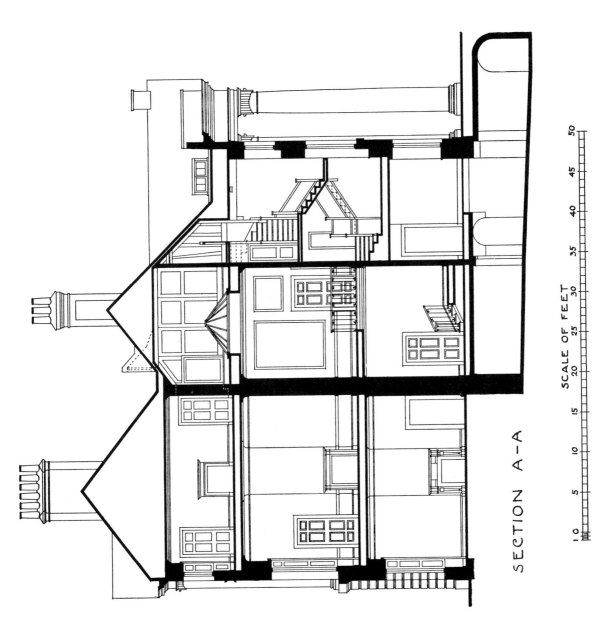

SECTION A—A

SCALE OF FEET

KEN WOOD. CROSS SECTION

PLATE 103

KEN WOOD. THE HALL (*p.* 115)

PLATE 104

KEN WOOD. THE ADAM LIBRARY (*pp.* 116 *ff.*)

PLATE 105

KEN WOOD. THE ADAM LIBRARY

PLATE 106

KEN WOOD. THE ADAM LIBRARY

PLATE 107

KEN WOOD
(a) THE ADAM LIBRARY FIREPLACE
(b) NORTH WALL (p. 117)

PLATE 108

KEN WOOD. THE LIBRARY CEILING (p. 117)

PLATE 109

KEN WOOD. THE ADAM LIBRARY. CENTRAL PANEL OF CEILING

PLATE 110

KEN WOOD. THE ADAM LIBRARY CEILING
(*a*) NORTH-WEST PANEL
(*b*) SOUTH-WEST PANEL

PLATE III

KEN WOOD. THE ADAM LIBRARY CEILING
(a) NORTH-EAST PANEL
(b) SOUTH-EAST PANEL

PLATE 112

KEN WOOD

(b) THE ADAM LIBRARY MIRRORS (p. 117)

(a) THE ADAM STAIRCASE (p. 115)

PLATE 113

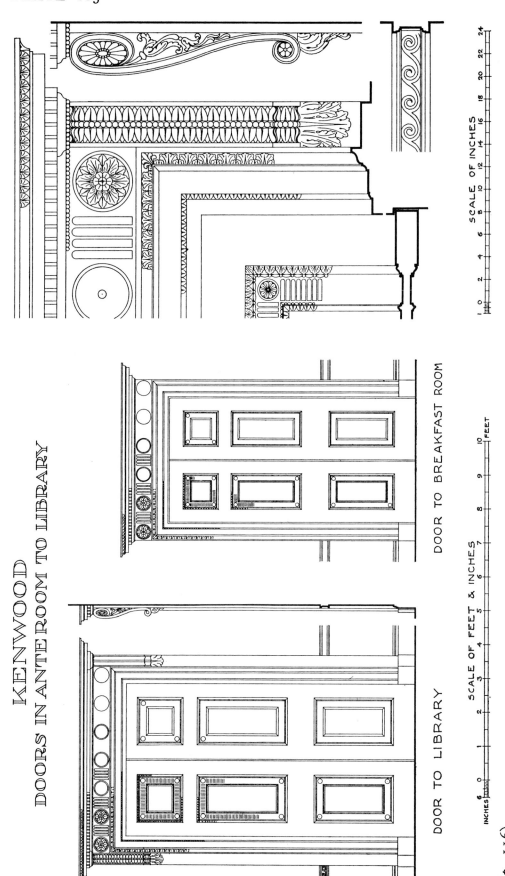

KENWOOD

DOORS IN ANTE ROOM TO LIBRARY

DOOR TO LIBRARY

DOOR TO BREAKFAST ROOM

SCALE OF INCHES

SCALE OF FEET & INCHES

PLATE 114

KEN WOOD
(*a*) THE VESTIBULE (*p.* 116)
(*b*) LORD MANSFIELD'S BEDROOM (*p.* 119)

PLATE 115

KEN WOOD
THE " MARBLE " HALL. ADDED *circa* 1795 (*p.* 116)

PLATE 116

KEN WOOD
(*a*) NORTH ROOM FIRST FLOOR (*p.* 119)
(*b*) ATTIC FLOOR. MANTELPIECE AND GRATE (*p.* 119)

PLATE 117

KEN WOOD
(*a*) THE STABLES
(*b*) THE DAIRY FARM (*p.* 121)

PLATE 118

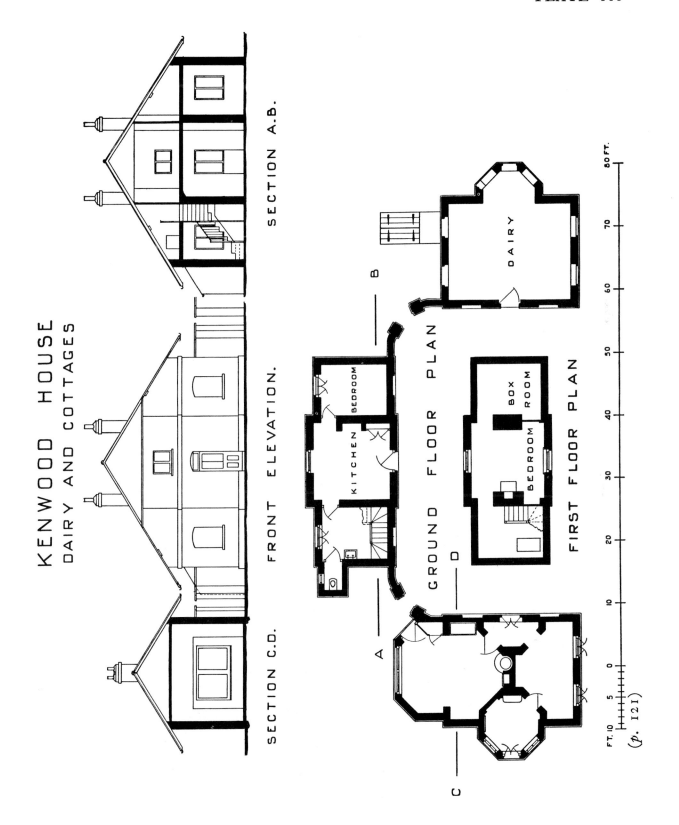

KENWOOD HOUSE
DAIRY AND COTTAGES

SECTION A.B.

FRONT ELEVATION.

SECTION C.D.

A

B

GROUND FLOOR PLAN

C

D

FIRST FLOOR PLAN

KITCHEN

BEDROOM

BEDROOM

BOX ROOM

DAIRY

FT. 10   5   0   10   20   30   40   50   60   70   80 FT.

(p. 121)

PLATE 119

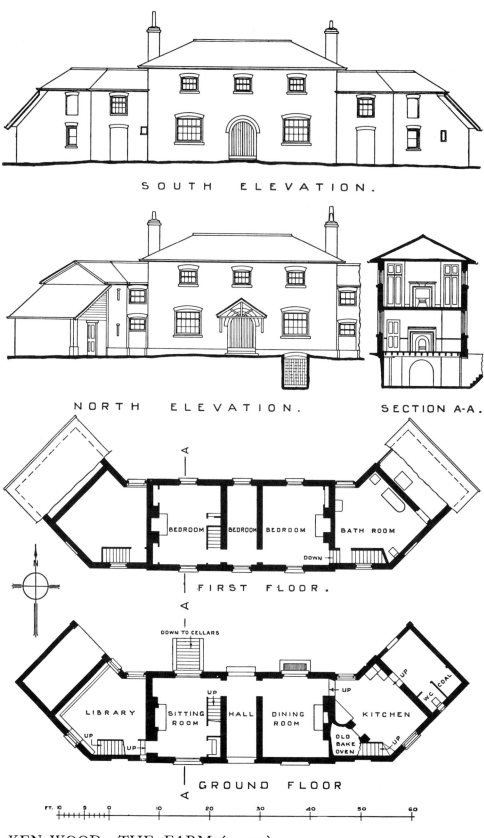

SOUTH ELEVATION.

NORTH ELEVATION.

SECTION A-A.

FIRST FLOOR.

GROUND FLOOR

KEN WOOD. THE FARM (*p.* 121)